THREE STUDIES IN
LOCALITY AND CASE

THEORETICAL LINGUISTICS

Chief Editor
Professor John Hawkins, University of Southern California

Consultant Editors
Professor Joseph Aoun, University of Southern California
Professor Bernard Comrie, University of Southern California
Dr Teun Hoekstra, University of Leiden
Dr Richard Hudson, University College, London
Professor James Hurford, University of Edinburgh
Professor Douglas Pulleyblank, University of Ottawa

The Theoretical Linguistics series does not specialize in any one area of language study, nor does it limit itself to any one theoretical approach. Synchronic and diachronic descriptive studies, either syntactic, semantic, phonological or morphological, are welcomed, as are more theoretical 'model-building' studies, and studies in sociolinguistics or psycholinguistics. The criterion for a work's acceptance is the quality of its contribution to the relevant field. All texts published must advance our understanding of the nature of language in areas of substantial interest to major sectors of the linguistic research community. Traditional scholarly standards, such as clarity of presentation, factual and logical soundness of argumentation, and a thorough and reasoned orientation to other relevant work, are also required. Within these indispensable limitations we welcome the submission of creative and original contributions to the study of language.

QUESTIONS OF INTONATION
Gillian Brown, Karen L. Currie and Joanne Kenworthy
THE SEMANTICS OF DETERMINERS
Edited by Johan van der Auwera
BINDING AND FILTERING
Edited by Frank W. Heny
THIRTY MILLION THEORIES OF GRAMMAR
James D. McCawley
COMPLEMENTATION IN MIDDLE ENGLISH
Anthony R. Warner
THE DEVELOPMENT OF WORD ORDER PATTERNS IN OLD ENGLISH
Marian C. Bean
THE SEMANTICS OF THE MODAL AUXILIARIES
Jennifer Coates
ANAPHORA AND SEMANTIC INTERPRETATION
Tanya Reinhart
WORD MEANING AND BELIEF
S. G. Pulman
HIERARCHIES, TARGETS AND CONTROLLERS
Grevill G. Corbett
CAUSALITY IN LINGUISTIC THEORY
Esa Itkonen
THE PASSIVE: A COMPARATIVE LINGUISTIC ANALYSIS
Anna Siewierska
DEPENDENCY AND NON-LINEAR PHONOLOGY
Edited by Jacques Durand

BASIC WORD ORDER: FUNCTIONAL PRINCIPLES
Russell S. Tomlin
ANAPHORIC RELATIONS IN ENGLISH AND FRENCH
Francis Cornish
THE ENGLISH IMPERATIVE
Eirlys Davies
STYLISTICS AND PSYCHOLOGY
Willie Van Peer
ALLOMORPHY IN INFLEXION
Andrew Carstairs
UNIVERSAL GRAMMAR
Edward L. Keenan
CONTEXT AND PRESUPPOSITION
R. A. van der Sandt
EXISTENTIAL SENTENCES
Michael Lumsden
THE SYNTAX OF COORDINATION
R. A. van Oirsouw
WELSH SYNTAX
Louisa Sadler
THE PHONOLOGY–MORPHOLOGY INTERFACE
Jolanta Szpyra
THEMATIC THEORY IN SYNTAX AND INTERPRETATION
Robin Clark
ACCESSING NOUN-PHRASE ANTECEDENTS
Mira Ariel
CATEGORIES, CONSTITUENTS AND CONSTITUENT
ORDER IN PITJANTJATJARA
Heather J. Bowe

THREE STUDIES IN LOCALITY AND CASE

Alexander Grosu

London and New York

First published 1994
by Routledge
11 New Fetter Lane, London EC4P 4EE

Simultaneously published in the USA and Canada
by Routledge
29 West 35th Street, New York, NY 10001

© 1994 Alexander Grosu

Typeset in Baskerville by
Ponting–Green Publishing Services, Chesham, Bucks
Printed and bound in Great Britain by
TJ Press (Padstow) Ltd, Padstow, Cornwall

All rights reserved. No part of this book may be reprinted or reproduced or utilized in any form or by any electronic, mechanical, or other means, now known or hereafter invented, including photocopying and recording, or in any information storage or retrieval system, without permission in writing from the publishers.

British Library Cataloguing in Publication Data
A catalogue record for this book is available from the British Library

Library of Congress Cataloging in Publication Data
A catalogue record for this book has been applied for

ISBN 0-415-10827-6

CONTENTS

Acknowledgements	ix
Introduction	xi

Study I The syntax of Free Relative Constructions

Introduction	3
1 THE CONFIGURATIONAL PROPERTIES OF REALIS FRCs AND THEIR INTERNAL SYNTAX EFFECTS: A CRITICAL REVIEW OF EARLIER LITERATURE	10
1.1 The WH-*head analysis*	10
1.2 The 'head by-pass' analysis	15
1.3 The pro *in governed positions analysis*	23
1.4 The internally-identified pro *analysis*	25
2 THE SYNTAX OF NULL-OPERATOR REALIS FRCs	44
2.0 Introductory remarks	44
2.1 FRCs with a reordered Null Operator	45
2.2 FRCs with resumptive pronouns in situ	46
2.3 FRCs with syntactic movement to a position other than [SPEC, C']	47
2.4 Head-internal relatives	49
2.5 Summary and conclusions	54
3 THE THEORY OF *pro*, **ANTI-PIED-PIPING EFFECTS AND NON-NOMINAL FRCs**	56
3.0 Introduction	56
3.1 The formal/content distinction in earlier work and a new theory of pro	57
3.2 Amount constructions, pro-*identification and the anti-Pied-Piping effects*	65
3.3 Towards a unified theory of pro	84
3.4 On non-nominal FRCs	89
3.5 Summary and conclusions	106

CONTENTS

4 COINDEXATION-DEPENDENT PF PROCESSES — 107
   4.1 The typology of processes — 107
   4.2 Attraction processes — 110
   4.3 Matching requirements — 113
   4.4 The theoretical status of matching effects: basic or derived? — 129

5 THE ANALYSIS OF NON-INDICATIVE/IRREALIS FRCs — 137
   5.1 Summary of results — 142

Study II Romanian determiners as functional categories

Introduction — 147

6 THEORETICAL BACKGROUND AND EARLIER RESULTS — 149
   6.1 Some facts of Romanian and their theoretical significance — 157
   6.2 The N-borne enclitic definite article as Case assigner — 159
   6.3 Genitive phrases as objects of complex prepositions — 163
   6.4 Genitives after adjectives — 170
   6.5 -L-bearing complex determiners — 178

7 ON THE ENCLITICIZATION PROCESS — 185
   7.1 Encliticization within the Government and Binding framework — 185
   7.2 Encliticization within the minimalistic framework — 190
   7.3 The linear order of genitive phrases and their licensers — 191
   7.4 Adjacency effects — 192
   7.5 Summary of results — 196

Study III On Null Operators in Romanian

Introduction — 201

8 *pro*-OPERATOR CONSTRUCTIONS — 203
   8.1 Cleft constructions — 203
   8.2 Comparative constructions — 204
   8.3 Relative clauses — 208
   8.4 Supine constructions with NOs — 217
   8.5 Too/enough constructions — 222
   8.6 Summary and conclusions — 223

Notes — 227
Bibliography — 250
Index — 255

ACKNOWLEDGEMENTS

There are more people to whom I am indebted for stimulating discussion and useful criticism than I can list here. None the less I wish to single out for special thanks Julia Horvath, whose sharp criticism has often prompted me to seek new and more interesting solutions. I am also grateful to Paul Hirschbühler, Maria-Luisa Rivero, Veneeta Srivastav, Jacqueline Guéron, Carmen Dobrovie-Sorin, Giuliana Giusti and Hubert Haider for useful discussion, as well as to audiences of colleagues and students at the universities of Tel-Aviv, Bar-Ilan, Beer-Sheva, Toronto, Montreal, Ottawa, Paris 7, Paris 8, Tübingen and Venice, where earlier versions of some of the material in this book were presented. The editors of the series, Jack Hawkins and Joseph Aoun, were very helpful and supportive. Last but not least I owe a special debt of gratitude to my wife Mariana, who has provided me with constant encouragement and support throughout the years that it took to see this project through.

This book is dedicated to my mother, wife and son.

INTRODUCTION

This work consists of three studies in the syntax of natural languages, which pursue related theoretical goals, assume common phrase structural and locality sub-theories and share some of the languages from which the supporting data are drawn.

A theme that is central to both the first and third studies and tangentially touched upon in the second study is that of the syntax of the null element *pro* in various contexts and with various roles, but first and foremost as Head of Free Relative Constructions and as Null Operator. Another theme of central importance, primarily in the first two studies, is that of the syntax of Case.

The theoretical framework assumed throughout this work is that of the Theory of Government and Binding (Chomsky 1981, 1982) augmented with a variety of proposals made in subsequent work (in particular Chomsky (1986a, 1986b); Abney (1987); Grimshaw (1991)). The analyses proposed are derived from, but also critically examine, central features of this theory, in particular its locality constructs such as government, adjacency and Extended Projection as well as processes operating within the limits defined by such constructs, for example feature spread, Case assignment, Case attraction, phi-feature and Case-transfer, identification of null categories, Head-Spec(ifier) agreement, Move-Alpha, and the like.

In view of the fact that this work was written and conceived before the publication of Chomsky's programme for a Minimalistic Theory (Chomsky 1992), no extensive exploration of the newer framework's potential with respect to the full range of issues addressed in this work was possible; none the less a comparison of the analyses made available by the older and newer frameworks was undertaken in respect to the facts discussed in Study 2. A result worth signalling in this connection is that one of the central proposals of Study 1 (the formulation and justification of a novel theory of *pro*), converges with the thrust of Chomsky's monograph in rejecting 'government' as a useful locality construct and in appealing instead to the notion of 'Minimal Domain'.

The first study addresses issues concerning the syntax of 'F(ree)

R(elative)' C(onstruction)s and their integration into a larger class of 'amount' relative constructions, under a broad construal of this term. These issues include: (i) the characterization of 'amount' relatives in contradistinction to restrictive relatives; (ii) the existence and nature of a null Head in realis FRCs; (iii) the principles which license *pro* in general and *pro* as Head of an FR in particular; (iv) the interacting principles which determine the 'anti-Pied-Piping' effects signalled in Grosu (1989), the complete exclusion of Pied-Piping with Null Operators, and certain 'surprising' Subjacency effects in Head-Internal Relatives; and (v) the typology of 'matching' effects (in respect to Case and category) in the world's languages. The data are drawn from a variety of Indo-European and non-Indo-European languages, first and foremost from Romance and Germanic languages.

Study 2 explores the descriptive and explanatory capabilities of the theory of functional categories in conjunction with various locality constructs in respect to the characterization of the internal syntax of nominal phrases and the syntax of Genitive Case assignment in Romanian, as well as the ways in which Romanian is similar to and different from three other languages in respect to these two subareas of grammar. The study also illustrates with new data the need for partial categorial neutralization within Extended Projections.

Study 3 takes as its point of departure the account of Null Operators developed in Study 1, and examines the distribution of overt and Null Operators in Romanian, contrasting it with the distributional patterns found in other languages. The central concern of the study is to motivate Null Operators in a number of comparative, relative and supine Romanian constructions, where homonymy of various sorts (potentially) 'masks' their presence.

Despite the connections between studies, each one is self-contained and fully comprehensible without reference to the others. To ensure this, a minimum of background information already provided in earlier studies has occasionally been repeated again in later ones.

It is to be hoped that this work will turn out to be of value both to researchers with a primary interest in linguistic theory and to scholars with a special interest in the grammars of Romance and Germanic languages, in particular of Romanian.

Study I

The syntax of Free Relative Constructions (FRCs)

INTRODUCTION

The central goal of this study is to further our understanding of F(ree) R(elative) C(onstruction)s, in particular of the properties they share with such relative constructions as Head-Internal relatives and correlatives, and of the ways in which they differ from restrictive relative constructions.

The comparison with restrictive relatives strongly suggests itself when one considers data like those in (1.1), where the bracketed constituent in the (a) subcase is an FRC and the one in the (b) subcase is a restrictive relative construction.

(1.1) a. [*What* John uttered] was blasphemous.
      b. [THE THINGS *which* John uttered] were blasphemous.

It may seem at first blush that (1.1a) is merely a reduced variant of (1.1b), the difference between them being limited to the fact that the relative clause has an overt antecedent in the latter case and a null or deleted antecedent in the former case. After all, the two subcases of (1.1) are essentially synonymous: the two relative clauses appear to have comparable gross internal-syntax properties (in particular, a *wh*-phrase in [SPEC, C']), and there is overwhelming evidence that (nominal) FRCs (see below) exhibit the overall distribution of restrictive relative constructions and more generally, of (uncontroversial) nominal phrases (for example, simplex DPs). The last point is demonstrated beyond any reasonable doubt with respect to FRCs by the complete parallelism between the various subcases of (1.2) and (1.3), the latter exhibiting FRCs in the contexts where the former exhibits overt simplex nominal phrases.

(1.2) a. [That rumour] was upsetting.
      b. Was [that rumour] upsetting?
      c. I dislike [that rumour].
      d. I consider [that rumour] scandalous.
      e. I am interested in [your ideas].
      f. Tell me about [that story]'s significance.
      g. He is [an engineer].

      h. What I find most upsetting is [that rumour].
      i. It is [that rumour] that I consider most upsetting.
      j. [His proposal], most of us disliked it.
      k. I never discussed it with Bill, [your proposal to me].
      l. She likes only one thing: [Bill's presents].

(1.3) a. [What I heard] was upsetting.
      b. Was [what you heard] upsetting?
      c. I dislike [what I heard].
      d. I consider [what I heard] scandalous.
      e. I am interested in [what you told me].
      f. Tell me about [what John said yesterday]'s significance.
      g. He is [what his father always wanted him to be].
      h. What I find most upsetting is [what you told me].
      i. It is [what you told me] that I find most upsetting.
      j. [What he had to propose], most of us disliked it.
      k. I never discussed it with Bill, [what you proposed to me].
      l. She likes only one thing: [what Bill gives her].

This point is reinforced by the observation that FRCs may occur in certain environments where 'bare' CPs have low acceptability (cf. (1.4a) and (1.4b) with (1.2b)/(1.3b) and (1.2d)/(1.3d) respectively), as well as by the observation that FRCs are excluded from environments where overt nominals are disallowed (cf. the ungrammatical versions of (1.5a) and (1.5b)).

(1.4) a. *Did [that Mary left him] greatly upset John?
      b. *John considers [that Mary abandoned her children] absolutely scandalous.

(1.5) a. [PRO]/[*Bill] to speak out now would be a mistake.
      b. [PRO]/[*Who(ever) had that crazy idea] to speak out now would be a mistake.

    Facts like the above have led those who addressed the syntax of FRCs to assume that they are nominal phrases of some sort, without however reaching a complete consensus on representational details. Thus, Chomsky (1973) assumed (without argument) that FRCs have the same gross representation as restrictive relative constructions, with the single difference that the antecedent undergoes deletion; Bresnan and Grimshaw (1978) argued that FRCs like the one in (1.1b) are headed by the initial *wh*-element; Groos and van Riemsdijk (1981) argued *contra* Bresnan and Grimshaw that FRCs are headed by a null category; and Jacobsen (1988) proposed to assume (without argumentation) that FRCs are CPs exhaustively dominated by a nominal phrasal node. The analysis that will be adopted and argued for in this study is a variant of the one put forward by Groos and van Riemsdijk, with one very important proviso: I believe, and will argue for this position directly, that it is wrong to view the null Head of an FRC as serving the same semantic function as the Head of a restrictive relative; in particular, I will

INTRODUCTION

endeavour to show that the Head of an FRC, in contrast to that of a restrictive relative, does *not* function as an *antecedent* (as various writers have explicitly or tacitly assumed), but, if anything, as a sort of anaphor or resumptive element. There are in fact a variety of indications that in spite of the synonymy of (1.1a) and (1.1b), FRCs differ significantly in their semantics from restrictive relative constructions, a state of affairs signalled by a variety of morphological and syntactic clues.

A first clue to this effect is provided by the observation that the *wh*-forms in (1.1a) and (1.1b) are distinct and – importantly – not interchangeable. Even more strikingly FRCs, but not restrictive relatives, allow *wh*-forms with *-ever,* and in fact full *wh*-nominal phrases, as illustrated in (1.1').

```
(1.1') a. [What(ever (things))) John utters] is/are blasphemous.
       b. [THE THINGS/THAT [which(*ever (things)) John utters]]
          are/is blasphemous.
```

The deviance of the fuller versions of (1.1'b) is in fact expected under the widely-held view that restrictive relative clauses are *predicated* of their antecedents, so that the *wh*-pronoun functions as a mere indicator of an *open* position. Now if the predication assumption is extended to free relatives, the well-formedness of the fuller versions of (1.1'a) is surprising.

Second, while restrictive relative constructions are, to the best of my knowledge, invariably of nominal category, free relatives appear to come in adjectival, adverbial and prepositional varieties, as suggested by the correspondence between the various subcases of (1.6) and (1.7).

```
(1.6) a. John will be [very tall].
      b. John will run [most quickly].
      c. John will live [in your city].

(1.7) a. John will be [however tall his father was].
      b. John will run [however quickly his father once did].
      c. John will live [in whatever city you choose to live].
```

Third, FRCs differ from restrictive relative constructions in that their *wh*-phrases are subject to (arguably universal) restrictions on Pied-Piping, as well as to (language-specific) restrictions which force them to 'match', to various extents, the (understood Head of the) FRC in respect to Case and category. As these two effects are extensively discussed and illustrated in ensuing sections of this study, illustration is postponed until then.

Fourth, FRCs exhibit a number of syntacto-semantic properties which are in general *not* found with restrictive relative constructions, but which *are* found with another kind of O(vertly) H(eaded) R(elative) C(onstruction), namely what Carlson (1977) proposed to call 'amount' relative constructions (for reasons that will become clear below). To bring this out, I will first exhibit and illustrate a number of differences between restrictive and amount OHRCs, and then show that the behaviour of FRCs is parallel to that of amount OHRCs. In constructing the ensuing illustrations, I am taking advantage of the English-specific fact that *wh*-pronouns, which are allowed in restrictive relative constructions, are disallowed in amount OHRCs, which can only be formed with N(ull) O(perators)s.

A first property which distinguishes restrictive from amount relatives is that in restrictives the syntactic operator (that is, the *wh*-pronoun or NO) may not originate in an environment that tolerates only indefinite nominals, while in amount clauses it may. This is illustrated in (1.8) in relation to the English presentational context 'there be ——', which – as pointed out in Milsark (1977) and subsequent works – brooks only *weak* nominals (which typically receive an indefinite interpretation).

(1.8) a. *The books which there are e on his desk need to be removed.
b. The books (that) there are e on his desk need to be removed.

A second difference is that, while relative OHRCs may exhibit either weak or strong determiners, amount OHRCs may exhibit only determiners which are both strong and non-partitive. This can be seen by comparing (1.9a) with (1.9b)–(1.9e) – observe that in the latter set, where an amount interpretation is forced by the 'there be ——' context, both the weak determiners *many*, *two* and *some* and the strong partitive determiner *most* are disallowed.

(1.9) a. The/most/many/two/some men who wore green suits left the party early.
b. The/*most/*many/*two/*some people that there were at the time lived only a few decades.
c. All there was in the shop has been sold out.
d. Every man there was on the island got sick.
e. Any beer there still is in the cooler is mine.

A third difference is that restrictive relatives may stack, while amount relatives may not, as illustrated in (1.10).

(1.10) a. The book which John likes (which Mary dislikes) has very thick covers.
b. The people that there were at your party (*that there had been at Bill's party) were dreadfully noisy.

Turning now to FRCs, (1.11)–(1.13) show that in respect to the three properties just listed, they behave just like amount rather than restrictive relative constructions.

(1.11) What(ever) there was in the closet can't have been very frightening.
(1.12) *There is what(ever) John bought on my table.
(1.13) What(ever) John found (*what(ever) scared Mary) can't have have been all that terrible.

Example (1.12) deserves special comment. FRCs obviously cannot exhibit overt determiners in Head position, since they have no overt Head. None the less, they are necessarily construed as definite (and thus as strong and non-partitive; cf. the grammatical version of (1.9b)), something brought out by their inability to occur in the context 'there be ——'.

What is then the fundamental semantic difference between restrictive and amount relative CPs? I submit that while the former are construed as *predicates*, the latter are construed in essentially the same way as *weak DPs*. That is while both types of clause intuitively designate entity-sets, the corresponding sets are different due to differences in the nature of the internal nominals which, at some level, occur in [SPEC, C'] and end up coindexed with CP. In restrictive clauses, that nominal is basically an abstraction operator over the predicate's open position, so that CP designates the set of entities which have the property expressed by the remainder of CP (in actual practice, the nominal may, if overt, contribute to the characterization of the set in question through its phi-feature specifications, in particular, specifications for number, gender and person; for the notion 'phi-feature' see Chomsky (1981: 330)). In amount clauses, on the other hand, the internal nominal is a weak DP, that is one which characterizes a set of entities *and* its cardinality/amount (a more precise characterization, as proposed by Rothstein (1988), is that a weak DP is interpreted as a set of sets of entities such that the member sets satisfy some cardinality condition). This fundamental property is moreover found not just in the amount constructions studied by Carlson (1977), but also in other constructions, in particular FRCs of various sorts and correlative constructions; for this reason, I propose to use from now on the term 'amount relative' in a broader sense to refer to any CP coindexed with an internal weak DP, where the latter is construed as taking CP-scope (hopefully, no confusion will arise between the broad and narrow uses of this term). An amount CP is interpreted as a set of sets whose properties are jointly expressed by the internal nominal and the remainder of CP; note that since CP is not a predicate, the internal nominal may be as informative as one wishes (hence, the contrast between the fuller versions of (1.1'a) and (1.1'b)). A crucial difference between the two types of relative clause is that a predicate presupposes a 'subject of predication', and is thus logically *subsequent* to that subject. In contrast, a weak DP typically constitutes 'novel information' and does not presuppose the existence of anything else; that is it constitutes a logically *primary* 'mention' of the set it designates. A consequence of this state of affairs is that there exist no restrictive relatives without some external nominal of which they are predicated, while there do exist amount relative constructions which consist exclusively of a CP.

As it happens, 'bare'-CP amount constructions are relatively infrequent, for reasons that will be made clear in section 3.2.1. The typical amount construction exhibits in addition a 'resumptive' (overt or null) CP-external weak DP, which may or may not form a constituent with CP, but which semantically combines with CP in the sense that the resulting semantic object designates a set of sets which must simultaneously satisfy the cardinality and other conditions expressed by CP and the external nominal. Just like simplex weak DPs, amount constructions, whether formed with or without an external nominal, need to be 'closed' by some overt or implicit quantifier (Heim 1982) – as we shall see, this is always the case.

The semantic distinction we have proposed with respect to restrictive/ amount relative clauses can go a long way in accounting for their distinct behaviour illustrated above. I reserve discussion and elucidation of the anti-Pied-Piping and matching effects for later on, and confine myself here to the three distinctions illustrated in (1.8)–(1.13). Thus the fact that the internal coindexed operators of amount, but not of restrictive clauses, may originate in the presentational context 'there be ——' is a consequence of the fact that only the former are *weak DPs* (by definition) in conjunction with the fact that the context at issue allows only weak NPs. The fact that the (complex constituent structurally headed by the) external weak DP must (explicitly or implicitly) be bound by a strong non-partitive D follows from the resumptive status of the external nominal. Note that this status is inconsistent with a weak determiner, which implies primary mention status, as well as with a partitive determiner, which defines a different set from the one that CP purports to designate (specifically, a proper subset of the latter). Finally, the inability of amount relatives to stack follows from their necessarily logically primary status, since only one purported mention (of a set) may be primary. Since restrictive relatives, and more generally predicates, have a logically subsequent status, stacking is permitted, because any number of objects may be subsequent to some primary object[1].

I hope to have established in this introductory section that FRCs belong to the broader class of amount relative constructions, and that the latter are significantly different from restrictive relative constructions. We may now turn to our main task, which is, essentially, to provide an enlightening analysis of the ways in which FRCs of the kind illustrated by (1.1b) differ in their syntactic properties from restrictive relative constructions, from amount constructions of the correlative type and from FRCs of other sorts. To this end, we shall proceed as follows.

In Chapter 1, we trace the historical evolution, during roughly the last fifteen years, of analytical approaches to the gross configurational properties of FRCs (in particular, to whether they are headed by *wh*-forms or by a null category) and to the special CP-internal properties alluded to earlier (that is, matching and anti-Pied-Piping effects). The FRCs considered in this first part of the chapter all exhibit a *wh*-phrase in [SPEC, C'] at S-Structure. Some old arguments for the null Head hypothesis are noted, and novel ones are adduced. It is concluded that FRCs of the kind under consideration are headed by *pro*. In Chapter 2, we examine a variety of types of FRCs which all contrast with those addressed in Chapter 1 in exhibiting an NO in [SPEC, C'] at S-Structure, rather than an overt *wh*-phrase. It is shown that these FRCs, just like the *wh*-type, exhibit the characteristic properties of amount constructions. A feature of special interest concerns the discussion of Head-Internal relatives in a number of languages, which in earlier literature were generally viewed as forming a homogeneous class. It is shown that some of them, in particular those of Quechua and Japanese (which exhibit no CP-external overt material, and are thus a kind of FRC), are *bona fide* amount constructions, while others, in particular those of Lakhota (which exhibit a CP-external determiner, and are thus a kind of OHRC), are restrictive constructions, and this despite the fact that their S-Structure internal Head is necessarily weak. Chapter 3 constitutes the 'centre of gravity' of the study, and deals with the following issues: first, it examines a number of earlier theories of *pro* which dealt with the formal and content licensing of this element in A-positions, and shows that none of them are naturally extendable to *pro* in FRC-Head position; a new theory of *pro* which successfully handles *pro* as FRC-head is then proposed, and its ability to tackle other *pro*-constructions, in particular *pro* as NO, is demonstrated. Second, it is shown in detail how the anti-Pied-Piping effects, as well as other effects found with NOs and in Head-Internal relative constructions, can be deduced from the assumption that *pro* needs to be identified at the level of S-Structure in conjunction with the ways in which the *antecedence* and *locality* conditions on *pro*'s identifier are defined. In this connection, it is demonstrated – among other things – that the failure of a linguistic element/phrase endowed with the appropriate feature specifications to satisfy either the constraints on antecedence or those on locality robs it of the ability to identify *pro*; that there can be no 'free restrictive relative' constructions; and, more generally, no 'free modifier' constructions. Third, the syntax of non-nominal FRCs is examined in detail, earlier analyses proposed in the literature are refuted, and a novel analysis is proposed and bolstered with evidence from several languages. Chapter 4 addresses various issues which concern matching effects in FRCs. On the descriptive level, cross-linguistic variation in the range of allowable non-matching options is provided with a tighter characterization than in earlier literature. On the theoretical level, it is proposed that the existence of matching effects is traceable to the FR's role as antecedent of *pro*; it is also proposed, in a more speculative vein, that the strictness/laxity of constraints on matching correlates, to a certain extent, with the morphological poverty/richness of the *wh*-phrase in respect to phi-feature specifications. Chapter 5 reinforces earlier proposals to relate properties of certain FRCs to the existence of a *pro*-Head by showing that other FRCs which demonstrably lack a *pro*-Head also lack the properties in question. Since these FRCs contrast with the amount constructions addressed in earlier sections of the chapter in exhibiting a verb in an irrealis form, I shall use 'realis' and 'irrealis' as pre-theoretical characterizations of amount constructions whose more basic distinction lies in their headed/headless status respectively. The chapter concludes with a summary of its major results.

1

The configurational properties of realis FRCs and their internal syntax effects
A critical review of earlier literature

1.1 THE *WH*-HEAD ANALYSIS

The first important attempt to come to grips with the properties of realis *wh*-FRCs was made by Bresnan and Grimshaw (1978). While these writers' ultimate interest was to argue for the existence of unbounded deletion rules in syntax (in addition to rules which move *wh*-phrases to COMP, or rather, to bring their proposal up to date, to [SPEC, C']), one of their major concerns was also the nature of the Head in FRCs of the kind under consideration. Their thesis was that, while 'true' FRCs (that is, constructions with null Heads) actually exist, the typical FRC is a special kind of OHRC.

This conclusion was argued for on the basis of certain 'matching effects' in respect to grammatical category and morphological Case which are not in general found in OHRCs. The effects in question consist of a requirement that the FRC as a whole and the *wh*-phrase that introduces it match in category/morphological Case. To illustrate the notion of 'matching' and the effects it induces, note that the FRC in (1a) is matching in category, since its initiating *wh*-phrase, 'what', is a nominal expression, and the FRC is moreover itself nominal in view of its distributional privileges (see the discussion of (1.2)–(1.3) in the Introduction). This FRC also happens to be matching in morphological Case, but only vacuously, since 'what' is not inflectable for Case. To illustrate non-vacuous Case-matching, we turn to the German example in (1.14).

```
(1.14) Ich vertraue, [wem   (immer) du   auch vertraust].
       I   trust      whom  ever    you  also trust
       'I trust whom(ever) you also trust.'
```

Note that the *wh*-phrase has the DAT(ive) form *wem*, rather than one of the NOM(inative), ACC(usative or GEN(itive) forms *wer*, *wen*, and *wessen* respectively, and that the bracketed FRC ought to receive DAT too, because the verb *vertrauen* ('to trust') assigns this particular Case to its object; accordingly, the FRC in (1.14) is matching in Case.

THE SYNTAX OF FREE RELATIVE CONSTRUCTIONS

That matching in the above sense constitutes a requirement is illustrated by the ungrammaticality of the English and German data in (1.15a) and (1.15b) respectively.

```
(1.15) a. *I have just met [about whom you spoke].
       b. *Ich vertraue, [wen (immer) du anstellst].
           I   trust       whom ever    you hire
          'I trust whom(ever) you hire.'
```

Note that the FRCs in (1.15) are (animate) verbal objects, and the natural analysis for them is thus as NPs bearing ACC and DAT Case respectively; the italicized *wh*-phrases in (1.15a) and (1.15b) are, however, a PP and an ACC NP respectively, and thus fail to match the corresponding FRCs in category ((1.15a)) and Case ((1.15b)).

It was earlier stated that matching requirements apply to *morphological*, rather than to *abstract* Case. To illustrate this point consider the following data (adapted from Groos and van Riemsdijk (1981)).

```
(1.16) a. *Ich hasse, [wer mich beleidigt].
           I   hate    who  me   insults
          'I hate who(ever) insults me.'
       b. Ich kaufe, [was dir gefällt].
          I   buy     what you pleases
          'I buy what(ever) pleases you.'
```

Note that (1.16a) and (1.16b) contrast in acceptability, although their corresponding FRCs and initial *wh*-phrases exhibit identical abstract Cases (that is, ACC and NOM respectively), so that both FRs are non-matching in respect to *abstract* Case. However, only (1.16a) is non-matching in respect to *morphological* Case, because its *wh*-phrase, *wer*, is unambiguously NOM; the *wh*-phrase in (1.16b), *was*, is interpretable as either NOM or ACC.

Matching effects of the kind illustrated above are not universal, as Bresnan and Grimshaw noted. For example, non-matching FRCs were permitted in Classical Greek (almost) freely; a few illustrative examples (from Hirschbühler (1976b), cited in Groos and van Riemsdijk (1981)) are provided below.

```
(1.17) a. Stugōn [hē (NOM) m'etikten].
          Hating who      to-me gave birth
       b. Egō (NOM) kai [hōn (GEN) egō kratō] menoumen    para soi.
          I (NOM)   and  who (GEN) I   command will-remain with you
          'I and whom I command will remain with you.'

(1.18) a. ... eidenai    tēn dunamin [eph'    hous an       iōsin].
              to-discover the strength against who  PARTICLE proceed
             '... to discover the strength (of those) against whom
              they are to proceed.'
```

11

```
b. ... dialegesthai    [par  hōn  laboien       ton misthon].
       to-give-lessons  from whom they-receive  the fee
'... to give lessons (to those) from whom they receive
     their fee.'
```

Note the contrast in grammaticality between (1.15b) and (1.17a, b). In (1.17a) the matrix verb selects an ACC object, while the italicized relative pronoun is in the NOM Case, as required by the subordinate verb; in (1.17b), the second conjunct of the matrix subject ought to be in the NOM Case, but the FRC begins with a GEN relative pronoun, as required by the subordinate verb. Note also the contrast between (1.15a) and (1.18). In (1.18a) and (1.18b) NPs occurring in place of the FRCs would receive GEN and DAT Case respectively; the FRCs begin instead with *wh*-phrases of category PP.

For ease of reference, I shall assume in what follows a descriptive tripartite typology of languages, consisting of: (i) languages that require matching under all circumstances ('matching languages'); (ii) languages that allow non-matching FRCs under certain circumstances only ('restricted non-matching languages'); and (iii) languages that allow non-matching FRCs under all circumstances ('unrestricted non-matching languages'); as we shall see in Chapter 4, the characterization in (iii) is probably too strong, there being apparently no totally non-matching languages, and the classes (ii) and (iii) will be reinterpreted in terms of whether non-matching constructions which violate certain hierarchically-defined Case restrictions are/are not permitted (for discussion see section 4.3.2). To illustrate, the contemporary stages of English, French, Italian, Russian and Hebrew appear to be of type (i); Finnish, a number of Modern Romance languages (Spanish, Catalan, Romanian) and Modern German appear to be of type (ii); and Latin, earlier stages of the Romance languages, Classical Greek, Old and Middle High German and possibly Gothic were of type (iii).

Bresnan and Grimshaw proposed the following account of matching FRCs: the initial *wh*-phrase occurs in Head, rather than in [SPEC, C'] position. Note that such an analysis, if tenable, elegantly accounts for matching effects, because a Head is expected to agree in Case and category with the construction it heads. None the less, there exist arguments based on a number of languages which show that it is not possible *in general* to account for matching effects in FRCs by appealing to the 'Head-hypothesis'. An argument based on Dutch and German data will be brought up in section 1.2.1, and one based on Hebrew data can be found in n. 9 to this study (see also Harbert (1990) for an argument based on Gothic). At this point, I should like to note two arguments against the Head-Hypothesis which rest on English data.

The first argument (which was independently discovered by Jacobsen (1988)) exploits the fact that in OHRCs whose subject has been gapped by operator movement, either a *wh*-phrase or an overt complementizer must be present (Bever and Langendoen 1971); as shown in (1.19a, b), this generalization applies to both restrictive and amount OHRCs.

(1.19) a. The man who/that/*∅ left was sick.
       b. All that/*which/*∅ pleases you pleases me.
       c. What(ever) pleases you pleases me.

If the initial *wh*-phrase of an FRC is in Head position, we may expect (1.19c) to be out; this, however, is not the case, and this state of affairs argues against the Head hypothesis. Note that no such problem arises if *what(ever)* is assumed to be in [SPEC, C'] position.

The second argument against the Head hypothesis exploits the constraints imposed by the 'focus' position of a cleft construction in English.

(1.20) a. I wonder what it is e that you saw?
       b. *Bob, who it is e that you saw, ...
       c. *The man who it is e that you saw ...
       d. *What it is e that you saw must have been scary.
       e. Whatever it is e that you saw must have been scary.
       f. *Anything (that) it is e that John buys is expensive.

The data in (1.20a)–(1.20d) suggest that a constituent that originates in the position at issue must be (emphatically, exclamatorily, etc.) stressable. Typically, interrogative, but not relative pronouns have this property; none the less, adding *-ever* to a relative pronoun makes it (exclamatorily) stressable, and (1.20e) is accordingly acceptable. Importantly, a stressable element in Head position does *not* ensure the acceptability of a relative construction whose operator is unstressable. This is shown by the unacceptability of (1.20f), where the Head *anything* is definitely stressable (cf. *ANYthing you buy is expensive!*), but where the operator moved from the focus position is null, and thus unstressable. The clear contrast between (1.20e) and (1.20f) is straightforwardly accounted for if *whatever* originates in focus position and is moved to [SPEC, C'], but not if it is assigned to the Head position.

The FRCs of Standard English are also unexpectedly different from OHRCs in disallowing complementizers after the (alleged) Head, as shown by *what (*that) he bought was expensive*. Bresnan and Grimshaw handled this fact by proposing that the relative is here an S (in current terminology, IP), rather than an S' (in current terminology, CP), which also enabled them to maintain that the 'gap' within the clause arises by deletion, rather than by movement.

With respect to non-matching FRCs, Bresnan and Grimshaw allowed for the possibility that at least some of these constructions are derived by movement of the initial *wh*-phrase to [SPEC, C'].

The Head-Analysis was put forward by Bresnan and Grimshaw not only with respect to nominal FRCs, but also for constructions like those in (1.7), which they viewed as headed by AP, AdvP or PP. An important feature of their analysis, which will be prominently addressed in section 3.4, is that in data like (1.7c) (in which, as Larson (1987) put it, a preposition is felt to be 'missing'), the initial overt P and the adjacent *wh*-phrase were assumed to be *sisters*. I provide more extensive illustration of the construction in question (which I shall henceforth call *missing-P FRC*) with data from French and English in (1.21) and (1.22) respectively.

(1.21)   a. Je le dis [*pour qui* je dois le dire].
              I it say for who I must it say
              'I say it (for the one) for whom I must say it.'
         b. Pierre s'   est battu [*avec qui* tu voulais qu' il sorte].
              Pierre self is beaten with who you wanted that he go-out
              'Pierre fought (with the one) with whom you wanted him
              to go out.'
         c. Je ne reviens pas [*de   chez qui* tu crois que je reviens].
              I not return not from at   who you believe that I return
              'I am not returning (from the one) from whom you think
              I am returning.'

(1.22)   a. I'll live [*in whatever town* you live].
         b. We'll move [*to whatever place* you think we should move].
         c. Mr. Brown died [*in whatever decade* Mr. Smith died].
         d. I'm leaving [*on whatever date* John arrives].

A feature of missing-P FRCs that I mention for the sake of completeness, even though I do not know of an interesting characterization of the phenomenon, is that not all languages permit them freely. For example, Bresnan and Grimshaw note that the English counterparts to the data in (1.21) are unacceptable. On this point, they write that missing-P FRCs are acceptable in English only when the initial *wh*-phrases have locative, directional or temporal import, as in (1.22a), (1.22b) and (1.22c, d) respectively. This characterization is however at best incomplete, because the feature which distinguishes between (1.22) and the English counterparts to (1.21) seems to be primarily the presence/absence of *-ever*; thus, a number of informants I consulted reported contrasts like the following *I (will) work for whom you work* vs *I (will) work for who(m)ever you work* (note that the *wh*-phrases are neither locative, nor directional, nor temporal). Bresnan and Grimshaw propose to account for what they take to be the correct generalization concerning cross-linguistic variation in missing-P FRCs as follows. Assuming that the in-clause gap bound to the *wh*-phrase arises not by *wh*-Movement (which is excluded by the absence of a COMP position in the clause that modifies the Head), but by the deletion of a proform of appropriate category (which may be overt or null), they attribute inter-linguistic variation to 'defective' proform-inventories in certain languages, for example, in English. This proposal is untenable if the controlling factor in English is presence/absence of *-ever* in the *wh*-forms.

THE SYNTAX OF FREE RELATIVE CONSTRUCTIONS

1.2 THE 'HEAD BY-PASS' ANALYSIS

1.2.1 Groos and van Riemsdijk's proposals

Bresnan and Grimshaw's analysis of matching effects (1978) was challenged by Groos and van Riemsdijk (1981). One particularly important objection that these writers raised was that the Head-analysis was not applicable to all instances of matching FRCs. In particular, such an analysis was argued to be insufficient in respect to matching constructions in Dutch and German for the following reasons: in subordinate clauses, simplex direct objects must occur in pre-verbal position; when a direct object is complex (in the sense of Ross (1967)), and, in particular, when it is an OHRC, the relative clause, but – crucially – not the entire complex NP, may follow the subordinate verb, as illustrated in (1.23b, c) (extraposition of the relative clause is not, however, obligatory, as shown by (1.23a)); when the direct object is an FRC, as in (1.23d), the entire (overt portion of the) FRC may extrapose, as shown by (1.23e). This state of affairs is incompatible with the assumption that *wen* in (1.23e) occupies the Head position, since it would imply a displacement of a (complex) NP across a verb, something which was seen in (1.23c) to be impossible for uncontroversial NPs. Accordingly, it appears necessary to assume that (1.23e) is parallel to (1.23b), in the sense that the clause alone has been extraposed, leaving a null Head in place.

```
(1.23) a.  Hans hat [den Boten, [den   Gretchen ihm geschickt hat],
           Hans has  the envoy  whom  Gretchen him sent        has
           empfangen.
           received
           'Hans has received the envoy that Gretchen sent him.'
       b.  Hans hat [den Boten] empfangen, [den Gretchen ihm geschickt
           hat].
       c. *Hans hat empfangen, [den Boten, [den Gretchen ihm geschickt
           hat]].
       d.  Hans hat, [wen   Gretchen ihm geschickt hat], empfangen.
           Hans has   whom  Gretchen him sent         has  received
           'Hans has received whom Gretchen sent him.'
       e.  Hans hat empfangen, [wen Gretchen ihm geschickt hat].
```

Groos and van Riemsdijk concluded that initial *wh*-phrases in German and Dutch FRCs need to be assigned to the [SPEC, C'] position and that matching effects in these languages must be accounted for in some other way (that FRCs in ACC object position are subject to at least some matching effects in German can be seen by inspecting (1.16a)). Groos and van Riemsdijk then go on to note that if a successful alternative analysis of matching effects can be found, the Head-analysis can be dispensed with in general (unless, of course, there is positive evidence to the contrary). Such an outcome, they stress, is desirable on independent grounds in view of certain additional questionable features of the Head-analysis for the constructions considered by Bresnan and Grimshaw. For example, Groos and van Riemsdijk point out that their assumption that the relative clause of matching FRCs is an S (= IP), rather than an S' (= CP), constitutes an *ad hoc* complication of the phrase-structure component of the grammar; this complication is a direct consequence of the Head-analysis and is needed, as already noted, to account for the absence of lexical complementizers or *wh*-phrases other than the one taken to be in Head position, as well as for the inability of the putative relative clause to extrapose (these properties are illustrated in (1.24), and to contrast with those of a clear case of complex NP headed by a *wh*-phrase, whose properties are illustrated in (1.25)).

(1.24) a. *What that Susan likes to eat is abominable.
       b. *What is abominable Susan likes to eat.

(1.25) a. What that Susan likes to eat is most tasty?
       b. What is most tasty that Susan likes to eat?

The alternative to the Head-analysis that Groos and van Riemsdijk put forward has the following main features: FRCs are always headed by a null category (which they do not further characterize), and the initial *wh*-phrase is always in [SPEC, C'], where it was placed by *wh*-Movement. The matching effects are attributed to a parameter, one value of which forces rules of 'regimen' (essentially, subcategorization and Case-assignment processes), to *by-pass the null Head of an FRC* and to apply to the phrase in [SPEC, C'] instead. The result of this operation is that the initial *wh*-phrase is treated by subcategorization and Case-assignment processes as if it were the Head of the FRC; hence, the matching effects in category and Case.[2] The other value of the parameter in question requires (or perhaps allows) rules of regimen to apply to specific *structural* positions, rather than to *lexically filled* positions. In languages which exhibit this value of the parameter, rules of regimen will apply to the null Head of an FRC, leaving the *wh*-phrase in [SPEC, C'] free to exhibit the category and Case of its trace; such languages will thus show no matching effects.

Groos and van Riemsdijk also turned their attention to the kind of data illustrated by (1.21)–(1.22), in connection with which they furthermore examined the status of missing-P FRCs in Dutch and German. According to them, these two languages allow no FRCs of this type, neither do they allow FRCs with a *full* nominal *wh*-phrase; in support of these contentions, they provided data like those in (1.26a) and (1.26b) respectively.

(1.26) a. *Das Buch liegt [*in was* /*worin*   auch die anderen Bücher liegen].
           the book lies   in what what-in also the other   books lie
           'The book lies (in that) in which the other books also lie.'
      b. *Ich mag [*welche Leute* du   auch magst].
           I   like which   people you also like
           'I like whatever people you also like.'

The solution which Groos and van Riemsdijk propose for data like (1.21), (1.22) and (1.26) attributes restrictions on missing-P FRCs to surface filters. According to this view, languages like French would have no filter at all, languages like English would (presumably) have a filter disallowing certain types of PPs in the [SPEC, C'] of FRs (they do not actually spell out what they have in mind for English), and languages like German and Dutch would have a filter excluding all types of missing-P FRCs; in relation to the last two languages, they also attempt to subsume the restrictions illustrated by (1.26a) and (1.26b) under a single filter (reproduced in (1.27)), which, note, also rules out non-matching nominal FRCs formed with the Pied-Piping of a preposition.

(1.27) *[e] [$_{COMP}$ W$_1$ wh W$_2$], unless W$_1$, W$_2$ = ∅

The major contribution made by Groos and van Riemsdijk to the understanding of FRCs is undoubtedly their having pointed out that not all matching effects can be accounted for in terms of the Head-analysis put forward by Bresnan and Grimshaw. Admittedly, the Head by-pass analysis is not without problems of its own, as will be seen in subsequent sections. At this point, I confine myself to noting that the filter in (1.27) does not seem to be the optimal analysis for the data it purports to cover, at the very least in so far as it seeks to bring facts like (1.26a) and (1.26b) under a single generalization. The two types of data need to be distinguished in at least some languages; for example, in English, where constructions like (1.26b) do not seem to be more restricted than FRCs with single-word *wh*-phrases, although constructions like (1.26a), while possible, are subject to certain restrictions (as noted in section 1.1). Furthermore, the two construction-types also need to be distinguished in German, because – contrary to what Groos and van Riemsdijk assert – German does *not* appear to have a blanket ban on data like (1.26a), but does seem to have a blanket ban on data like (1.26b). Thus, while my informants rejected data of the latter type, the data in (1.28) were judged basically acceptable.

(1.28) a. Achte,   [*worauf* ich dich aufmerksam mache]!
          pay-attention what-on I   you attentive   make
          'Pay attention (to that) which I draw your attention to.'
     b. Schneide das Brot, [*womit*   ich es geschnitten habe]!
          cut   the bread what-with I it cut   have
          'Cut the bread (with that) which I [earlier] cut it with!'
     c. Ich spreche [*wovon*   auch du sprichst].
          I   speak   what-from also you speak
          'I am talking (about that) which you, too, are talking about.'
     d. Ich habe nachgedacht, [*worüber*   du gesprochen hast].
          I   have reflected   what-about you spoken   have
          'I reflected (about that) about which you spoke.'
     e. Er stürzt sich [*auf wen* er sich nur   stürzen kann].
          he rushes REFL on whom he REFL only rush   can
          'He collars whoever he can.'

There is also another objectionable aspect of Groos and van Riemsdijk's proposals, in particular, the view that the Head of FRCs like those in (1.21) and (1.22) is a null *NP*, and thus that such FRCs constitute complex NPs rather than complex PPs, as Bresnan and Grimshaw had assumed; this point will be elaborated on below, when we consider the proposals in Harbert (1983).

1.2.2 Hirschbühler and Rivero's proposals

The Head by-pass analysis and other aspects of Groos and van Riemsdijk's proposals were subjected to close scrutiny in a number of subsequent studies. Two attempts to sharpen and refine the by-pass approach to matching will be presented and discussed (in respect to the points that are relevant in the present context) in this and the next section.

Hirschbühler and Rivero (1981, 1983) pointed out that the bi-valued parameter proposed by Groos and van Riemsdijk was unable to provide, by itself, a full account of linguistic variation, since, as noted in section 1.2.1, languages appear to fall into at least three groups (that is, matching, non-matching and partly non-matching). Furthermore, these writers showed that the by-pass value of the parameter is potentially capable of characterizing partially, rather than fully, non-matching languages, because not all NP positions are the targets of rules of regimen.

Specifically, Hirschbühler and Rivero pointed out that the fact that French and English exhibit category-matching effects in the position of Left-Dislocation remains unexplained, since the position in question is not a subcategorized one; furthermore, if the subject position is also viewed as outside the range of subcategorization processes (a view held by many earlier scholars), matching effects in subject position remain equally unexplained. What Hirschbühler and Rivero had to propose for fully matching languages (such as Modern French and English) is, as far as I can see, of little theoretical interest (they proposed an *ad hoc* filter). Of interest was, however, their contention that Groos and van Riemsdijk's proposals are just what is needed to account for the effects found in certain *restricted* non-matching languages; in particular Spanish and Catalan, which – according to them – exhibit category-matching effects in the positions of verbal and prepositional object, but not in the positions of subject or Left-Dislocation. Their claim was based on contrasts like those found in the following Spanish data (adapted from Suñer (1984)):

(1.29) a. [*Con quien* me quiero casar] vive a la vuelta.
       with whom me want to-marry lives at the corner
    '(The one) who I want to marry lives around the corner.'
  b. [*Con quien* me quiero casar], ése ni me da la hora.
       with whom me want to-marry that not-even me gives the time
    '(The one) with whom I want to get married, that one doesn't even give me the time of day.'

c. *Andrea tiene [de quien María tanto se burlaba] en su
    Andrea has   of whom Maria so-much self mocked in her
    clase.
    class
    'Andrea has (the one) who Maria was making so much fun of in
    her class.'
d. *Andrea salió   con [de quien María tanto se burlaba].
    Andrea went-out with of whom Maria so-much self mocked
    'Andrea went out with (the one) Maria was making so
    much fun of.'

From a historical perspective, Hirschbühler and Rivero's primary contribution to the understanding of matching phenomena lies – in my view – in their articulation of the need to distinguish between fully and partially non-matching languages and in their demonstration that Groos and van Riemsdijk's analysis did not accomplish this goal. At the same time, they did not propose a unified analysis of partial non-matching effects. In Chapter 4, I shall argue that such a unified analysis *is* possible, and that the correct analysis is *not* of the kind that Hirschbühler and Rivero proposed with respect to Romance languages.

1.2.3 Harbert's proposals

A further attempt to sharpen and improve on Groos and van Riemsdijk's Head by-pass analysis was made in Harbert (1983). Harbert considered more closely the nature of null elements in Head position, and furthermore sought to derive the presence/absence of matching requirements in various languages from general principles of linguistic theory in conjunction with independently attested properties of individual languages, rather than attribute them to an FRC-specific parameter, as Groos and van Riemsdijk did.

In relation to the status of the null Head, Harbert proposed that (at least in FRCs of category NP) this Head can only be either PRO or *pro*, but not an anaphor or variable, as there are no appropriate A- or Ā-binders. To derive the distribution of matching requirements in various languages, Harbert made a slight, but crucial modification in Groos and van Riemsdijk's assumptions. Thus instead of viewing the by-passing of a null Head as a necessary consequence of a particular fixing of a parameter, he assumed that this move constitutes an option available to government, and thus to rules of regimen (which, he assumed, depend on government), in every language. This option, together with the restriction that the Head can be only PRO or *pro*, enables the matching/non-matching effects to be derived as follows: if no mechanisms are available for identifying a *pro*-Head in some position, a PRO-Head remains the only alternative; but since PRO may not be governed, external governors of the FRC are forced to make use of the by-pass option, with the result that rules of regimen necessarily apply to the *wh*-phrase in [SPEC, C'], inducing matching effects. If, on the other hand, a *pro*-Head can be identified in some position, external governors do not need to by-pass it, since *pro* may be governed; in such a case, no matching effects will be found. Note that in a context where *pro* may not be identified *and* no governor for the FRC exists, the Head of the FRC will be PRO, but matching effects will not be found, since the absence of government implies that no rules of regimen are applicable. Harbert assumes that such a state of affairs is found in the position of left-dislocated phrases in German, in view of the acceptability of non-matching FRCs in this position (illustrated in (1.30)).

```
(1.30)  [Wonach      man eifrig    strebt], das bleibt  oft    unerreicht.
        what-after one eagerly    aspires    that remains often  unattained
        '(That) towards which one eagerly aspires, that remains often
        beyond reach.'
```

But since some languages, in particular English and French, do exhibit matching effects in the position of Left-Dislocation (as shown in (1.31)), Harbert is forced to assume that languages may vary according as the position of left-dislocated elements is governed or not.

```
(1.31) a. *[With whom you spoke], I don't want to see him any more.
       b. *[A qui    tu  as     parlé], je ne veux plus le  voir.
             to whom you have spoken   I  not want more him to-see
             (same meaning as (1.31a))
```

I find this particular proposal concerning matching effects in Left-Dislocation position quite unappealing. As far as one can tell, the position of left-dislocated phrases seems to be, in all the languages from which the examples in (1.30) and (1.31) are taken, 'higher' than [SPEC, C'], in view of data like the following, in which left-dislocated constituents are followed by a reordered *wh*-phrase (which occupies the [SPEC, C'] position).

```
(1.32) a. Maria, wer kennt sie besser als    ich?
          Maria  who knows her better than  I
       b. Marie, qui la  connaît mieux  que  moi?
          Marie  who her knows    better than me
       c. Mary, who knows her better than me?
```

In fact, note that if the alleged governor is assumed to be the verbal inflection, this element is – according to current views – even more 'remote' from the left-dislocated element at S-Structure in (1.31) than in (1.30) (in respect to V2 languages, such as German, but not in respect to French or English, it is usually assumed that the inflectional elements together with V raise to C°). The assumption of a distinction in government properties, especially in the direction conjectured by Harbert, thus seems quite implausible.

It is perhaps appropriate to note at this point that matching effects in fully matching languages are also found in A'-positions other than that of Left-Dislocation, for example, in the positions of the bracketed constituents in (1.33).

(1.33) a. *I don't like him at all, [with whom you were speaking].
       b. *Mary pursues only one kind of man: [with whoever her sister happens to go out].

Such data may seem to compound the implausibility of Harbert's proposal, in that they appear to force him into an apparently incorrect view, namely the view that the positions of the bracketed constituents in (1.33) are governed. However, these constituents seem to need to be 'reconstructed' into the direct object position in the main clause.[3] Since matching/non-matching possibilities are determined by the *pro*/PRO distribution, that is by the Binding Theory, and since the latter needs to apply after Reconstruction (as shown by data like *it's himself that John admires most*), the data in (1.33) are not problematic for Harbert.

In section 1.4.3.3, we shall see that there are strong empirical reasons against accounting for matching/non-matching contrasts in the position of Left-Dislocation in terms of a distinction in government status. An alternative which avoids these various difficulties will be presented in Chapter 3.

Let us now turn to Harbert's views on the ways in which a *pro*-Head may be identified, which are of considerable interest. He proposes two major mechanisms for Head-*pro* identification, both of which assume *FRC-external* identifiers; however, in certain cases, *FRC-internal* identifiers are also appealed to. The proposed FRC-external identifiers are governors, in particular, the AGR element of the verbal inflection and any lexical element capable of assigning Case. To achieve identification, AGR(eement) and Case must moreoever be 'sufficiently rich' morphologically (note that in respect to Case assigned by, say, a verb or preposition, morphological richness is in general *potential* richness, since Case is typically not overtly realized on FRCs).

More specifically, Harbert assumes that whenever AGR is able to identify *pro* in some position, it is also capable of identifying the *pro*-Head of an FRC that occurs in that position, in virtue of the widely held assumption that government, and features assigned or transmitted under government, 'percolate' to the Heads of governed phrases. He thus predicts that null subject languages always allow non-matching subject FRs. The claim that (unrealized) 'rich' Case can identify the Head of an FR is based on more indirect considerations. Thus as Harbert himself notes, *pro*-arguments are not automatically permitted in all Case-assignment positions. The reason for this, he suggests, is that Case alone is not sufficient for *pro* identification, number and gender being also required. Unlike AGR, which can in principle not only assign Case to *pro*, but also identify it in respect to number and gender, other Case-assigners (in particular, verbs and prepositions) cannot in general effect such identification; accordingly, argument-*pro* is not automatically licensed by verbs or prepositions, even in Case-rich languages. In the case of Head-*pro*, however, Harbert considers that, in a Case-rich language, the assignment of Case is sufficient for identification, because information on such features as number and gender is automatically provided by the *wh*-phrase with which *pro* is coindexed; in this case, then, identification is viewed as jointly effected by FRC-external and FRC-internal factors.

Harbert also considers the distribution of missing-P FRCs, such as those in (1.21) and (1.22), and criticizes Groos and van Riemsdijk on a number of points. First, he notes that (1.27) incorrectly excludes PP-initiated FRCs in left-dislocated position in German (see (1.30)); as it happens, such constructions are also incorrectly excluded in other situations (see (1.28)). Second, acceptable data like those in (1.21) are permitted, under the analysis assumed by Groos and van Riemsdijk, to violate the Projection Principle, since verbs which subcategorize for a PP fail to have this requirement satisfied at *all* syntactic levels of representation, in particular, at D-Structure; this conclusion follows directly from a somewhat curious assumption of Groos and van Riemsdijk's, namely, that FRCs overtly initiated by a *wh*-phrase of category PP are headed by a *nominal* null category, and thus constitute complex *NP*s (as can be inferred from their examples, which are reproduced as (1.34c) and (1.34d) below). This is particularly mystifying in view of the fact that they did not make such an assumption in relation to FRCs overtly initiated by APs or AdvPs, as indicated by their examples, reproduced here as (1.34a) and (1.34b).

(1.34) a. He'll grow [$_{AP}$ e [$_{AP}$ however tall] his father was].
       b. I'll word my letter [$_{AdvP}$ e [$_{AdvP}$ however] you word yours].
       c. I'll move [$_{NP}$ e [$_{PP}$ to whatever town] you move].
       d. I'll talk [$_{NP}$ e [$_{PP}$ to whoever] you talk].

To correct this defect, Harbert proposes that, at D-Structure, FRCs like those in (1.21) or (1.22) are not simply complex NPs with a null Head, but complex NPs which are furthermore objects of a preposition that is morphologically identical to the one which initiates the *wh*-phrase; this preposition is assumed to undergo a (late) deletion rule. Concerning the cross-linguistic variation in respect to the distribution of the kind of construction under consideration, Harbert proposes to assume that languages may differ in the range of applicability of the preposition-deletion rule. Thus the rule is assumed to be applicable everywhere in French; in some, but not all, environments in English; and nowhere in German (it appears that Harbert was, just like Groos and van Riemsdijk, unaware of the existence of acceptable data like those in (1.28)). Observe, however, that Harbert's analysis raises some difficulties that did not arise in connection with Groos and van Riemsdijk's analysis: non-application of the proposed deletion rule invariably yields an ungrammatical result, as illustrated with French, English and German data below (cf. (1.35a) with (1.21a) and (1.35d) with (1.26a)).

(1.35) a. *Je le dis pour [*pour qui* je dois le dire].
           I it say for   for who I must it say
   b. *I'll live in [*in whatever town* you live].
   c. *I'll work for [*for whom* you also work].
   d. *Das Buch liegt in [*in was/worin* auch die anderen Bücher liegen].
        the book lies in in what   also the other books lie

Such data cannot be accounted for by assuming that the proposed deletion rule is *obligatory*, since this would lead to a contradiction in cases like (1.35c, d) (recall that the deviance of such data *without* the leftmost prepositions was attributed by Harbert to the *inapplicability* of the rule in question). It thus appears that distinct stipulations are needed to rule out data like (1.35c, d) *with* and *without* the leftmost prepositions.

Harbert's analysis has a noteworthy feature which distinguishes it from Bresnan and Grimshaw's: he assumes that missing-P FRCs are headed by a P, but not by a PP; that is to say, he assumes that the initial P is a sister of a 'complex NP', not of a simplex one. This view was later espoused on different grounds in Larson (1987), who at the same time insisted on retaining Bresnan and Grimshaw's Head-hypothesis for the 'complex NP'. In view of the complexity of the issues involved, and also of the fact that Larson is almost exclusively concerned with non-nominal FRCs, presentation and discussion of his proposals are postponed until section 3.4.

1.3 THE *pro* IN GOVERNED POSITIONS ANALYSIS

In this section and the next, we will consider two additional approaches to the syntax of FRCs which rejected the Head by-pass mechanisms on principled grounds, while modifying and building on some of Harbert's insights; in particular, on the view that the Head of an FRC may be *pro* and that this *pro* may be (partly) identified by FRC-internal mechanisms.

This section is devoted to a review of the proposals in Suñer (1984), where the Head by-pass mechanism is rejected on grounds of inconsistency with fundamental assumptions of the GB theory, in particular, with the assumption that subcategorization entails theta-marking (that is, the assignment of thematic roles to arguments) in accordance with the Theta-Criterion (which holds that there is a 1:1 correspondence between arguments and thematic roles; for a more rigorous definition of 'Theta-Criterion' see Chomsky (1987: 335)). Note that this implies that the *wh*-phrase is assigned a theta-role in those cases where subcategorization by-passes the null Head and applies to it. But the *wh*-phrase is also part of a chain formed by movement, and thus receives the theta-role of the variable that it binds. What this means is that the *wh*-phrase receives *two* theta roles, which is inconsistent with the Theta-Criterion.

Suñer's account of the structure of FRCs and of the matching parameter, while retaining many features of Harbert's account, also makes certain small, but crucial, modifications in it. The features she retains are:

(1.36) a. The Head of an FRC is either PRO or *pro*.
     b. Non-matching FRs are found either in ungoverned positions, or when governed by 'rich' AGR or by a lexical Head capable of assigning 'rich' Case.
     c. The analysis of missing-P FRCs.

Where Suñer's account significantly differs from Harbert's is in the analysis of matching FRCs in governed positions. Such FRCs are assumed to be headed by *pro*, just like their non-matching counterparts (an assumption necessitated by the rejection of the Head by-pass option), and the matching effect is attributed to an extension of Harbert's observation that the Head of an FRC (and of restrictive/amount relatives in general, for that matter) can derive some of its feature-content (such as gender, number and person) from coindexed features on the *wh*-phrase. What Suñer in effect proposes is that, in addition to these coindexed features, which automatically exhibit identical values on *pro* and on the *wh*-phrase, agreement in respect to (morphological) Case is sufficient to effect identification of the Head-*pro*. To account for matching in category, Suñer extends the notion of *Case* to encompass prepositions as well, a move for which there is considerable empirical support (as we shall see in later sections). This extended notion of Case – which, following Grosu (1989), I shall call 'Kase' from this point on – predicts, in conjunction with Suñer's other assumptions, that whenever a Head-*pro* may not be identified by some FRC-external element, Pied-Piping of a preposition is excluded, except where the FRC is introduced by an identical preposition (as assumed in connection with (1.21)–(1.22)). To sum up, Kase-agreement of *pro* with a *wh*-phrase replaces in Suñer's account Harbert's mechanism of Head by-pass by subcategorization and Case marking rules.[4]

In addition to the kind of FRCs that we have focused on so far, and which are characterized by the fact that their verb is in a realis (in particular, the indicative) mood, Suñer also turns her attention to a type characterized by irrealis verbal forms (she in fact, somewhat incorrectly, limits her attention to infinitival constructions), and which is *not subject to matching requirements*. Some of Suñer's illustrations of the latter type (with Spanish data), which also bring out the non-matching option, are provided below.[5]

(1.37) a. Briana no encuentra [con quien salir].
     Briana not finds   with whom to-go-out
     'Briana does not find (anyone) with whom to go out.'

b. Briana no encuentra [de quien fiar-se].
   Briana not finds   of whom to-trust-self
   'Briana does not find (anyone) whom to trust.'
c. Andrea tiene [de quien burlar-se] en su clase.
   Andrea has   of whom to-mock-self in her class
   'Andrea has (someone) of whom to make fun in her class.'
d. Andrea tiene [con quien votar].
   Andrea has   with whom to-vote
   'Andrea has (someone) for whom to vote.'

The gist of Suñer's account of the two types of FRCs finds expression in the following filter, which she assumes holds at PF:

(1.38) Given the structure:

   . . . [$_{NP}$ [$_N$ pro] [$_S$, [WH-phr] [$_S$ . . . +tn . . .

then:

   pro must be non-distinct in Kase[6] from WH-phr.

As pointed out in Grosu (1989), this filter does not correctly reflect Suñer's presumed intentions, since its last line has the unintended effect of requiring that all tensed FRCs in all languages be matching. I shall assume in what follows that what Suñer really had in mind was something more like (1.39).

(1.39) Given the structure:

   . . . [$_{NP}$ [$_N$ pro] [$_S$, [WH-phr] [$_S$ . . . +tn . . .

then:

   Wh-phr can identify pro only if it is non-distinct in Kase from the latter.

This filter expresses the distinction in matching requirements between finite and non-finite FRCs by mere stipulation. In Chapter 5, it will be shown that the distinction at issue (more exactly, a distinction in matching requirements between realis and irrealis FRCs) need not be stipulated, and that it follows straightforwardly from an independently motivated structural difference between the two types.

1.4 THE INTERNALLY IDENTIFIED *pro* ANALYSIS

In Grosu (1989), I argued for a number of crucial modifications in Suñer's proposals outlined in section 1.3, and, most importantly, for the conclusion that the *pro*-Head of indicative FRCs is *always* identified (that is, licensed for content) FRC-internally. This section is a substantially expanded version of the arguments for and against specific aspects of Suñer's proposals marshalled in that earlier work.[7] Only those parts of Suñer's proposals which concern realis FRCs will be addressed here. Those concerning irrealis FRCs will be taken up in Chapter 5.

THREE STUDIES IN LOCALITY AND CASE

1.4.1 The Notion 'Kase'

As noted in section 1.3, Suñer proposes to regard prepositions as a sort of Case, which in effect means viewing both Ps and Case as special instances of a more general category, which I proposed to call 'Kase'; note that 'P(repositional) Kase' needs to be viewed as 'complex Kase', because P-objects always carry Case. I find myself in strong agreement with this view for the following reasons.

First, the notion 'Kase' has a certain initial naturalness in that Case and Ps serve essentially parallel syntactic and semantic roles in natural languages. In this connection, note that both simplex and complex Kase may be semantically empty or semantically significant; for example, the marking of *direct objects* (usually a semantically non-significant situation) may be effected either by some Case, (typically, Accusative or Partitive) or (also) by some P (such as Spanish *a* or Romanian *pe*); conversely, the marking of locatives (a semantically significant situation) may be effected either by Ps (as in English, French, etc.) or by some Case (a state of affairs found in Ugro-Finnic languages). This parallelism is, incidentally, implicitly recognized by the names of these categories in Hebrew, where 'Case' and 'preposition' are, respectively, *yaxasa* and *milat-yaxas* (note that both terms include the root *yaxas* 'relation').

Second, as Harbert (1983: 269) observes, matching effects in Case and category seem to be found either together or not at all in specific positions within various languages; this is captured naturally if matching is stated in relation to Kase.

Third, it appears that morphological identity is in general sufficient for the satisfaction of matching requirements *both* in respect to Case *and* in respect to prepositions; that is to say, identity in respect to abstract syntactic features does not seem to be necessary in either type of situation. In relation to Case, the point has already been demonstrated in (1.16). In relation to prepositions, the point is illustrated by the following Spanish data.

```
(1.40) a. Soñaba    [con  quien tú  saliste    ayer].
          I-dreamed with who   you went-out  yesterday
          'I dreamed (about the one) with whom you went out yesterday.'
       b. Escribí [a   quien viste    ayer].
          I-wrote ACC who   you-saw yesterday
          'I wrote (to the one) whom you saw yesterday.'
```

In (1.40a), which is reproduced from Suñer (1984) together with her acceptability judgements, *con* is an idiosyncratic marker required by the matrix verb *soñar* 'to dream', and at the same time serves a comitative function with respect to the *wh*-phrase; it thus arguably has distinct grammatical functions in the two clauses. In (1.40b), the matrix verb *escribir* requires an indirect object, which is marked by *a*; *a* can, however, also mark direct objects under certain circumstances, and the *wh*-phrase has a direct object role. The acceptability of the data in (1.40) suggests that, in respect to both Case and prepositions, matching need not take morphologically unrealized *syntactic* distinctions into account (however, differences in *semantic* content may cause problems; see section 4.1 for discussion of some variability in acceptability judgements with respect to (1.40a), but not (1.40b)).

Fourth, parallel behaviour of Case and prepositions is sometimes found in the phenomenon traditionally known as 'inverse Case-Attraction', which consists in the 'transmission' of the Case of the *wh*-phrase to the Head of an OHRC. A number of examples from Middle High German, cited in Paul (1904; § 345), are reproduced below.

```
(1.41) a. [Den(ACC) schatz    den(ACC) sin vater  lie],  der(NOM) wart
          the       treasure whom      his father left   that     was
          mit ir geteilt.
          with her shared
          'The treasure that his father left, that was shared with her.'
       b. [Dem(DAT) gote dem(DAT) ich da   dienen soll],  den(ACC)
          the       god  whom     I  there serve  should  that-one
          enhelfent si   mir so nicht loben.
          NEG-help  they me  so not   praise
          'The god whom I must serve, they do not thus help me
          worship him.'
       c. [Fuer alle die si    komen], die(NOM) muosen in  des      jehen.
          for  all  who they   come    those    must   them of-that tell
          'All those for whom they come, those must tell them about it.'
```

All the subcases of (1.41) exhibit a complex NP in Left-Dislocation position. Simple NPs in this position typically exhibit either the 'default' NOM Case, or the Case of the 'resumptive pronoun' in the ensuing clause, as illustrated in (1.42).

```
(1.42) Dieser Mann(NOM)/diesen Mann(ACC), den(ACC) würde ich gern
       this   man          this   man        him      would I   gladly
       einladen.
       invite
       'This man, I would gladly invite him.'
```

In (1.41a, b), however, the Head of the complex NP exhibits the Case of the *wh*-phrase, rather than NOM or the Case of the resumptive pronoun, in virtue of the (optional) application of reverse Case-Attraction. Now, observe that in (1.41c), the preposition *fuer* occurs with the Head, even though it is construed with the *wh*-phrase (as indicated by the translation). This suggests that the phenomenon under consideration is one of 'inverse *Kase*-Attraction', rather than simply one of 'inverse *Case*-Attraction'.

Fifth, the notion 'Kase' can be given a theoretical interpretation within a recent development in the theory of phrase structure, namely, the theory of Extended Projection (Grimshaw 1991). Basically, an Extended Projection consists of the projections of a *lexical* Head H plus some 'segment' of the maximal uninterrupted sequence of *functional* categories that immediately dominates the maximal projection of H (excluding the specifiers of functional categories); furthermore, the functional projections of an Extended Projection possess a 'functional rank', which corresponds directly to their hierarchical 'height'. If we view Case as a functional category (as Lamontagne and Travis (1986) proposed), then Kase constitutes, within this framework, simply the 'top' sequence of (functional) categories of a maximal nominal Extended Projection, which may be either simplex, or complex,[8] as noted above.

Sixth, an extremely important phenomenon which requires appeal to Kase is that of the anti-Pied-Piping effects to which I alluded in the Introduction to this work. These effects, which will be the object of extensive discussion below, amount roughly to the following: in *wh*-FRCs, Pied-Piping of material not included in an Extended Projection of the *wh*-element is disallowed. Thus, Kase may pied-pipe, but, for example, elements in [SPEC, D'], such as *whose*, may not.

Seventh, as will be illustrated in section 4.3.2, the P-Object position imposes far stricter constraints on non-matching than other positions, and these restrictions concern both non-matching due to Case and non-matching due to the presence of a preposition. See section 4.3.2.1 for a rationalization of this state of affairs in terms of notions to which we turn directly.

Having argued for the notion 'Kase', I now proceed to a close review of Suñer's account of matching constructions, of non-matching constructions, and of contrasts which she attributes to the occurrence of FRCs in governed vs non-governed positions.

1.4.2 Matching constructions

As noted in section 1.3, Suñer's analysis of matching FRCs purports to be expressed by the filter in (1.39), which is reproduced for convenience as (1.43) below.

(1.43) Given the structure:

    ... [$_{NP}$[$_N$ *pro*] [$_{S'}$[WH-phr] [$_S$ . . . +tn . . .

then:

    WH-phr can identify *pro* only if it is non-distinct in Kase from the latter.

In the body of her text, however, Suñer makes certain remarks which characterize the mechanism for Head-*pro* identification in a somewhat different way:

(1.44) In essence, the agreement rule (9ii) [which says '*pro* is non-distinct in Case from *WH*-phr', where 'Case', as already noted, stands for 'Kase'; A.G.] fulfills the same mission that the rule of subject–verb agreement achieves with respect to the empty subject position of null subject languages. Both rules ensure that the content of the empty category *pro* is determined [that is, identified, or licensed for content; A.G.]. This outcome unifies *pro*-determination by claiming that agreement (in person, gender, number and Case) is the crucial factor for *pro* identification. Note that in both instances the empty category is, at some level of structure, coindexed with the element that helps in its determination; in one case coindexation is with INFL, in another with the *WH*-phrase.

Observe that, according to the passage in (1.44), the identifier of *pro* is *the element coindexed with it*. But according to (1.39), the identifier is *the wh-phrase in* [SPEC, C']. While the elements characterized by the italicized expressions are coextensive in the cases Suñer (and others before her) considered, they need not be coextensive in general, in particular, in cases involving Pied-Piping, a phenomenon whose significance appears to have been largely overlooked in earlier literature. Now, in situations of this type, neither the element coindexed with *pro* nor the *wh*-phrase in [SPEC, C'] can identify *pro* under identity in Kase, as illustrated by the data in (1.45) and (1.46) respectively (the data in (1.45a) and (1.46a) are from German, the datum in (1.45b) is from Romanian).

(1.45) a. *Ich bedarf [pro$_i$(GEN) [wessen$_i$(GEN) Bild du verloren
      I need   whose   picture you lost
      hast]].
      have
      'I need (the one) whose picture you lost.'
   b. *Ion merge înaintea [pro$_i$(GEN) [a cui$_i$(GEN) poză/
      Ion walks before   whose   picture
      poză   cui$_i$(GEN) se află pe masă]].
      the-picture whose   self finds on table
      'Ion walks before (the one) whose picture is lying on the table.'

(1.46) a. *Ich bewundere [pro(ACC) [[wessen Bild](ACC) du verloren
      I admire   whose picture   you lost
      hast]].
      have
   b. *I admire [pro(ACC) [whose picture/the picture of whom] (ACC) you lost]].

Note that the result is ungrammatical even when both kinds of phrases agree in Kase with *pro*, as shown by (1.47).

(1.47) *Ich bedarf [pro(GEN) [wessen(GEN) Bildes](GEN) du auch
I need whose picture you also
bedarfst].
need
'I need (the person) whose picture you also need.'

It thus emerges that Suñer's analysis fails to account for the fact that the two kinds of phrases MUST be coextensive for *pro* to be successfully identified. One might think that empirical adequacy can be achieved by modifying Suñer's filter as follows:

(1.48) Given the structure:

... [$_{NP}$ [$_N$ *pro*$_i$] [$_{S'}$ [Y WH-phr$_i$ Z]] [$_S$ ... +tn ...

WH-phr$_i$ can identify *pro*$_i$ only if
(i) the former has the same Kase as the latter, and
(ii) Y, Z = ∅.

This may be so with respect to the data that we have examined so far; we will see, however, in section 1.4.3 that (1.48) is empirically inadequate with respect to data of another sort. I also note that (1.48) – and in particular (1.48(ii)) – is purely stipulative and not obviously related to conditions needed for *pro*-identification in other constructions; a more motivated solution will be put forward in Chapter 3.

The anti-Pied-Piping effects illustrated in (1.45)–(1.47) (and further illustrated in the next section) are not only problematic for the kind of approach adopted by Suñer with respect to internal-syntax restrictions in FRCs. It also reveals a serious empirical inadequacy in the Head by-pass approach put forward by Groos and van Riemsdijk (1981) and subsequently espoused by Hirschbühler and Rivero (1981) and by Harbert (1983) (see section 1.2). Thus that approach is unable to rule out data like (1.46), where the phrases in [SPEC, C'] satisfy both the subcategorization and the Case requirements of the corresponding matrix verbs.

Furthermore, data like (1.46) would also appear to require some special stipulation within the kind of approach advocated by Bresnan and Grimshaw (1978) (see section 1.1), which would place the entire italicized *wh*-phrases in (1.46) in Head position. They assume that the derivation of matching FRCs involves the deletion of a pronominal anteceded by the Head, as well as an empty category coindexed with a c-commanding antecedent in the output to *both movement and deletion processes* (see their rules for 'Controlled *pro* Deletion' and '*Wh*-Movement' on pp. 370 and 372 respectively). Therefore, given rules of interpretation that can apply to outputs of movement with Pied-Piping, it is unclear what would in principle prevent their application in the derivation of constructions like those in (1.46).

1.4.3 Non-Matching Constructions in A-Positions

The anti-Pied-Piping effects of which some illustrations were provided in the preceding section will be used in this section to lay bare certain empirical inadequacies in Suñer's views on Head-*pro* identification. This proposal, recall, held essentially that non-matching options are found whenever a *pro*-Head can be licensed by some *FRC-external* identifier, in particular, by 'sufficiently rich' verbal AGR or by a governor capable of assigning 'sufficiently rich' Case; such a state of affairs eliminates, according to Suñer's account, the need for Head-*pro* to be identified through *FRC-internal* mechanisms. This analysis makes a clear prediction: identification of *pro* by an external governor should enable the *wh*-phrase in [SPEC, C'] to be subject to no other constraints than those which apply to *wh*-phrases in [SPEC, C'] in OHRCs. As we shall see, however, this prediction is falsified by (at least) two types of facts. These results, in conjunction with certain considerations of a conceptual nature, will lead us to the conclusion that Head-*pro* is always identified FRC-internally. I discuss the consequences of identification by AGR and by (external) Case in separate sections, and in that order.

1.4.3.1 AGR as FRC-external Identifier

A first prediction made by the hypothesis that AGR can identify the Head of, say, a subject coindexed with it is that in positions where subject *pro* is acceptable, non-matching FRCs should in general be no less acceptable. This, however, does not appear to be the case.

Adams (1987) proposes that English has *pro* subjects in imperative constructions, the absence of ('rich') AGR being in this case irrelevant because the feature [PERSON] has a constant value (that is, '2'). Since English imperative constructions also allow overt subjects, and since FRCs, and thus their Heads, are invariably [3PERSON], we may expect, under Suñer's proposals, that non-matching FRCs should have the same acceptability as matching ones. However, as shown in (1.49), the contrast between matching and non-matching FRCs is as strong as elsewhere in the language.

(1.49) a. [Whoever I happen to look at] stand up!
      b. *[At whoever I happen to look] stand up!

The prediction we are investigating is also disconfirmed with respect to a language where *pro* subjects are more widely allowed than in English, that is, Modern Hebrew. Borer (1989) notes that *pro* subjects are freely permitted in the first and second persons of the past and future tenses, and typically require a 'controller' in the superordinate clause in the third person of the tenses just mentioned (because AGR is apparently not sufficiently 'rich' to effect identification unaided); in the present tense, where AGR is morphologically defective for [PERSON], *pro* subjects are disallowed, except in generic constructions, where the subject is necessarily [3PERSON], as illustrated in 1.(50).

(1.50) a. *pro* nidme li še   hu xole
              seems me that   he sick
        'It seems to me that he is sick.'
     b. *pro* omrim   še hu xole
              say.PRES.PL   that he sick
        'They say (i.e., it is said) that he is sick.'

Borer's claim that third person *pro* subjects in the past or future tense require an antecedent is perhaps too strong, since informants accept data like (1.51) in appropriate contexts, for example, as a reply to 'where is your secretary?' (for additional counterexamples to Borer's characterization of the distribution of subject *pro*'s in Hebrew, see Ariel (1990: § 6.1)).

(1.51) *pro* itaxen še *pro* taxzor   be-karov.
            likely that   return.FUT.3.SG.F. in-close
       '(It) is likely that (she) will return soon.'

But even if we discount such data, the feature [PERSON] – which, when insufficiently 'rich', prevents *pro* subjects, – should cause no problems in respect to the Head of an FRC, which, as noted above, is always [3PERSON]. Accordingly, we may expect non-matching FRCs to occur freely in subject position. However, this is definitely not so, not even in the past or future tenses, as illustrated in (1.52).

(1.52) a. Itaxen še [mi še   xipsa   otxa]   taxzor
          likely that who-that sought.F. you.SG.M. return.FUT.2.SG.F
          be-karov.⁹
          in-close
          'It is likely that (the female person) who was looking for you
          will return soon.'
       b. *Itaxen še [et -mi -še   xipasta]   taxzor be-karov.
          ACC -   who - that   you-sought.M.
          'It is possible that (the female person) whom you were looking
          for will return soon.

Finally, the prediction we are investigating is also sometimes problematic in respect to (unrestricted) *pro*-subject languages which tolerate non-matching subject FRCs, in particular Spanish and Romanian. Thus, null subject sentences like the reduced versions of (1.53a) and (1.53b) are perfectly natural, in fact preferred to the full versions in cases which do not require emphasis on the parenthesized subjects.

(1.53) a. (Ellos) salieron hace dos minutos.
              they   went-out makes two minutes
          'They went out two minutes ago.'

b. (Ei) abia au plecat.
   they just have left
   'They have just left.'

Non-matching subject FRCs are admittedly possible, as illustrated by (1.29b) (repeated below) and (1.54).

(1.29) b. [Con quien me quiero casar], ése ni   me da   la hora.
          with whom me want to-marry that not-even me gives the time
          'The one) with whom I want to get married, that one doesn't
          even give me the time of day.'

(1.54) a. [Cui   i   se dă   de mîncare]
          who.DAT him.DAT self give of food
          trebuie să muncească.
          must   SP work.3
          '(He) to whom food is given must work.'
       b. [Cu   cine iese   Maria] e deobicei un om de nimic.
          with who goes-out Maria is usually   a   man of nothing
          '(He) who Maria goes out with is usually a no-good.'

None the less, such constructions have marginal status for many speakers. Suñer (1884: n.2) notes this fact in relation to Spanish ('some native speakers feel ill at ease with non-matching FRs'), and many Romanian speakers I consulted also accepted data like (1.54) only after some initial hesitation. Furthermore, such marginality is more pronounced with certain Kase-markers than with others; for example, with locative Kase, as illustrated below.

(1.55) a. Casa   [unde/ în care locuieşte Maria] nu se   poate vinde.
          the-house where in which lives   Maria not self can   sell
          'The house where/in which Maria lives cannot be sold.'
       b. ?*[Unde/ în ce locuieşte Maria] nu se poate vinde.
          where in what

In fact, it seems to be mostly in proverbs, such as the one in (1.56), that all speakers of Romanian feel completely comfortable with non-matching FRs.

(1.56) [Pe cine nu -l   laşi   să   moară] nu te lasă
       ACC who not-him let.2.SG. SUBJ die.3. not you let.3.
       să   trăieşti.
       SUBJ live.2.SG.
       'Whom you won't allow to die will not allow you to live.'

Potentially significant in this connection is the fact that Hirschbühler and Rivero (1981) provide only proverbs as illustrations of their claim that Catalan is non-matching in subject position (one such illustration is reproduced in (1.57)).

(1.57) [A qui l'adulació   halaga], si la pren la paga.
       to who the-flattery pleases if her takes her pays
       '(He) who likes flattery and accepts it, pays for it.'

All in all, non-matching subject FRCs in Romanian and Spanish (and possibly in Catalan) seem to have the status of marked constructions, which may well be in the process of disappearing (see section 4.2.2 for discussion of this point). Suñer herself suggests in the footnote referred to above that the somewhat marginal status of Spanish non-matching FRCs may reflect a tendency for non-matching FRCs to drop out of the language. If so, the marginality of non-matching subject FRCs in Spanish and Romanian is unexpected under the hypothesis that *pro* is identified by AGR, since – as already noted – null subjects (which, by hypothesis, are identified by AGR) are perfectly natural for everybody.

We now proceed to investigate the predictions made by the hypothesis that AGR can identify Head-*pro* with respect to Pied-Piping constructions, that is, the prediction that Pied-Piping need not be more restricted than in restrictive OHRCs. As it turns out, this prediction is strongly disconfirmed. In fact, Pied-Piping of material not included in an Extended Projection of the *wh*-element appears to be systematically excluded even in contexts where matching is not required. To see this, compare Pied-Piping possibilities in subject restrictive OHRCs and in FRCs in Romanian.

(1.58) a. Individul   [al cărui cîine/cîinele căruia muşcă trecătorii]
          the-individual whose   dog the-dog whose bites the-passers-by
          trebuie amendat.
          must   fined
          'The individual whose dog bites those who walk by must be fined.'
      b. *[Al cui cîine/cîinele cui muşcă trecătorii]   trebuie amendat.
           whose dog   the-dog whose

(1.59) a. Individul   [cu ale cărui tablouri/cu   tablourile
          the-individual with whose   pictures with the-pictures
          căruia a fugit Maria] a depus   plîngere la poliţie.
          whose has run   Maria has deposited complaint at police
          'The individual with whose pictures Maria ran away has
          complained to the police'
      b. *[Cu ale cui tablouri/ cu   tablourile   cui a fugit
           with whose pictures with the-pictures whose
           Maria] a depus plîngere la poliţie.

(1.60) a. Elevul   [mîndru de care nu e nici un profesor]
          the-pupil proud of who not is no a teacher
          n- are ce   căuta în şcoala   noastră.
          not has what look-for in the-school our
          'The pupil that no teacher is proud of has no
          place in our school.'
      b. *[Mîndru de cine nu e nici un profesor] n-are ce
           proud of who
           căuta în şcoala noastră.

Note also that similar contrasts arise in Spanish, as illustrated below.

(1.61) a. El tipo [con cuya foto María se fué]
         the guy with whose picture Maria self went
         es muy simpático.
         is very pleasant
         'The guy with whose picture Maria went away is very pleasant.'
      b. *[Con la foto de quien María se fué] es muy simpático.
          with the picture of who

As a final piece of disconfirmation of the hypothesis we are testing, observe that Pied-Piping of an NP is excluded in imperative subject position in English (where, as noted above, *pro* subjects are allowed).

(1.62) *[Whose clothes I look at] stand up!

Summarizing the results of this section, the acceptability of *pro* subjects in some context in no way implies that non-matching or pied-piped FRCs are (equally) acceptable in that context, nor does a non-matching option in some context imply a Pied-Piping option in the same context. This state of affairs casts serious doubt on the hypothesis that AGR can identify the *pro*-Head of an FRC, and points to the possibility – which will be extensively argued for in Chapter 3 – that the *pro*-Head needs to be identified by the FR in some way.

1.4.3.2 Rich Case as FRC-external identifier

We now proceed to test the predictions of the Harbert/Suñer view that, in the absence of coindexation with AGR, rich Case assignable by an FRC's governor can identify the FRC's *pro*-Head (in conjunction with FRC-internal mechanisms). Recall that a *pro* argument is not necessarily possible in just any rich-Case position, so that the presumption concerning the (partial) identifying ability of rich Case arises solely from the availability of the non-matching option. The prediction we wish to test is then that, in rich-Case positions where non-matching is allowed, Pied-Piping of material other than Kase is also allowed. As we shall see, this prediction fares no better than the one we investigated in section 1.4.3.1.

We begin by a consideration of a number of restricted non-matching languages. First, consider Finnish, a language with an exceptionally rich Case system, which Harbert explicitly cites in support of the proposal at issue. As reported on in Bresnan and Grimshaw (1978), Finnish permits non-matching in object position subject to a Hierarchy of Case-Markedness, in the sense that the Case of the *wh*-phrase cannot be less 'marked' than that of *pro*; the unmarked Cases of Finnish are NOM, ACC, and PART(itive) (possibly, the structurally assigned Cases); the marked Cases are all the others, in particular EL(ative).[10] A grammatical non-matching construction cited by Bresnan and Grimshaw is reproduced in (1.63).

(1.63) Valitsen [pro(PART) [mistä(EL) sinä pidät]].
I-choose   what   you like
'I choose what you like.'

The hypothesis under investigation predicts that, in unmarked-Case positions, Pied-Piping should be no more restricted in FRCs than it is in OHRCs. As can be seen by comparing (1.64a) and (1.64b), this prediction is false.

(1.64) a. Valitsen kalan [minkä väristä sinä pidät].
          I-choose fish   whose colour you like
          'I choose a fish whose colour you like.'
       b. *Valitsen [pro(PART) [minkä   väristä](EL)
                                whose(INANIM) colour
          sinä pidät].
          you like
          'I choose (something) whose colour you like.'

Significantly, the bracketed string of (1.64) *minkä väristä sinä pidät* is acceptable when used as a question meaning 'which thing's colour do you like?', and is perceived as deviant only when used as an FRC.

A second language which provides counter-evidence to the hypothesis under investigation is Romanian. Romanian has some morphological Cases, in particular, a distinction between NOM/ACC and DAT/GEN in animate *wh*-pronouns, further distinctions by means of the dummy ACC preposition *pe* and the dummy GEN preposition *a* being sometimes possible. As we shall see in more detail in Chapter 4, non-matching in Romanian is also governed by a Hierarchy of Case-Markedness (more exactly, Kase-Markedness), in particular, by the hierarchy 'NOM<Other'. Since inanimate direct objects are morphologically indistinct from NOM, non-matching is basically acceptable in inanimate direct object position, as illustrated in (1.65).

(1.65) a. Nu vom   putea obţine
          not will-we can   obtain
          [cu ce   plănuiam   să   ne construim o nouă casă].
          with what planned-we SUBJ us build   a new house
          'We will not be able to get (that) with which we
          were planning to buy a new house.'
       b. Nu aş   dori să   retrăiesc
          not would-I wish SUBJ relive
          [la ce   ai   făcut aluzie mai înainte].
          at what have.2.SG. made allusion more before
          'I would not like to relive (that) which you
          hinted at a few moments ago.'

Since Romanian does not have verb–object agreement, a proponent of the Harbert/Suñer hypothesis would have to assume that the Heads of the FRs in (1.65) are licensed by Case. This in turn gives rise to the prediction that

THE SYNTAX OF FREE RELATIVE CONSTRUCTIONS

Pied-Piping in FRCs should be as free as in OHRCs; this prediction is disconfirmed by contrasts like those in (1.66) and (1.67).

(1.66) a. Propun   să   discutăm situaţia   [mîndru de care
       I-propose SUBJ discuss the-situation proud of which
       ˌnu e niciunul dintre noi].
       not is none   among   us
       'I propose that we discuss the situation which none of us is proud of.'
    b. *Propun să discutăm [mîndru de ce nu e niciunul dintre noi].
       'I propose that we discuss (that) which none of us is proud of.'

(1.67) a. Ţi -am   adus   articolul   [nişte comentarii despre care
       you-have.1 brought article-the   some   comments   about which
       au   apărut în presă].
       have   appeared in press
       'I have brought you the article some comments about which have appeared in the press.'
    b. *Ţi-am adus [nişte comentarii despre ce au apărut în presă].
       'I have brought you (that) some comments about which have appeared in the press.'

A third language that provides counterevidence to the hypothesis at issue is Modern German. As we shall see in Chapter 4, Modern German is – contrary to what Groos and van Riemsdijk (1981) and Harbert (1983) asserted (see sections 1.2.1 and 1.2.3 respectively) – a restricted non-matching language, where non-matching is governed by the Hierarchy of Kase-Markedness 'NOM<ACC<Other'; the possibility of non-matching in ACC object position is illustrated by the following datum (from Pittner (1991)).

(1.68) Sie lädt   ein, [pro(ACC) wem(DAT) sie
       she -vites in-   whom   she
       zu Dank   verpflichtet ist]
       to thanks obligated   is
       'She invites (those) towards whom she has obligations.'

The hypothesis we are testing makes the prediction that, so long as the *wh*-phrase (and perhaps the *wh*-word) is not NOM, Pied-Piping in ACC object position should be as free for FRCs as it is for OHRCs; the contrast in (1.69) shows that this prediction is incorrect.

(1.69) a. Sie lädt   diejenigen(ACC) ein, deren Freunden(DAT)
       she -vites those   in- whose friends
       sie zu Dank   verpflichtet ist.
       she to thanks obligated   is
       'She invites those, towards whose friends she has obligations.'
    b. *Sie lädt   ein, [pro(ACC) [wessen Freunden](DAT)
       she -vites in-   whose   friends

```
        sie zu Dank    verpflichtet ist.
        she to thanks  obligated    is
        'She invites (those) towards whose friends she has
        obligations.'
```

Let us now consider how the prediction we are investigating fares in respect to the kind of languages that I proposed to call, with certain reservations, 'unrestricted non-matching'. For presumably fortuitous reasons, all the languages of this type that I have seen mentioned in the literature (Latin, Classical Greek, Gothic and earlier stages of German, French and Spanish) appear to be dead languages, which makes it naturally difficult to obtain direct disconfirmation of the hypothesis, if it is false. None the less, a thorough search through compendious reference grammars of Latin, Greek and Middle High German has failed to yield a single mention of Pied-Piping of anything other than Kase in any *governed* position, although various possibilities involving non-matching were abundantly illustrated. In fact, Hermann Paul (1920: IV, § 411) makes the following statement, which in effect rules out Pied-Piping of material other than Kase in governed FRCs: 'Ein von einem Subst. abhängiger Gen. FORDERT, weil er erst mit dem Subst. zusammen ein Satzglied bildet, IMMER RUECKBEZIEHUNG, vgl. *wes Brot ich esse, des Lied ich singe*, wo *des* unentbehrlich ist' (a genitive dependent on a noun *always requires a subsequent resumptive pronoun,* cf. *whose bread I eat, his song I sing,* where *his* is indispensable) [my emphasis A.G.]; in modern terminology, Paul's statement says that Pied-Piping induced by the re-ordering of an adnominal genitive (i) was not permitted in governed positions, but (ii) was permitted in a position of Left-Dislocation. The need for a resumptive pronoun in Paul's particular example is probably due to independent reasons, since a gap induced by the reordering of the FRC from the position of the resumptive pronoun was undoubtedly ruled out by whatever principle excludes data like (1.70).

```
(1.70) *Wessen isst du [e Brot]?
        whose  eat  you  bread
      '*Whose do you eat [e bread]?'
```

None the less, Paul's statement, viewed against the background of his extremely rich illustration of a variety of non-matching and Case-Attraction possibilities, can certainly be construed to imply the points (i) and (ii) above.

Things being as they are, I feel justified in making the strongest assumption consistent with the available evidence, and I thus put forward the claim that the following descriptive statement holds:

(1.71) In governed positions,[11] realis FRCs formed by reordering a *wh*(-like) element to the FR's [SPEC, C'] *universally* disallow Pied-Piping of material not included in an Extended Projection of the element coindexed with the *pro*-Head.

THE SYNTAX OF FREE RELATIVE CONSTRUCTIONS

The statement just made qualifies the restriction on Pied-Piping by reference to 'material included in an Extended Projection of the element coindexed with the Head', because Pied-Piping is not disallowed *in general*, as can be seen from the following data:

(1.72) a. I will hire [pro$_i$ [[whatever people]$_i$
          you want to work with]]
     a'. I will hire [pro$_i$ [[whatever friends of John]$_i$ you
          want to work with]].
     a". I will hire [pro$_i$ [[whatever people that you
          manage to assemble]$_i$ you want to work with]].
     b. *I will hire [pro$_i$ [[with [whatever people]$_i$] you want
          to work]]
     c. *I will hire [pro$_i$ [[[whatever worker]$_i$'s wife] does
          not make too much trouble]]

In all the subcases of (1.72), the *wh*-word is, under most current analyses (but see section 2.4), the D(eterminer) of a nominal expression which also includes a noun (in fact, an N^2 complement to D, if the latter is analysed as a functional Head). Mere Pied-Piping of the complement of a *wh*-D (which is included in all the projections of the latter) causes no problems, as shown by the perfect acceptability of (1.72a); nor do problems arise when the complement of a *wh*-D has itself a complement or a sister relative clause, as shown by (1.72a') and (1.72a") respectively. It is only the Pied-Piping of material *not included in an Extended Projection of the wh-word* which leads to unacceptability, as illustrated by (1.72b) and (1.72c).

1.4.3.3 FRCs in ungoverned positions

As noted in sections 1.2.3 and 1.3, Harbert (1983) and Suñer (1984) address the fact that (realis) FRCs in a position of Left-Dislocation sometimes exhibit matching effects and sometimes do not. I reproduce below some of the earlier examples which illustrate this state of affairs, adding the Romanian data in (1.73).

Non-matching disallowed

(1.17) a. *[With whom you spoke], I don't want to see him any more.
     b. *[A qui tu as   parlé], je ne veux plus le voir.
          to whom you have spoken I not want more him to-see
            (same meaning as (1.17a))

Non-matching allowed

(1.15b) [Con quien me quiero casar], ése   ni
         with who   me want   marry   that-one not-even
         me da   la hora.
         me gives the hour

39

'(The one) with whom I want to get married, that one wouldn't even give me the time of day.'

(1.30) [Wonach   man eifrig strebt], das bleibt oft
        what-after   one eagerly aspires   that remains often
        unerreicht.
        unattained
        '(That) towards which one eagerly aspires, that remains often beyond reach.'

(1.73) a. [Cui(DAT) i   se   dă   de mîncare], ăla
          who   him self it-gives of food   that-one
          să muncească!
          SP eat.3.
          '(The one) to whom food is given, let him work!'
       b. [Cu   cine iese   Maria], ăla   e deobicei
          with whom goes-out Maria   that-one is usually
          un om de nimic.
          a man of nothing.
          '(The one) with whom Maria goes out, that one is usually a no-good.'

In section 1.2.3, I raised conceptual objections against the mechanism envisaged by Harbert as responsible for contrasts like the above, specifically against the view that the presence/absence of matching effects in the position under consideration is due to its being, respectively, governed/ungoverned (I argued that this position is ungoverned in general). Since Suñer's view of such data is basically the same as Harbert's, with the additional twist that she allows for the alternative possibility that the absence of matching effects in null-subject languages like Spanish or Romanian might be due to government by the 'rich' AGR, the same objections hold against her account as well. Also in section 1.2.3, I promised to provide additional empirical evidence against the view that the kind of contrast just illustrated can be accounted for in terms of a difference in government status; we are now in a position to fulfil this promise.

The proposal to account for non-matching effects in the Left-Dislocation position by assuming either that a *pro-* Head is licensed by 'rich' governing AGR or that a PRO-Head (which is presumed not to need local identification) is licensed by non-government leads to the expectation that Pied-Piping in this position should be as free in FRCs as it is in OHRCs. However, this prediction is in general not fulfilled, as can be seen in relation to the following data from Romanian and Spanish (I omit any demonstration of the fact that the kind of Pied-Piping displayed in the various bracketed FRCs is permitted in comparable OHRCs).

(1.74) a. *[A cui fotografie/fotografia cui   atîrnă pe perete],
          whose picture   the-picture whose hangs on wall
          ăla   nu mă poate suferi.
          that-one not me can   bear

'(The one) whose picture is hanging on the wall,
that one can't stand me.'
b. *[Cu a cui carte/cu cartea cui a fugit
with whose book with the-book whose has run-away
Maria], ăla se va plînge poliţiei.
Maria that-one self will complain to-the-police
'(The one) with whose book Maria ran away, that one will
complain to the police.'
c. *[Mîndru de cine nu e nici un profesor], ăla va
proud of who not is no a teacher that-one will
trebui să părăsească şcoala.
must SP leave the-school
'(The one) that no teacher is proud of, that one
will have to leave this school.'

(1.75) *[Con la foto de quien María se fué],
with the picture of who Maria self went
ése es muy simpático.
that-one is very pleasant
'(The one) with whose picture Maria went away,
that one is a very pleasant person.'

The clear deviance of (1.74) and (1.75) refutes the view that FRCs in the position of the bracketed constituents are headed by an externally identified *pro* or by a PRO which needs no external or internal identification.

In section 1.2.3, I noted that FRCs occurring in certain ungoverned positions at S-Structure may none the less be viewed as governed following reconstruction (see data in (1.33)). Such FRCs exhibit, as expected, the essential tolerance for non-matching and the intolerance for unrestricted Pied-Piping that characterizes the position 'into which' reconstruction operates (see (1.76) and (1.77)), and are thus neutral with respect to the point considered in the preceding paragraph.

(1.76) a. Maria e întotdeauna dispusă să cumpere aşa ceva
Maria is always ready to buy so something
(adica): [la ce se uită copiii ei
i.e. at what REFL looks children-the her
cu jind].
with craving
'Maria is always ready to buy this sort of thing (i.e.):
what her children stare at cravingly.'
b. Pe Maria o interesează un singur bărbat
ACC Maria her interests one single man
(şi anume): [cu cine s -a încurcat
and specifically with whom REFL-has involved
sora ei].
sister-the her
'Maria is interested in one man only (specifically):
who her sister got involved with.'

(1.77) a. *Maria e întotdeauna dispusă să cumpere așa ceva (adică):
Maria is always ready to buy so something
[reclamele despre ce le -a atras
the ads about what them-has attracted
atenția copiilor ei].
attention-the children.DAT her
'Maria is always ready to buy this sort of thing (namely):
(that) the ads about which has attracted her
children's attention.'

b. *Pe Maria o interesează un singur bărbat
ACC Maria her interests one single man
(și anume): [al cui frate îi face curte
and specifically whose brother her makes court
soră -sii] /[cu al cui frate s -a
sister-her.DAT/with whose brother REFL has
încurcat sora ei].
involved sister her
'Maria is interested in one man only (i.e.)
(the one) whose brother is courting her sister/ with whose
brother her sister got involved.'

The data brought up so far in this section (except for (1.76)–(1.77)) indicate that lack of government cannot confer on FRCs the internal–syntax privileges of OHRCs any more than 'rich' AGR or 'rich' Case can. This result also casts doubt on the claim that these various notions, that is, 'rich' AGR, 'rich' FRC-external Case and/or lack of government, are the factors responsible for non-matching possibilities.

The facts presented so far in this section suggest that the descriptive statement (1.71) is true even if the initial qualification 'in governed positions' is eliminated. There is however one type of construction which represents a *prima facie* counterexample to the generalized version of (1.71), and which was brought up in the quotation from Herman Paul in section 1.4.3.2 (I reproduce his example in (1.78)).

(1.78) Wes Brot ich esse, des Lied ich singe.
whose bread I eat his song I sing
'(He) whose bread I eat, it is his song that I sing.'

Example (1.78) is obviously a proverb, but such constructions can be formed productively in Modern German as well; for example, (1.79) was judged fully acceptable by my informants.

(1.79) [Wessen Frau du verführst], dessen Zorn muss du fürchten.
whose wife you seduce his anger must you fear
'(He) whose wife you seduce, it's his anger that you must fear.'

Some informants were slightly uncomfortable with comparable constructions where the *w*-pronoun and the R(esumptive) P(ronoun) were not in structurally parallel positions (as, for example, in (1.80a)), but none the less rated such data as vastly better that comparable ones with an FRC in subject position (for example, (1.80b)).

(1.80) a. (?) [*Wessen Frau* du verführst], der wird dich immer hassen.
              whose wife you seduce   he will you always hate
           '(He) whose wife you seduce, that one will always hate you.'
    b. *[*Wessen Frau* du verführst] wird dich immer hassen.
       '(He) whose wife you seduce will always hate you.'

In Grosu (1989), I proposed to regard (relatively) acceptable data like those in (1.80) as exhibiting instances of PRO-headed FRCs. At this stage, I no longer wish to maintain this analysis, and this for both empirical and principled reasons.

On the empirical side, we would expect PRO-headed FRCs to occur precisely where PRO may occur. This seems, in any event, to be the prediction made by the Harbert/Suñer account, which assumes that PRO-headed FRCs are possible in some Left-Dislocation positions precisely because those positions are ungoverned (they evidently assume that PRO may not be governed, as maintained, for example, in Chomsky (1981)). However, as was seen in the Introduction, FRCs are *not* possible in the typical PRO-positions (I reproduce the relevant data below).

(1.5) a. [PRO]/[*Bill] to speak out now would be a mistake.
    b. [PRO]/[*Who(ever) had that crazy idea] to speak
       out now would be a mistake.

The contrasts in (1.5) are in fact hardly surprising, if we note that the various approaches to PRO-licensing have assumed that the conditions which license PRO and those which license overt nominal expressions are mutually exclusive (data like *John wants PRO to go* and *John wants Mary to go* have in general been handled by assuming two homophonous verbs *want* with slightly different properties). For example, Chomsky and Lasnik (1991) argue convincingly that PRO is a 'minimal argument' bearing 'null Case'; an FRC, on the other hand, is undoubtedly an overt expression, in fact, an R-expression, and thus ought to bear non-null Case. Since the conditions on PRO and on R-expressions are mutually incompatible, a PRO-headed FRC would be a self-contradictory construction; accordingly, it cannot exist.

For these various reasons, I propose to regard realis FRCs as invariably headed by *pro*. As for the (surprising) acceptability of data like those in (1.79) and (1.80a), I suggest in section 3.2.6 that the left-dislocated amount relatives are not FRCs, but 'bare' correlative-like clauses, which, as will be seen, are consistent with unrestricted Pied-Piping.

2

The syntax of Null-Operator realis FRCs

INTRODUCTORY REMARKS

In Chapter 1, we discussed in detail the properties of realis FRCs characterized by the presence at S-Structure of an overt phrase in the FR's [SPEC, C']. We have seen that these are amount, rather than restrictive constructions, that their external syntax appears to be essentially the same as that of homocategorial simplex expressions, and that their internal syntax exhibits two special features: (i) (presumably) universal anti-Pied-Piping effects, and (ii) language- and construction-specific Kase-matching effects. In this chapter, we will briefly examine a number of FRC-types which, descriptively, share the property of *not* exhibiting an overt phrase in the FR's [SPEC, C']; it will be proposed, and further argued for in Chapter 3, that in all these FRC-types, an NO is present in [SPEC, C'] at S-Structure. All constructions known to me that have this property are of the *nominal* kind; accordingly, only such constructions will be discussed and illustrated in this section.

In respect to the semantic status of these constructions, they appear to belong to the amount type, just like *wh*-FRCs. This point is easiest to demonstrate in relation to Head-Internal relatives (discussed in section 2.4), where all three properties noted in the Introduction can be detected. The constructions discussed in sections 2.1–2.3. exhibit one clearly verifiable property, that is, necessary construal as a definite nominal. The remaining two properties are difficult to check, for objective reasons that will become clear below (see section 2.5), but the one verifiable property still supports an amount analysis.

As far as their syntactic properties are concerned, they seem to have, much like nominal *wh*-FRCs, the typical distribution of (uncontroversial) nominal phrases. In respect to their internal syntax, the fact that they are formed with an NO excludes any kind of Pied-Piping, and thus rules out on independent grounds any possible violation of matching or anti-Pied-Piping requirements.

2.1 FRCs WITH A REORDERED NULL OPERATOR

The NO strategy is used in English to form OHRCs of both the restrictive and the amount variety, and both with and without an overt complementizer, as shown in (1.81).

(1.81) a. The cat [*NO* (that) I told you I found *e* outside] . . .
      b. All [*NO* (that) I told you I found *e* outside] . . .

In some languages, this strategy is used not only for OHRCs, but also for FRCs. Illustrations of such FRCs are provided in the (b) subcases of the following sets of data (the (a) subcases exhibit corresponding OHRCs). The data in (1.82)–(1.83) are from Turkish and are taken from Kornfilt (1984: Ch. 5); the data in (1.84) are from Chinese and are taken from Huang (1984), with inconsequential adaptations; the data in (1.85) are from (an elevated register of) Modern Hebrew. The Turkish and Chinese data exhibit no overt complementizer, the Hebrew data (necessarily) do. The analysis of the ensuing data in terms of NOs is based on the existence of a 'gap', as well as on usual diagnostics for movement to [SPEC, C'] (such as Subjacency effects; illustration omitted).

(1.82) a. [[[Bu   hava   -da e_i deniz-e gir -en   -ler]
          this weather-LOC   sea -in enter-PARTIC-PL
          NO_i] çocuk-ler$_i$] fazla   açıl -na -stn(lar).
          child-PL   too-much open -NEG -IMPER (PL)
          'The children who go into the sea by such weather shouldn't swim too far.'
    b. [[[Geçen yaz   ada   -da e_i gör-düğ   -üm] NO_i] kişi -ler]
        last summer island-LOC   see-PARTIC-1 -SG   person-PL
        bu   yaz   gel -ne -di(ler).
        this summer come-NEG-PAST(3.PL)
        'The people who(m) I saw on the island last summer didn't come this summer.'

(1.83) a.   [Bu   hava- da *e* deniz-e gir- en-   ler]
          this weather-LOC   sea -in enter-PARTIC-PL
          fazla   açıl -na-   sın(lar).
          too-much open- NEG-   IMPER(PL)
          '(Those) who go into the sea in such weather shouldn't swim too far'.
    b.   [Geçen yaz   ada- da   *e* gör-dük- ler- in]
        last summer island-LOC   see-PARTIC-PL- 1.SG
        bu   yaz   gel- ne- di(ler).
        this summer come-NEG-PAST(3.PL)
        '(Those) who(m) I saw on the island last summer didn't come this summer.'

(1.84) a.   [[ni   mai *e* de]   *NO*] shu. . . .
          you buy   PARTICLE   book

'The book that you bought ...'
```
       b. [[ni    mai e de]      NO]   pro
           you buy   PARTICLE
          'That which you bought ...'

(1.85) a. Bo    nidaber       al     ha -davar [ašer raita      e].
          come we-will-talk about the-thing   that you-saw
          'Let's talk about the thing that you saw.'
       b. Bo    nidaber       al    [ašer raita       e].
          come we-will-talk about   that you-saw
          'Let's talk about what you saw.'
```

As far as I can tell from the literature, such FRCs have the essential distribution of simplex NPs. In relation to their internal syntax, note that mismatches in morphological Kase cannot in principle arise, because NOs bear no morphological Kase; we may say either that these constructions are necessarily vacuously matching, or that the issue of (non-)matching is inapplicable here. In relation to Pied-Piping, it is also invariably excluded, because NOs *in general* (that is, not just in FRCs) cannot trigger Pied-Piping of *any* kind, not even of a preposition (Bresnan 1977; Chomsky 1977; Browning 1987); in general, displaced null elements seem unable to 'drag along' overt material, a point to which I return in section 3.2.3.

2.2 FRCs WITH RESUMPTIVE PRONOUNS *IN SITU*

Another type of FRC uses RPs *in situ*, rather than extraction, a relativization strategy that is well-known in so far as OHRCs go. In particular, Hebrew permits both OHRCs and FRCs which superficially differ from those in (1.85) in exhibiting an RP where the latter exhibit a 'gap' (the RP option is, I understand, also resorted to in Turkish and Chinese when extraction would violate Subjacency or the ECP). I provide in (1.86) an illustration from Modern Hebrew of an FRC of the kind at issue.

```
(1.86) Bo    nidaber       al [pro_i [ašer af exad
       come we-will-talk on         that no one
       lo  mit'anyen       be txunot-av_i]].
       not interests-self in features-his
       'Let's talk about (that which) no one is interested
        in its properties.'
```

As shown by the contrast between the two subcases of (1.87), the construction of (1.86) contrasts with the one in (1.85b) by permitting relativization 'into' an extraction island.

```
(1.87) a. *Bo    nidaber       al ašer eyneni makir af exad še
           come we-will-talk on that I-not know no one that
           ma'arix e.
           values
```

'Let's talk about (that which) I don't know anyone
that values (it).'
b. Bo   nidaber   al ašer eyneni makir af exad še
   come we-will-talk on that I-not know no one that
   mit'anyen   be txunot-*av*.
   interests-self in features-his
   'Let's talk about (that which) I don't know anyone who is
   interested in its properties.'

Safir (1986: § 6) argues that RPs are Ā-bound from [SPEC, C']. If so, whenever RP dependencies are free from Subjacency effects, the Ā-binder needs to be viewed as an NO inserted directly in its surface position (presumably at D-Structure). Since the operator is not moved from a lower position, Pied-Piping cannot in principle arise. As for Kase-matching, it is vacuously ensured by the absence of overt Kase (what was said in section 2.1 concerning reordered NOs extends straightforwardly to base-generated NOs).

One may in principle ask whether the RP is subject to requirements of Kase-matching with the FRC's Head (anti-Pied-Piping effects cannot arise, because the RP does not move). As far as I know, such matching effects have not been reported. In relation to Hebrew, (1.88a) – in which the RP has P-Object Case (which is morphologically distinct from NOM) – shows that mismatching is allowed in a position in which non-matching FRCs formed by movement to [SPEC, C'], as in (1.88b), are not permitted (see n. 9, p. 228).

(1.88) a. [*pro* ašer kol exad hit'anyen   b -*o*] mehave   basis
           that all one interested-self in-it constitutes basis
           xašuv   le-hitpatxuyot nosafot.
           important to-developments additional
        '(That which) everyone was interested in constitutes an
        important basis for additional developments.'
      b. *[*pro* be ma še kol exad hit'anyen]   mehave
           in what that all one interested-self constitutes
           basis xašuv   le-hitpatxuyot nosafot.
           basis important to-developments additional
           (same purported meaning as (1.88a))

2.3 FRCs WITH SYNTACTIC MOVEMENT TO A POSITION OTHER THAN [SPEC, C']

A third type of FRC which provides an important hint as to the nature of anti-Pied-Piping effects is a variant of the one described in section 2.2. and illustrated in (1.86). In addition to relative constructions with RPs *in situ*, Hebrew has OHRCs and FRCs in which RPs are reordered (subject to Subjacency), but end up in a position *distinct from* [*SPEC, C'*]. Illustrations

of OHRCs and FRCs of this type and of their sensitivity to Subjacency are
provided in (1.89)–(1.90).

(1.89) a. Bo   nidaber   al ha -inyanim ašer *itam*$_i$
         come we-will-talk on the-issues   that *with them*
         af exad lo roce   le-hit'asek e$_i$
         no one not wants to-deal
         'Let's talk about the issues *with which* no one
         wants to deal.'
      b. Bo   nidaber   al [pro ašer *ito*$_i$ af exad
         come we-will-talk on   that *with-it* no one
         lo roce   le-hit'asek e$_i$].
         not wants to-deal
         'Let's talk about (that) *with which* no one wants to deal.'

(1.90) a. *Bo   nidaber   al ha -inyanim ašer *itam*$_i$
         come we-will-talk on the-issues   that *with them*
         eynenu makirim anašim še   rocim le-hit'asek e$_i$.
         we-not know   people that want to-deal
         '*Let's talk about the issues with which we do not know
         people who want to deal.'
      b. *Bo   nidaber   al [pro ašer *ito*$_i$ eynenu makirim
         come we-will-talk on   that *with it* we-not know
         anašim še   rocim le-hit'asek e$_i$].
         people that want to-deal
         '*Let's talk about (that) with which we do not
         know people who want to deal.'

The claim that the final landing site of the italicized pronouns in (1.89) and
(1.90) is different from (and lower than) [SPEC, C'] is based on the
following considerations: in the Hebrew counterpart to *wh*-FRCs, the *wh*-
phrase *precedes* an overt complementizer (see n. 9, p. 228); on the assumption that *wh*-phrases move to [SPEC, C'], the italicized pronouns in (1.89)–
(1.90) must occupy a different position, because they follow an overt
complementizer (see Reinhart (1981) for a detailed discussion of this
phenomenon).

The particular interest of the FRC type just described is that the
movement of the reordered phrase makes it possible to check whether the
latter is subject to anti-Pied-Piping and Kase-matching effects *specific to FRCs*
(in contradistinction to the constructions discussed in sections 2.1 and 2.2,
where such effects turned out to be excluded on independent grounds).
Example (1.89) shows that Kase-matching effects are absent (cf. (1.88b));
while (1.91b) shows that anti-Pied-Piping effects are likewise absent.

(1.91) a. Bo   nidaber   al ha -munaxim ašer *be txunotei -hem*
         come we-will-talk on the-concepts that *on properties-their*
         af exad lo mit'anyen e.
         no one not interests-self

48

'Let's talk about the concepts such that no one
is interested in their properties.'
b. Bo   nidaber   al [pro ašer be txunot   -av
come we-will-talk on   that in properties-his
af exad lo mit'anyen e].
no one not interests-self
'Let's talk about (that) such that no one
is interested in its properties.'

This state of affairs, which is in sharp contrast to what we saw to be the case in FRCs formed by movement to [SPEC, C'], and, first and foremost, to the invariable presence of anti-Pied-Piping effects, points to the conclusion that anti-Pied-Piping effects do not simply arise whenever FRs are formed by movement, but only when the ultimate target of such movement is *the FR's [SPEC, C']*.

2.4 HEAD-INTERNAL RELATIVES

The final type of construction we will look at is commonly known as a 'Head-Internal relative'. Basically, it differs from *wh*-FRCs in having the superficial appearance of a canonical clause, the internal nominal coindexed with CP occurring *in situ* and exhibiting no special morphological markings. Illustrations from Ancash Quechua and Japanese are provided in (1.92a) and (1.92b), which are taken, with inconsequential adaptations, from Srivastav (1991b), and Watanabe (1991) respectively; the italicized constituents are the 'internal Heads'.

(1.92) a. [nuna *ishkay bestya*-ta ranti-shqa-n]
         man   two   horse-ACC buy- PERF-3
         alli bestya-m   ka-rqo -n.
         good horse- VALIDATOR be-PAST-3
         'The two horses that the man bought were good horses.'
         '*Two (of the) horses that the man bought were good horses.'
     b. [John -ga (*sono) *ronbun*-o   kaita-no] -ga
        John NOM   that paper   ACC wrote-NM NOM
        LI-ni notta.
        LI-LOC appeared
        'The paper that John wrote appeared in *LI*.'

Head-Internal relative constructions are usually not viewed as a kind of FRC, apparently because their internal Head is generally a full nominal. However, in *wh*-FRCs, the phrase coindexed with CP may also be a full nominal, as was shown in (1.72). Accordingly, if the pre-theoretical term 'FRC' is used to designate amount relatives which typically occur in A-positions and which exhibit no overt Head, as we have implicitly done so far, there is no reason for not applying it to the kind of construction illustrated in (1.92). The only difference between *wh*-FRCs and the constructions under consideration here which needs to concern us is, I submit, that the latter are formed through the reordering to [SPEC, C'] of an *NO*, rather than of an *overt phrase*. I will now proceed to show that, apart from the distinction just noted (and whatever follows from it, for example, absence of Pied-Piping), Head-Internal relatives exhibit the major characteristic properties of FRCs.

Concerning semantic status, the constructions in (1.92) appear to possess all three distinguishing features of amount constructions. First, as illustrated in (1.92b), the 'internal Head' may not exhibit a strong determiner. Second, as Srivastav (1991b) explicitly notes, the bracketed construction in (1.92a) is necessarily construed as a definite (and thus strong non-partitive) DP (a point brought out in the English translation); concerning (1.92b), I was unable to consult a native informant, but the English translation provided by Watanabe is consistent with the extension of this generalization to Japanese. Third, as G. Hermon kindly informed me (personal communication), Quechua Head-Internal relatives do not stack, which is furthermore in contrast to the behaviour of Quechua relatives with an external Head which do stack, and must thus be viewed as restrictive relatives.

Concerning the hypothesis that the constructions in (1.92) are formed through movement to [SPEC, C'] prior to S-Structure, Cole (1987a) and Watanabe (1991) note that the constructions they discuss exhibit Subjacency effects; that is to say, the internal Heads may not occur within such extraction islands as complex NPs or subordinate interrogative clauses. This state of affairs suggests that an NO of some sort is moved out of the internal Head and into [SPEC, C'].

Finally, concerning the distribution of Head-Internal relative constructions, it appears to be that of uncontroversial nominal phrases. This points to the conclusion that they are headed by *pro*, just like *wh*-FRCs. In section 3.2.4 we shall bring up additional evidence from Japanese which reinforces this conclusion.

Let us briefly return to the NO which we posited and consider its possible 'launching site'. A hint is provided by certain languages where internal Heads exhibit *wh*-elements that undergo overt reordering. Thus, alongside languages like English, where an entire full internal Head needs to be reordered to [SPEC, C'] (as in (1.72a)), there exist languages like Classical Greek, where *wh*-elements alone may be reordered out of the internal Head, leaving 'behind' a remnant comparable to the italicized sequences in (1.92a) and (1.92b); this is illustrated in (1.92c).

(1.72) a. I will hire [pro$_i$ [[whatever people]$_i$ you want to work with]]

(1.92) c. oichetai pheugōn [hōn   eicheis *martura*]
       is-gone fleeing   which.ACC you-had witness.ACC
       'The witness whom you had has run away.'

Elements like *which* and *what(ever)* are usually viewed as Ds, not DPs (at least, when they co-occur with an N(P)). It therefore appears necessary to assume that in constructions like (1.92c) – and correlatively (1.92a) and (1.92b) – some process separates D from NP prior to reordering to [SPEC, C'], so that what is reordered is a DP, rather than a D; this assumption is necessitated by the requirement for structure preservation, since specifiers are maximal projections.[12]

An alternative view is put forward in Watanabe (1991), where it is proposed that the NO in constructions like (1.92c) originates in the *specifier*, rather than the *Head* position of a (weak) DP, and thus constitutes a DP at all levels of representation. If we extend this analysis to the overt *wh*-elements in (1.92c) and – importantly – to those in data like (1.72a), (1.72a'), (1.72a"), and, for that matter, (1.1a), the descriptive statement in (1.71) is no longer strictly accurate, since it fails to distinguish between acceptable data like (1.72a, a', a") on the one hand and unacceptable data like (1.46b) on the other. However, as indicated in n. 22 (p. 235), this type of contrast can be straightforwardly captured regardless of whether *wh*-elements are assumed to occupy a X^0 or a [SPEC, X'] position (let X signify a functional category).

Whichever of the two analyses just envisaged is adopted, the Subjacency effects are accounted for in a manner which contributes to the unification of *wh*-FRCs with Head-Internal relative constructions in terms of movement to [SPEC, C'] prior to S-Structure.[13]

Just as in other constructions which employ NOs, violations of the anti-Pied-Piping constraint are independently prevented from arising. Mismatches in morphological Kase that concern *pro* and the NO also cannot arise (for the reasons indicated in section 2.1). As for constraints on non-matching involving *pro* and the 'internal Head', as far as I can tell none have been reported in the literature; in (1.92a), for example, the 'internal Head' has ACC Case and the 'complex NP' has NOM Case; until proof to the contrary, I shall assume that they never arise.

We have now concluded the presentation of the major types of realis FRCs. However, before also concluding Chapter 2 of this study, it will be instructive to examine an additional type of relative construction, which is Head Internal in the commonly accepted sense, that is, it exhibits a canonical clause with the distribution of a nominal phrase and coindexed with an internal nominal, and which in past literature (for example, Williamson 1987; Cole 1987a) has not been carefully distinguished from constructions like those in (1.92a, b). The construction in question is found in Lakhota, and is superficially distinct from those in (1.92a, b) only in exhibiting a CP-external D of which CP appears to be the complement; all my information about it comes from Williamson.

This construction is interesting in that it provides justification for one aspect of the characterization of amount relative clauses which was proposed in the Introduction. The characterization in question was that an amount relative exhibits a coindexed weak internal nominal *which is construed as taking CP-scope.* While the necessarily weak status of the internal nominal was abundantly illustrated and some of its consequences were pointed out, the reason for adding the italicized part to the characterization has so far not been made clear. The Lakhota relative constructions provide the needed justification, as I propose to show directly.

That the construction under consideration contains a coindexed *weak* internal nominal is beyond doubt; Williamson shows with numerous illustrations that the class of nominals that can serve as internal Heads is exactly the class of weak DPs (1987: § 7.1.4). I reproduce one of her examples in (1.92d), which shows that an internal Head may be indefinite, but not definite.

(1.92) d. [[Mary *owiža wa/*ki* kağe] ki] he ophewathu.
          Mary quilt a   the make the DEM I-buy
          'I bought the quilt that Mary made.'

However, Lakhota Head-Internal relatives exhibit two additional features which are completely unexpected for amount constructions. First, the entire construction need not be definite (more generally, strong non-partitive), as shown in (1.92e) (it may, of course, be definite as well, as shown by (1.92d)). Second, the construction permits the stacking of relative clauses, as illustrated in (1.92f).

(1.92) e.   [[Mary *owiža wa* kağa] cha] he ophewathu.
          Mary quilt a make Ind DEM I-buy
          'I bought a quilt that Mary made.'
     f.   [[[[Wowapi wa Deloria owa] cha] blawa] cha] ...
          book   a Deloria write Ind I-read Ind
          'A book that Deloria wrote that I have read ...'

This is in stark contrast to the behaviour of amount OHRCs and realis *wh*-FRCs (see the Introduction), as well as to that of the Head-Internal relatives of, for example, Quechua, as shown above (see p. 49). What can be the reason for the apparently 'schizophrenic' behaviour of Lakhota Head-Internal relatives?

The solution to this puzzle is provided, I submit, by the italicized portion in the characterization of amount relatives which was discussed above. Thus, while in the Quechua and Japanese constructions there is no indication that the internal Heads are construed otherwise than as taking scope from the position marked by an NO at S-Structure, there is abundant evidence that the internal Heads of the Lakhota constructions are construed as taking scope outside of CP and immediately under the CP-external D (Williamson 1987: § 7.2); this point is brought out with particular force in stacked constructions, where the internal Head, which occurs within the *most deeply* embedded clause, is construed as taking scope over the *highest* clause. Accordingly, the Lakhota relatives do not fit our proposed definition of amount constructions. I propose to regard them as *bona fide* restrictive relatives, which differ from the restrictive relatives of languages like English in their S-Structure configurational properties, but not in their semantics.

Let us elaborate on the foregoing: we need to distinguish two types of situation, according to whether the CP-external D is strong or weak (as, for example, in (1.92d) and (1.92e) respectively). In the former case, the internal Head is construed as a complement to a strong CP-external D, much like the bracketed constituents in *the* [*many boys*], *all* [*hundred boys*] or *any* [*two boys*]; in the latter case, the internal Head is construed as though it had occurred in place of the CP-external element *cha*. While Williamson glosses *cha* as 'Ind(efinite)', it seems clear enough from the translations she provides for various data (in particular, (1987: 176) and the example reproduced as (1.92e) above) that *cha* makes no contribution to meaning; this is especially clear in stacked constructions, where non-maximal relative CPs obligatorily exhibit an (obviously meaningless) token of *cha* (see (1.92f), where two tokens of *cha* occur). Whether the CP-external D is a strong determiner or the dummy (weak) element *cha*, the relative clause is construed as a predicate whose open position corresponds to the superficial position of its internal Head, such that the predicate is applied to the internal Head; in stacked constructions, each relative is construed as a predicate whose open position corresponds to the superficial position of its own internal Head.

How should the scope of the internal Head be captured by the grammar of Lakhota? Williamson (1987: § 7.2.2) proposes that the internal Head undergoes raising in the LF component (Logical Form) and is adjoined to CP. Williamson also notes that internal Heads may take scope out of constituents which normally constitute extraction islands (such as Complex NPs; see her examples, 1987: 177), and proposes to account for this state of affairs by assuming that LF-movement is free from the constraints that apply to pre-S-Structure movement (that is, the Subjacency condition). This type of approach does not clarify the role of dummy weak Ds in constructions like (1.92e) and (1.92f), and is furthermore difficult to reconcile with the more recent minimalistic framework of Chomsky (1992), where LF is an (interface) level of representation, but not a well-defined component of rules, so that it is unclear that Subjacency-insensitive movement processes can be defined in a principled way. An alternative approach which avoids such pitfalls can be constructed along the following lines: suppose that each relative CP is sister to a weak D which projects a (weak) DP, and that the 'highest' weak DP may or may not serve as complement to a strong D. Assume furthermore that when no such strong D is present, the highest weak D is overtly realized as *cha*, and when a strong D is present, the hierarchically adjacent weak D is phonologically unrealized. Finally, assume that all the weak Ds of a relative construction are coindexed, the lowest only being an item with content, and the remainder, (overt or covert) dummies. Given these assumptions, we may simply view the highest dummy as marking the scope of the internal Head (and in stacked constructions, of all internal Heads). This gives the right result both when a strong D is present and when it is not, and permits a straightforward account of the fact that the scope of internal Heads is not constrained by Subjacency, since scope-marking is achieved without movement.

Observe that the insensitivity to Subjacency of Lakhota Head-Internal relative constructions constitutes another way in which these constructions differ from the corresponding ones in Quechua and Japanese. This contrast can be straightforwardly captured by assuming that the former, unlike the latter two, involves no NO-Movement from the specifier of the internal Head to [SPEC, C'] (in fact, if such movement did occur, it would assign an incorrect scope to the internal Head).

To conclude, the definition of amount constructions must take into account the logical scope of CP-internal coindexed weak nominals co-indexed with CP, the mere presence of such a nominal at S-Structure (or at any level of representation, for that matter) not being decisive. It thus emerges that the pre-theoretical term 'Head-Internal relative construction' does not characterize a natural class.

2.5 SUMMARY AND CONCLUSIONS

In this chapter we have considered four types of realis FRCs which contrast most immediately with those discussed in Chapter 1 in exhibiting no overt phrases in [SPEC, C'] at S-Structure; in each case, justification was provided for assuming an NO in that position at that level.

The examination of these constructions has yielded the following results:

(1) Their distribution is essentially the same as that of *wh*-FRCs; accordingly, a comparable gross structure is justified, that is, a complex nominal category headed by *pro*.

(2) In view of the null status of the operator in [SPEC, C'], which rules out any kind of Pied-Piping or morphological Kase, the constructions at issue are vacuously (and irrelevantly) consistent with the most stringent matching and anti-Pied-Piping constraints.

(3) The constructions under consideration exhibit the typical properties of amount constructions endowed with an external nominal. This was exhaustively demonstrated with respect to the subtype discussed in section 2.4. Concerning the subtypes discussed in sections 2.1–2.3, they are, just like realis *wh*-FRCs, invariably construed as definite; for example, (1.85b) may not be construed as 'let's talk about something that you saw', but only as 'let's talk about that which you saw'. I am unable at this stage to provide positive evidence for the remaining two properties, that is, weak internal coindexed nominal and inability to stack. In particular, a demonstration of the latter property is rendered difficult by the fact that the various FRs are superficially indistinct from restrictive relatives, so that it is unclear how to

'force' an amount reading on multiple clauses (that is, how to avoid readings comparable to, say, (1.72a'')).

(4) A contrastive analysis of Head-Internal relatives in a number of languages has established that a weak CP-internal nominal coindexed with CP induces amount properties only of it is construed as taking scope from [SPEC, C'].

3

The theory of *pro*, anti-Pied-Piping effects and non-nominal FRCs

INTRODUCTION

In the preceding two chapters of this study, I established certain gross properties of FRCs, namely, that they consist of a Head-*pro* and a sister amount relative clause which, at S-Structure, exhibits in [SPEC, C'] either a *wh*(-like) phrase or an NO. In this third chapter, I propose to achieve a number of goals, in particular: (i) to account for the fact that FRCs have essentially the *external syntax* (that is, distribution) of the properly contained categories with which they are coindexed; (ii) to provide an account of the ways in which FRCs differ from OHRCs in respect to *internal syntax*, in particular, in exhibiting (apparently) *universal anti-Pied-Piping effects*, as well as *language-specific Kase-matching effects* subject to systematic variation – these effects being moreover restricted to FRCs with an overt wh(-like) phrase in [SPEC, C'] (at S-Structure); and (iii) to provide an analysis of FRCs of *non-nominal* category, first and foremost of those with a 'missing preposition'.

Central to enterprises (i) and (ii) will be the refining of existing theories of *pro* which assume that *pro*, just like null categories of other types, needs to be *conjunctively* licensed in *two* distinct ways, that is, *formally* and *for (syntactic) content* (content licensing, usually referred to as 'identification', is, of course, needed just in case *pro* has content). By and large, I will propose that the formal licensing component of my refined theory of *pro* provides an answer to (i) above, and that the identification component, in conjunction with a number of assumptions that I will put forward separately, provides an explanation for the anti-Pied-Piping phenomenon, as well as for the fact that Kase-matching effects arise only when anti-Pied-Piping effects are present (a direct and detailed discussion of Kase-matching effects is however reserved for Chapter 4). My proposed refinements in the theory of *pro* are, however, not solely aimed at accounting for properties of FRCs; accordingly, one of the ensuing sections will examine its consequences with respect to other *pro* constructions as well.

This chapter is broken down as follows. In section 3.1, I examine critically three representative *conjunctive* theories of *pro*, and propose an alternative theory which builds on some of their insights while rejecting others; in a nutshell, I shall argue that *pro* is formally licensed by Case (however it may be assigned) and identified by a 'local antecedent', a notion which will be made precise in section 3.1.3. The formal licensing component of this proposal provides an answer to (i) above (since nominal phrases in general require Case). Both the formal and the content licensing proposal put forward below are of independent theoretical interest in that they deny the usefulness of 'government' and appeal instead to the construct 'Minimal Domain', thus converging with proposals made, on entirely independent grounds, by Chomsky (1992). In section 3.2, I show how the assumption that the FR is the local antecedent of *pro* yields, in conjunction with independently motivated assumptions, an explanation for the Pied-Piping effects; a welcome bonus of this analysis is that it also yields insight into certain otherwise 'unexpected' Subjacency effects found in Japanese Head-Internal relatives. In constructing an account of the anti-Pied-Piping constraint, a number of issues of independent interest are addressed, in particular, the *raison d'être* of external nominals in amount constructions, the status of requirements which 'anticipate' Rizzi's *wh*-Criterion at S-Structure, and the conditions under which feature specifications may be conveyed from one Extended Projection to another. In section 3.3, I consider the implications of my theory of *pro* for some *pro*-constructions other than FRCs. Finally, in section 3.4, I address the issue of non-nominal FRCs. The centre of gravity of that section consists in a critical examination of the major attempts in the past to come to grips with missing-P FRCs, and in an argument for a novel alternative to all of them.

3.1 THE FORMAL/CONTENT DISTINCTION IN EARLIER WORK AND A NEW THEORY OF *pro*

Clearly, licensing of some sort is necessary in respect to *all* categories, whether overt or null, a state of affairs which Chomsky (1986b) proposed to capture by means of a Principle of Full Interpretation. None the less, the licensing mechanisms needed for null categories cannot be identical to those which apply to overt categories, since the distribution of the former and of the latter differs, at least sometimes. As hinted at above, a variety of earlier studies have argued for a *conjunctive* approach to the licensing of null categories; important landmarks in this orientation are, in respect to *non*-pronominal null categories, Lasnik and Saito (1984), Chomsky (1986a), Aoun *et al.* (1987), Rizzi (1989), and in respect to *pro*, Rizzi (1986) and many of the studies in Jaeggli and Safir (1989a). It is important to note that these earlier studies of *pro* concentrated primarily on *pro* in A-positions, that is as subject, verbal object and, to a lesser extent, prepositional object.

As a preamble to deciding on a formal licensing procedure for *pro* as FRC-Head, I shall outline and critique three earlier theories of *pro*, which differ significantly from each other and which seem to encapsulate most of the current views on the topic, paying special attention to the feasibility of their extension to *pro* in Head-of-FRC position.

3.1.1 Three earlier theories of *pro*

In this section, I outline the major features of the theories of *pro* put forward in Rizzi (1986), Jaeggli and Safir (1989b) and Authier (1992).

3.1.1.1 Rizzi (1986)

Rizzi states, in relation to the formal/content approach to null categories in general that 'formal licensing appears to involve some kind of .... government relation, and the recovery procedure [that is, identification; A.G.] involves some kind of binding relation, in an extended sense' (1986: 519).[14]

In relation to *pro*, Rizzi proposes the following three necessary conditions for formal licensing:

(1.93) a. a Head-governor;
        b. case assigned by the Head-governor;
        c. a positive specification of a parameter, whose values
           may differ from governing category to governing category
           and from language to language.

Concerning identification, he proposes that it is achieved either through coindexation with certain features borne by an identifying element, or by some pragmatic procedure (the latter is intended for languages like Chinese, Japanese, etc.); in the former case, the features borne by the identifier are required to be 'sufficiently rich' (a notion which has so far resisted precise quantification).

A notable and curious feature of Rizzi's theory of *pro* is the assumption that in situations where identification is achieved by feature-coindexing, the identifier is *necessarily* the formal licenser (that is, the Case-governor; see (1.93a, b)). This proposal is curious in that comparable 'linkage' assumptions have not in general been entertained in relation to null categories other than *pro*; for example, Rizzi's own version (1989) of the (*non*-pronominal) E(mpty) C(ategory) P(rinciple) makes no such assumption. It should be noted, however, that the linkage in question does not eliminate the distinction between formal and content licensing, which Rizzi views as necessary to account, for example, for the licensing of an expletive *pro* (where identification is inapplicable).

3.1.1.2 Jaeggli and Safir (1989b)

Jaeggli and Safir differ – as already hinted at above – from Rizzi in respect to the proposed formal licensing mechanism. While they do assume the components (1.93a, b) (which they 'reassign' to identification), they consider that (subject) *pro* is formally licensed just in case the AGR reflex is, from a morphological viewpoint, either *uniformly* realized or *uniformly* unrealized throughout the verbal paradigm. Their identification procedure is, apart from the 'reassignment' of (1.93a, b) noted above, not substantially different from Rizzi's.

3.1.1.3 Authier (1991)

Authier differs radically from the two earlier proposals in assuming that *pro* is formally licensed by *absence* of Case. Specifically, he adapts an idea put forward in Safir (1985) (and no longer maintained in Jaeggli and Safir (1989b)) to the effect that Case may be obligatorily or optionally assigned to certain positions in certain languages. Unlike Safir, however, who proposed to parametrize this distinction, Authier attempts to derive it from a property of AGR, in particular, from its 'strength'/'weakness' (in the sense of Pollock (1989)). According to Pollock, strong AGR is transparent for the purpose of theta-marking of the argument coindexed with AGR by a Verb which has raised and adjoined to AGR (weak AGR is, of course, opaque under such circumstances). Authier extends this proposal in the sense that strong, but not weak, AGR can optionally absorb the Case-assignment property of the Verb. When Case has been absorbed, *pro* may appear in the Caseless A-position. Concerning the identification of definite *pro*, Authier does not significantly differ from Rizzi (he does, however, refine the identification of 'arbitrary' *pro* in assuming binding by a 'non-selective' (possibly null) operator).

3.1.2 A Critique of the three earlier Theories of *pro*

We shall now take a critical look at the three views of *pro* outlined above, paying attention both to their merits *per se* and to the feasibility of their extension to *pro* as FRC-Head. We will consider the proposals in reverse order.

3.1.2.1 Authier (1992)

Authier's view of AGR as capable of absorbing Case was prefigured in works such as Rizzi (1982), where strong AGR was viewed as 'pronominal'. While this mechanism can certainly account for subject and object *pro*, it is not very plausible for *pro* as a P-object. In French, for example, bisyllabic prepositions allow *pro*-objects, as illustrated by the following data (note that the null P-object is both internal to a Complex NP and A-bound, so that an analysis as a variable bound by a Null Operator, of the kind proposed by Huang (1984) with respect to null objects in Chinese, is here excluded):

(1.94) Ce   collier$_i$ m'inspire   le   désir de m'enfuir avec pro$_i$.
      this necklace me-inspires the desire of me-flee with
      'This necklace makes me feel like running away with (it).'

None the less, there are no grounds known to me for assuming an AGR coindexed with the P-object, let alone a 'strong' one; why Case should not be assigned here thus remains mysterious. To extend Authier's theory to FRCs, one might propose that Case percolation, in contrast to Case assignment, is an optional process, which needs to apply only when an NP has an overt Head. What such an account does not explain is the impossibility of PRO-headed FRCs (see section 1.4.3.3), since, under the envisaged analysis, both the requirement that the FRC (an R-expression) receive Case and the requirement (assumed by Authier) that PRO not receive Case would be satisfied. Furthermore, it is unclear how to make sense of Kase-matching effects under the assumptions here considered, since it seems hardly possible to maintain that the Case of the *wh*-phrase needs to be morphologically consistent with the one that *pro* does *not* have. I thus do not see that a Caseless approach to *pro* is promising in respect to FRCs.

3.1.2.2 *Jaeggli and Safir (1989b)*

Let us now turn our attention to Jaeggli and Safir's proposals. As the authors themselves admit, these are problematic in respect to expletive *pro* as the subject of a small clause, as can be seen in relation to the data in (1.95).

(1.95) a. Jean considère [*pro* scandaleux que Marie soit partie].
        John considers   scandalous that Mary be   gone
     b. *John considers [*pro* scandalous that Mary left].

Thus, the English object-AGR is invariably null, so that the *pro* in (1.95b) is predicted to be licensed, contrary to fact. Furthermore, note that French has overt object agreement (under certain circumstances), but only in participial forms; this means that the paradigm is non-uniform, which predicts, contrary to fact, that (1.95a) is ungrammatical.

I wish to add that the proposal under consideration is also problematic in relation to certain subject-*pro* constructions. Thus Romanian exhibits overt Subject–Verb agreement in the various tenses of the indicative and in the present subjunctive, but not in the past subjunctive. This leads to the prediction that Romanian can have no *pro* subjects of any kind, when in fact both expletive and definite *pro* are possible in all the forms of the indicative and of the subjunctive. This is illustrated in the subjunctive data below, in which *pro* is an expletive in (1.96) and a definite expression in (1.97): the (a) subcases exhibit present subjunctive forms within the bracketed clauses; the (b) subcases, past subjunctive forms;[15] note that the null subjects in (1.97) are A-bound and internal to a Complex NP, which excludes an analysis in terms of variables bound by NOs.

(1.96) a. E   posibil [*pro* să   fie adevărat că   Ion s   -a   sinucis].
           is possible   SUBJ be true   that Ion SELF-has killed
           'It is possible that (it) is true that Ion committed suicide.'
       b. E   posibil [*pro* să   fi fost adevărat că   Ion se
           is possible   SUBJ be been true   that Ion SELF
           sinucisese].
           had-self-killed
           'It is possible that (it) was true that Ion
           had committed suicide.'

(1.97) a. Gică se   va   căsători cu   fata   pe care e posibil
           Gică SELF will marry   with girl-the ACC who is possible
           [*pro* s   -o angajez /angajezi/angajeze/angajăm/angajaţi
                  SUBJ-her hire.1.SG/2.SG   /3.   /1.PL. /2.PL.
           ca secretară săptămína viitoare].
           as secretary week-the next
           'Gică will marry the girl who it is possible that (I/you/
           /(s)he/we/they) will hire as secretary next week.'
       b. Gică se   va   căsători cu   fata   pe care e posibil
           Gică SELF will marry   with girl-the ACC who is possible
           [*pro* s   -o fi angajat ca secretară acum cîţiva ani].
                  SUBJ-her be hired   as secretary now several years
           'Gică will marry the girl who it is possible that (I/you/
           (s)he/we/they) hired as secretary several years ago.'

In addition to the difficulties just noted, it is highly unclear how to extend the proposal at issue to *pro* as FRC-Head. Should one require uniformity in the realization of the AGR which is coindexed with a subject or object FRC? If we do, we predict that subject or object FRCs are excluded when the matrix verbal paradigm is non-uniform (that is, in subject position in English), which is patently false. Furthermore, which paradigm should be considered relevant with respect to the Heads of left-dislocated FRCs? Plainly, it is hard to see how this approach can get off the ground.

3.1.2.3 *Rizzi (1986)*

Let us finally address the theory of *pro* as put forward by Rizzi. We will not consider its merits in respect to the constructions that Rizzi directly addressed and will proceed to a consideration of the feasibility of extending it to FRC-Heads. I see (at least) three difficulties with such an extension. First, the requirement that *pro* should be governed incorrectly predicts that

FRCs may not appear in non-governed positions, in particular in Left-Dislocation position. Second, the requirement of a positive setting for the language- and category-specific parameter which Rizzi assumes incorrectly predicts that FRCs are excluded when their governor carries a negative value for that parameter; for example, it is wrongly predicted that English verbs admit no FRCs as direct objects (recall that object arbitrary *pro* is not possible in English, according to Rizzi). And third, the 'linkage' requirement, which entails that identification is necessarily effected by a governor, that is, an FRC-external element, leaves us without an explanation of the fact that FRCs are subject to anti-Pied-Piping effects even in positions where they are governed by an element capable of licensing and identifying an argument *pro*.

3.1.3 An alternative theory of *pro*

It emerges from the preceding discussion that none of the three approaches to argument-*pro* can in any obvious way be extended to Head-*pro*. I shall now outline an alternative theory of *pro*, which builds on some of the insights in Rizzi (1986), and which, while adequate for the constructions Rizzi addressed, can also cope with additional constructions that he did not address. In proposing this alternative, we will demonstrate its ability to account for *pro* as FRC-Head; its applicability to additional *pro* constructions will be discussed in section 3.3.

What, then, can be the mechanisms responsible for the licensing and identification of *pro* as FRC-Head? It seems to me that the licensing mechanisms, that is, those that identify the existence of *pro* in some position, should be able to account for the fact that it occurs exactly where OHRC-Heads occur; as sister to a CP, the constituent they form together having in addition the distribution of overt NPs. Clearly, OHRC-Heads bear (possibly abstract) Case; I propose that Case constitutes the basic mechanism for the (formal) licensing of an FRC-Head.[16] Whether or not stipulations in the sense of (1.93c) need to be added is an issue I leave open.

As for identification, it seems clear that it cannot be limited to government configurations in which some X^o functions as identifier (I am here concerned with identification by an *antecedent* and under *locality*; for identification without an antecedent or without locality, see section 3.3). I propose to attack this problem by separating the issue of the *local domain* in which *pro* may be identified from the issue of which elements within such a domain may serve as *antecedents*.

A glaring defect of the government proposal is that it predicts identification *into the Head* of a governed XP, something which leaves the anti-Pied-Piping effects found in FRCs mysterious; in this respect then, government is too strong a notion. Government is also unnecessarily strong in that E(xceptional) C(ase) M(arking) configurations are not possible identification configurations (on this, see Rizzi (1986)). We may thus reduce the local domain for identification, in those instances where the antecedent is an X^0, to what Chomsky (1992) calls the the *Minimal Domain* of X^0, that is, the complement and specifier of X^0 plus the constituents adjoined to X^0 and to its projections. Chomsky's more formal definition takes the *Domain* of a Head H to be the set S of nodes contained in the least full-category maximal projection dominating H that are distinct from and do not contain H; the *Minimal Domain* of H is the smallest subset K of S such that for any member A of S, some member B of K reflexively dominates A. Note that restricting *pro* identification by some X^0 to the latter's minimal domain is adequate for all the constructions addressed by Rizzi in the manner he envisaged, while at the same time correctly disallowing identification into the Head of an FRC.

To devise an identification procedure for the Head of an FRC, we need to generalize Chomsky's definition of Minimal Domain in a rather natural way, and at the same time face the issue of what constitutes a possible antecedent. Observe that, when *pro* is the Head of some maximal projection, something other than the Head of that projection must be the identifier.

The extension just alluded to concerns constructions which are headed by some X^n, $n > 0$, as is the case in FRCs, which have, I assume, the structure [$_{DP}$ [$_{DP}$ *pro*] CP] (for more discussion of this point, see section 3.2). All that is needed is to allow 'Minimal Domain' to be defined (in the manner proposed by Chomsky) not only in respect to Heads of rank 0, but also in respect to Heads of higher rank. Given this extended definition of Minimal Domain and the proposal that *pro* must be identified within its Minimal Domain, CP is the only possible candidate for this role. However, it turns out that not every CP coindexed with *pro* is a possible identifier in the configuration at issue, since realis FRCs appear to be invariably amount constructions, as we saw in Chapters 1 and 2. That is to say, an amount relative may be taken to have the ability to identify *pro*, but not a restrictive relative, since there are apparently no restrictive FRCs. This leads us to a consideration of the notion of 'possible antecedent'.

Implicit in Rizzi's view that *pro* must be identified by a Head is the assumption that the antecedent must bear a significant asymmetric linguistic relation to *pro*, in which it is moreover the 'primary' member. Clearly, there is a significant relation between a Head on the one hand and its complement, specifiers and adjuncts on the other. Just as clearly, the Head is logically primary with respect to each of the other three, since a (differentiated) maximal projection may consist of just a Head, but may not lack one. The implied view is, I believe correct, but it does not force us to allow only Heads as antecedents. As noted in the Introduction to this work, a significant relation also holds between an amount relative and its 'resumptive' Head and in this case, it is the relative that is the primary member. The primacy in question is semantic in nature, since restrictive and amount relatives are both *syntactic adjuncts* of their Heads (note that, in both cases, the entire construction is *nominal*, not *verbal*). None the less, on the semantic level, the Head of an amount relative, but not of a restrictive one, is a sort of 'semantic adjunct' of CP. Since the structural primacy of a Head is irrelevant in those cases where *pro* itself has Head status, the suitability of structural adjuncts in general and of CP adjuncts in particular as antecedents of *pro* is decided on semantic grounds. We are thus led to the correct prediction that *pro*-headed FRCs are necessarily amount constructions.

I note that a stronger prediction is in fact made, namely that any nominal construction which consists exclusively of a *pro* Head and an adjunct that does not have semantic primacy over *pro* is excluded. While I have not extensively checked this prediction across languages, the facts that most immediately come to mind appear to support it. For example, English allows no nominal arguments of the form *poor or *from the hills, which presumably include a *pro*-Head, although it does allow comparable constructions with an overt nominal, for example, *poor people, people from the hills*, as well as comparable constructions with *pro* and an overt D that can identify it, for example, *the poor, those from the hills* (on *pro* identification in these last examples, see section 3.2).

Before concluding this section, I wish to compare briefly the proposal on formal licensing made above with an earlier proposal made in Grosu (1989), according to which the Head-*pro*'s formal licenser is the *wh*-phrase in [SPEC, C']. I can see at least two reasons for preferring the proposal made here to my earlier one.

First, the justification for the earlier proposal came entirely from Rizzi's 'linkage' condition between fomal and content licensing (it was assumed in my earlier paper that *pro*'s identifier is the *wh*-phrase in [SPEC, C']), and Rizzi had not himself offered any justification for it. Furthermore, the linkage condition is far from conceptually attractive, since nothing of the kind has ever, to the best of my knowledge, been contemplated with respect to any other type of null categories (as already pointed out in section 3.1.1.1). Thus those who maintain the *pro*/PRO distinction view PRO as licensed by some negative condition, such as lack of Case or lack of government, and identified by some antecedent or covert quantifier. As for non-pronominal null categories, current versions of the ECP view some form of Head-government as responsible for formal licensing, and the (closest trace of) the antecedent which, through movement, gave rise to the null category as responsible for identification (see Rizzi (1989)); the two kinds of licensers are thus never the same for non-pronominal null categories of type X^{max}, and are not necessarily identical even for null categories of type X^o (Rivero 1991). One would thus want to have strong empirical grounds for adopting the *pro*-specific linkage put forward by Rizzi, over and above the fact that the two sources of licensing appear to coincide in the cases discussed by Rizzi. However, as already noted, no other support for the linkage hypothesis was given.

Second, my earlier proposal complicates the task of unifying the licensing conditions for *pro* in various constructions, because the configurational relation that was assumed to be relevant for the formal licensing of FRC-Heads is quite different from the configurations that exist elsewhere (for example, when *pro* occurs in A-positions). In contrast, the proposal made here, which does not rely on specific configurations but on Case alone, is straightforwardly applicable to the various *pro* constructions (I return to this issue in section 3.3.1).

To sum up, I view the proposal made here as superior to my earlier one on (at least) conceptual grounds.

3.2 AMOUNT CONSTRUCTIONS, *pro* IDENTIFICATION AND THE ANTI-PIED-PIPING EFFECTS

We now turn to the issue of how *pro* is identified in FRC-Head position, which, I believe, holds the key to an understanding of the Pied-Piping effects. In a nutshell, I propose to build on the result that the FR alone is fit to function as local antecedent of the Head-*pro*, and to show that the restrictions on Pied-Piping follow from this assumption in conjunction with other independently justifiable ones (in particular, the view that *pro* must be identified at S-Structure).

3.2.1 On the syntax and semantics of amount relative constructions

Before proceeding to the task just outlined, it will be useful to address two points which will provide a better perspective on amount relative constructions in general and on *pro*-headed amount relative constructions in particular. These points are: (i) the *raison d'être* of a (null or overt) external nominal in amount constructions; and (ii) the properties of correlative constructions, in particular the ways in which they resemble and the ways in which they differ from the various amount constructions discussed so far.

In the Introduction to this work, I argued that amount relatives include a weak DP which ends up coindexed with CP. The details of such coindexation, which have not been spelled out so far, are straightforward. In those instances where either the weak DP, or an NO bearing its index move to [SPEC, C'] prior to S-Structure, coindexation with CP is already possible at that level through the independently motivated mechanisms of Spec-Head agreement (which carries the operator's index to C^o) and percolation through a(n Extended) Projection (which carries the index to CP). In certain instances of Pied-Piping, essentially, those barred by the descriptive statement in (1.71), the transfer of the weak DP's index to [SPEC, C'] is not possible at S-Structure, but only after the application of certain LF operations (for justification of this point and a consideration of its implications, see section 3.2). The transmission of the weak DP's index to CP makes it possible for the latter to be interpreted in the way in which weak DPs typically are, as noted in the Introduction. This view of amount CPs creates the expectation that they may serve as input to the kind of logical operations that typically apply to weak DPs, in particular, Existential Closure (Heim 1982). In other words, one may expect – so long as no other considerations are taken into account – that 'bare' CPs coindexed with a weak internal DP should occur in all the contexts where (weak) DPs are allowed. This expectation is, however, not fulfilled. While there exist situations where a 'bare' CP of the kind under consideration alternates with a weak DP, such situations are far from typical (for discussion of an actual case, see Chapter 5). The typical situation is for the CP to 'combine' in some way with an external nominal.

Why should this be so? I suggest that the reason is that 'bare' CPs which designate entity-sets of some sort are *non-canonical* linguistic objects; in the spirit of Grimshaw, we may call them 'concealed entity-sets'. Thus, just as propositions, questions and exclamations are typically expressed by CPs, not by DPs, so are entity-sets typically expressed by DPs, rather than by CPs; correspondingly, just as any verb which s-selects a proposition, question or exclamation automatically allows such semantic objects to be realized as CPs, but not necessarily as DPs (see Grimshaw (1979) for discussion and illustration), so does any verb which s-selects an entity-set automatically allow it to be realized as a DP, but not necessarily as a CP. The *raison d'être* of the external nominal is thus, I submit, to enable a non-canonical construction to achieve canonical status (of course, the external nominal must agree on cardinality specifications with the CP-internal nominal coindexed with it; the specifications may in principle be provided by one of the nominals, or redundantly by both).

Before turning to my next point, I wish to elaborate slightly on the fact that the internal and external weak DPs may exhibit any of the realizations that are in principle available for weak DPs; in particular, each of them may be either a full nominal, or an overt pronominal, or a null pronominal. To illustrate, a full nominal realization for the external DP is found in such amount OHRCs as those of (1.9d) and (1.9e), a null pronominal realization in the various kinds of FRCs discussed in Chapters 1 and 2. A null pronominal realization for the internal DP is found in English amount OHRCs, an overt pronominal realization in FRCs like (1.1b), and a full nominal realization in FRCs like those in (1.72a), (1.72a') and (1.72a"). A simultaneous full nominal realization for both DPs, while not found in the OHRCs known to me, is found with correlative constructions, to which we now turn.

THE SYNTAX OF FREE RELATIVE CONSTRUCTIONS

In all the amount constructions that have been discussed so far, CP and the weak external DP form a constituent. Thus, the gross (S-Structure) representation for amount OHRCs is, I assume, the full version of (1.98a). For realis FRCs, I assume the reduced structure of (1.98a), with the external weak DP realized as *pro*; I further assume that a definite binder is provided by an LF rule of closure (in the ensuing representations, 'D(P)$_s$' and 'D(P)$_w$' stand for 'strong D(P)' and 'weak D(P)' respectively).

(1.98) a.

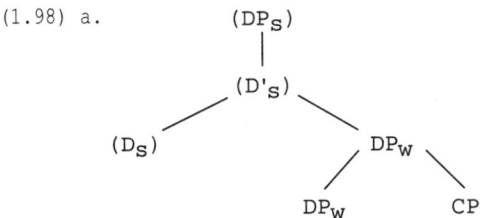

A complex DP such that the weak external DP is a sister of CP is, however, not the only way in which an amount construction can achieve canonicity. An alternative possibility is encountered in correlative constructions, where CP is typically left-adjoined to IP and an external nominal, which includes the overt strong non-partitive D (when there is one), occurs in some A-position within IP, as schematically represented in (1.98b). These constructions are discussed in considerable detail in relation to Hindi in Srivastav (1991a, 1991b), where a large number of their properties are exhibited and justified. Among these, I note the following: correlatives may also be left-adjoined to the strong external DP, as in (1.98b'); the dependency between CP and the external nominal is unbounded, but constrained by Subjacency (for an illustration, see (1.102) below); correlatives exhibit *wh*-phrases which may occur either *in situ* or left-adjoined to IP, but not in [SPEC, C'], and whose distribution is constrained by Subjacency. Observe that in (1.98b) and (1.98b'), CP c-commands the external weak DP, just as in (1.98a).

A comparison of Hindi correlatives with the headed amount constructions discussed in earlier sections reveals no difference in respect to amount status. Thus, the CP-internal *wh*-nominal may exhibit weak determiners, but not strong ones, as illustrated in (1.100); this may be taken as an indication that correlatives are amount constructions. Second, the CP-external nominal is either interpreted as definite (if it is *pro*), or else exhibits only strong non-partitive Ds, as illustrated in (1.101). Third, correlatives do not stack (personal communication from Srivastav; demonstration omitted). To sum up, the three distinctive properties of amount OHRCs and realis FRCs which were expounded in the Introduction are also found with correlatives. A fourth factor which points to the amount nature of correlatives is that the *wh*-like element *jo* may cooccur with the particle *bhii* '-ever', just like the *wh*-forms of English realis FRs (and unlike the *wh*-forms of English restrictive relatives).

(1.98) b.

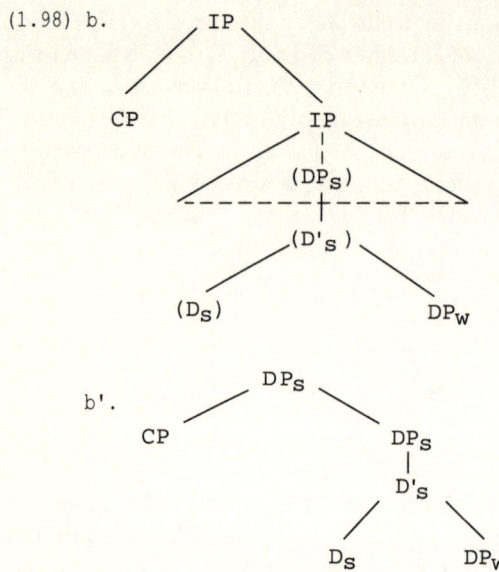

b'.

I note in passing that Hindi correlatives allow virtually every possible combination of *wh*-phrases and external nominals. Thus, the *wh*-phrase may be either a full nominal, as in (1.99a, b), or a pronominal, as in (1.99c), and the external nominal may be *pro*, an overt definite pronoun, or a full DP, as illustrated in (1.99). Note that (1.99b) instantiates the combination of external and internal full nominals which was announced earlier in this section.

(1.99) a. [jo laRkii khaRii hai] *pro*/ vo lambii hai.
          REL girl standing is   DEM tall is
    b. [jo laRkii khaRii hai] vo laRkii lambii hai.
          REL girl standing is DEM girl tall is
    c. [jo khaRii hai] vo laRkii lambii hai.
          REL standing is DEM girl tall is
      'Which girl is standing, that girl/she is tall.'

(1.100)   [jo do /kuch/*ve/ *dono/   *sab laRke khaRe   hãĩ]
         REL two/few/   those/both/ all boys standing are
         ve   lambii hãĩ.
         those tall are
        'Which two/few/*those/*both/*all boys are standing,
         they are tall.'

(1.101)   [jo laRke khaRe   hãĩ] *pro*/ ve/ dono/ sab/ *do /*kuch/
         REL boys standing are   they/those/both/all/ two/ few
        *adhiktam lambii hãĩ.
        most   tall   are
       'Which boys are standing, they/those/both/all/*two/*few/*most
       are tall.'

(1.102) *[jo vahāā rahtaa hai] māĩ yeh baat
　　　　REL there lives　　　 I this matter
　　　ki　 (vo) nahīī ayaa jaantii hūū.
　　　that he　 not　 came know
　　　'Who lives there, I know the fact that *pro*/he
　　　did not come.'

Pursuing our comparison of correlatives with headed amount constructions, there is one type of situation where a difference in behaviour is expected, namely, when the external nominal is *pro*.[17] The reason is that FRs satisfy the locality conditions on *pro* identification (see section 3.1.3), while correlatives do not. Accordingly, we may expect *pro* in correlative constructions to be licensed by whatever factors license it in constructions without correlatives. This prediction is confirmed in respect to Hindi, as Srivastav kindly informed me (personal communication). That is to say, *pro* has exactly the same distribution in correlative constructions that it has outside them; in particular, it may occur as subject and direct object (where it is arguably licensed by AGR), but not, for example, as a P-object. The proposed irrelevance of correlatives to *pro* identification also makes another prediction: if overt movement to [SPEC, C'] takes place within the correlative, such movement should be free from anti-Pied-Piping constraints (this prediction assumes the correctness of the argumentation in section 3.2.4, which relates anti-Pied-Piping effects to *pro* identification). This prediction is unfortunately not testable in respect to Hindi, where there is no overt movement to [SPEC, C'] in correlatives (as noted earlier in this section); it is however arguably testable in relation to certain German data, with confirmatory results (see section 3.2.6).

Returning to the amount status of correlatives and the three distinctive properties it shares with headed amount constructions, the proposals I made in my Introduction with respect to the latter generalize straightforwardly to the former, as far as I can see.

It is perhaps worth pointing out that the analysis of amount constructions which has been put forward here differs in certain respects from the analysis proposed by Srivastav. Her view was that realis FRCs are headless NPs which exhaustively dominate CP, are interpreted as definite generalized quantifiers, and undergo Quantifier-Raising (QR) at LF. Concerning correlative clauses, she assumed that, even though they are not dominated by NP, they are none the less interpreted as definite generalized quantifiers owing to a 'lifting' operation which applies at LF (QR is unnecessary, since correlatives are already in a scope position in overt representation). FRCs and correlatives are assumed to bind distinct kinds of variables; FRCs bind the trace left by Quantifier-Raising, while correlatives bind the external nominal when it is an overt definite pronoun or *pro*, and some null definite complement of the external nominal when the latter exhibits a strong D with universal import (for example, *dono* and *sab* in (1.101)). Concerning the restrictions on the Ds that may occur with the external nominal, Srivastav suggests, relying on Sportiche (1988), that only floating quantifiers license null partitive constructions, and that the class of Ds permitted in cases like (1.101) is exactly the class of floating quantifiers.

I see (at least) two respects in which Srivastav's approach is less satisfactory than the one put forward in this study. First, the definiteness of FRCs and of correlatives that bind *pro* is achieved by stipulation; on my account, this was motivated by the logically subsequent status of *pro*. Second, the assumption that the overt Ds that occur with the external nominals of correlatives and with amount OHRCs are exactly the floating quantifiers is far from obviously correct. Glaring *prima facie* counterexamples are provided by the English elements *every* and *any*, which are allowed in OHRCs (see (1.9d)–(1.9e)), but do not float (cf. *every man died* with **the men died every (one)*, and *any beer pleases me* with **(the) beer pleases me any*). It thus seems that Srivastav has no account of the restrictions under consideration; in my analysis, a motivated account based on the logically subsequent status of the external nominal was offered.

3.2.2 FRs and the Typology of Clauses

Having espoused the view that amount relatives in general and FRs in particular designate sets of sets of entities with logically primary status, let us attempt to determine how they fit into a general typology of clauses. Such a typology was recently proposed in Rizzi (1989: § 2.7.), and it made no provisions for amount relative clauses. Rizzi's typology uses two bi-valued features, one morphological ([wh]) and one semantic ([PRED]). The feature combinations [+*wh*, +PRED], [–*wh*, +PRED], [+*wh*, –PRED] and [–*wh*, –PRED] purport to characterize clauses like English *wh*-restrictive relatives, *that*- and 'bare' restrictive relatives, interrogative complements, and declarative complements respectively. Note that this taxonomy, when applied, for example, to English, cannot distinguish FRs from interrogative complements, since it characterizes both as [+*wh*, –PRED], nor can it distinguish between overtly headed amount relatives and declarative complements, because it characterizes both as [-*wh*, -PRED]. In addition, the taxonomy appears to mix semantic criteria ([+/–PRED]) with morphological ones ([+/–*wh*]); thus, the interrogative/relative contrast is semanto-syntactic, while the *wh*-/'bare' restrictive relative contrast is basically morphological. Since there exists (at least) a quadri-partite semanto-syntactic distinction, illustrated by the contrast among declaratives, interrogatives, restrictive relatives and amount relatives, we need *two* binary features with syntacto-semantic content, while retaining the [+/–*wh*] feature to characterize certain distinctions (noted in Chapter 2) between constructions with NOs and constructions with *wh*-operators.

I propose the following modified cross-classification of clauses. On the one hand, we may distinguish between clauses which designate abstract objects, such as propositions, questions or exclamations, and clauses which are interpreted as a set (of sets) of entities in virtue of coindexation with a nominal they properly contain. The former category includes declaratives, interrogatives and exclamatives, the latter restrictive and amount relatives. To distinguish between these two classes, let us use a feature [+/−COIND], which indicates whether CP is/is not coindexed with a phrase it properly contains; note that [+COIND] is also an appropriate characterization for FRs coindexed with non-nominal contained phrases (in particular, AP, PP and AdvP). On the other hand we may distinguish between clauses formed with a non-anaphoric operator, and clauses which are not so formed. The former class includes amount relatives and interrogatives, the latter, restrictive relatives (which are formed with an anaphoric operator) and declaratives (which exhibit no operator at all). To this end, I introduce the feature [+/−N(on)A(naphoric)OP(erator)]. The four types illustrated by declarative complements, interrogative complements, amount relatives, and restrictive relatives are thus characterized as, respectively, [−COIND, −NAOP], [−COIND, +NAOP], [+COIND, +NAOP] and [+COIND, −NAOP]. The proposed system predicts that there may be clauses with NOs that correspond to the three semantic types [−COIND, +NAOP], [+COIND, +NAOP] and [+COIND, −NAOP]; plausible English realizations of these types are, I submit, comparative clauses, amount relative clauses with overt Heads and *that-/*'bare' restrictive relatives respectively.

To avoid misunderstandings, I hasten to stress that the two semanto-syntactic features just proposed do not purport to capture all the necessary distinctions among clauses. Additional features will undoubtedly be needed to characterize, for example, exclamatory clauses.

3.2.3 The upper and lower bounds of Pied-Piping, and the *wh*-Criterion

As a preamble to tackling the issue of anti-Pied-Piping effects, we will attempt to clarify the factors that determine the upper and lower bounds of Pied-Piping in general.

We begin by taking a closer look at the import of the morphological feature [*wh*]. We are only interested in those instances where this feature indicates that the element bearing it needs to be interpreted as a logical operator of some sort (we thus ignore uses of *wh*-words in echo questions). Actual interpretation as an operator depends, within the framework assumed here, on a *wh*-element's achieving CP-scope at LF, one possibility (but not the only one), being its displacement to [SPEC, C'].

In the above discussion of clausal types, we proposed to retain Rizzi's view that clauses – and their Heads – may be (non-overtly) marked as [+*wh*] (see Rizzi (1991) on how this specification on C° is licensed in various situations). The import of such a feature on some C° is, according to Rizzi, that the corresponding CP must serve at LF as the scope of an operator with appropriate content; Rizzi assumes that this requires [SPEC, C'] to include such an operator at LF. With a view to capturing this generalization, Rizzi (1991) introduces the ((b) subcase of the) 'wh-Criterion'.

(1.103) The wh Criterion

    a. A wh operator must be in a Spec-Head configuration with a [+wh] X°.
    b. A [+wh] X° must be in a Head-Spec configuration with a wh operator.

In addition, Rizzi proposes that the *wh*-Criterion can serve as a basis for the characterization of a certain aspect of natural language variation, namely, that in *some*, but not *all* languages, certain types of *wh*-phrases must be moved to a scope position by S-Structure. Rizzi's analysis of such states of affairs rests on the assumption that the 'LF-driven' *wh*-Criterion must be satisfied in certain languages at S-Structure as well. This assumption, in conjunction with certain auxiliary hypotheses,[18] enables Rizzi to account for a significant range of data.

Still, Rizzi's conception of the *wh*-Criterion is a far cry from full adequacy. First, as alluded to above, LF scope may need to be achieved in ways other than by movement to [SPEC, C']. Second, language-specific 'anticipations' of the *wh*-Criterion at S-Structure are *not* simple *calques* of their LF counterparts. Third, anticipatory movement to [SPEC, C'] at S-Structure appears to be necessary even in certain languages with *wh*-phrases *in situ*, particularly in those where such *wh*-phrases exhibit Subjacency effects. I proceed to illustrate these three possibilities.

An illustration of the first two points just noted is provided by what Pesetzky (1987) calls 'D(iscourse)-linked' *wh*-phrases, that is, phrases which assume a contextually known set, for example, *which books*. Pesetzky points out that such phrases appear to be free of ECP effects at LF, as illustrated, for example, by the contrast between **what did* WHO say? and *what did* WHICH PEOPLE say?, and concludes on this basis that D-linked *wh*-phrases are not operators, and thus do not need to undergo LF-movement to a clausal-scope position. To account for the fact that such phrases are none the less construed as the 'target' of interrogation with clausal scope, Pesetzky proposes that [SPEC, C'] is filled at LF not by the *wh*-phrase, but by a (null) 'unselective' operator with interrogative force, which binds the *wh*-phrase *in situ* and thereby signals the construal scope of the latter. Dobrovie-Sorin (1987, 1990) adds a refinement to this proposal by proposing that D-linked *wh*-Determiners such as *which*, do occupy a scope position at LF, but only within their maximal projection (that is, they have DP-scope, rather than CP-scope). This illustrates the first point in the preceding paragraph. The second point in the preceding paragraph is illustrated by the observation that, even if D-linked *wh*-phrases do not need to move to [SPEC, C'] at LF, they must move overtly in languages with overt *wh*-Movement, for example, English. To illustrate, note that **I wonder [John likes which girl]* is just as ill-formed as **I wonder [John likes whom]*. In general, in contexts where non-D-linked *wh*-phrases must undergo overt movement, so must D-linked *wh*-phrases.

The situation described above shows that S-Structure requirements on *wh*-phrases may be stronger than LF requirements. The converse state of affairs is also encountered, in particular in constructions where material not contained within the Extended Projection of the wh-element has undergone Pied-Piping. Under such circumstances, the *wh*-element must achieve CP-scope at LF (unless it is D-linked, in which case it needs to be bound by an unselective interrogative operator with CP-scope). At S-Structure, however, this is not necessary; that is to say, the *wh*-element may remain *in situ* within the Pied-Piped phrase. To illustrate the point, observe that *whose book do you like best?* is a well-formed sentence, but one which needs to be construed as a question about book-authors, book-owners, etc., rather than as a question about books. In constructions of this type, additional LF manipulations are needed to ensure that non-D-linked *wh*-phrases achieve CP-scope (for proposed implementation mechanisms, which achieve this goal, see, for example, Chomsky 1977, 1992, Safir 1986).

What has been said in the two preceding paragraphs clearly shows that the S-Structure conditions which hold in languages with overt movement to [SPEC, C'] do not have the function of ensuring that the appropriate LF representations already exist at S-Structure. Rather, they arguably have the function of signalling in some way that well-formed LF representations *will* arise. The mechanism which carries out the signalling function is, we may assume, the (covert) 'spread' of the [*wh*] feature to [SPEC, C'], the position from where *wh*-elements must ultimately take scope or be unselectively bound. In cases of Pied-Piping, the [*wh*] feature can reach [SPEC, C'] only if the phrase which occupies that position includes a *wh*-element. Furthermore, the transmission of the [*wh*] feature from the position occupied by the element which overtly bears it must be permitted by the grammar of the language. The latter point is addressed in Grimshaw (1991: § 3.2.2), to which we now turn.

Grimshaw's proposal for (covert) feature transmission assumes the theory of Extended Projection that was mentioned in section 1.4.1. Recall that the projections of a *lexical* Head H together with the (maximal) uninterrupted sequence of *functional* projections that immediately dominates the maximal projection of H, but excluding the Specifiers of functional categories, are assumed to form H's (maximal) *Extended Projection*. Extended Projections are taken to define the domain within which features may percolate. In addition, there may be mechanisms for transmitting features from one Extended Projection into another, for example, Spec-Head agreement. To illustrate the (in)ability of the [wh] feature to spread from certain positions, consider the data in (1.104).

(1.104) a. I wonder [$_{DP}$ which book] he read.
       b. I wonder [$_{PP}$ with whom] they spoke.
       c. I wonder [$_{DP}$ which friend's book] they read.
       d. *I wonder [$_{DP}$ a book about whom] they read.

Example (1.104a) is a straightforward instance of feature-percolation within a 'perfect', that is, non-extended, X^{max} (from D^0 to D^{max}). (1.104b) is an instance of percolation within an extended projection (from D to P^{max}, the latter being viewed as a *nominal* functional category, and thus a member of the extended projection to which *whom* belongs). In (1.104c), both percolation and Spec-Head agreement are involved; thus, the [wh] feature is transmitted by percolation from *which* to *which friend*, by Spec-Head agreement from *which friend* to *'s*, and again by percolation from *'s* to DP. The deviance of (1.104d) is attributed by Grimshaw to the non-existence of mechanisms which would enable [wh] to spread beyond PP.[19]

It is of some interest to note that the kind of discrepancy which exists between LF and S-Structure requirements in [wh]-marked clauses is also found in negative constructions. Rizzi (1991) proposes that the *wh*-Criterion generalizes naturally to negative constructions, and Haegeman and Zanuttini (1991) construct an account of a variety of effects found in certain negative constructions of a number of languages (most particularly, West Flemish) in terms of the following extension of the *wh*-Criterion:

(1.105) The Neg-Criterion

       a. Each NegP must be in a Spec-Head relation with a Neg X°.
       b. Each Neg X° must be in a Spec-Head relation with a NegP.

West Flemish has a Neg X° which is optionally realizable as *-en*.[20] On the assumption that the Neg-Criterion (also) holds at S-Structure in West Flemish, its (b) subcase correctly predicts that (1.106a) and the full version of (1.106b) contrast in grammaticality in the way indicated, because the former only exhibits a NegP in [SPEC, C']; in the latter example, the phrase in [SPEC, C'] merely includes a NegP as a proper subpart. By making comparable assumptions about English, the essentially parallel contrast between (1.106c) and (1.106d) is also correctly predicted.

(1.106) a. [$_{NP}$ Niets]   (en)-deeg Valère.
               nothing *en* -did Valère
            'Valère did not do anything.'
       b. [$_{VP}$ Niets zeggen] (*en)-durft Valère zeker.
               nothing say   *en* -dares Valère certainly
            'To say nothing, Valère wouldn't dare.'
       c. [No women] has John (ever) treated so badly.
       d. *[The women with no children] has John (ever)
               treated so badly.

Now, observe that the well-formedness of (1.106e)–(1.106g) appears to contradict the (b) subcase of the Neg-Criterion, since the phrases in [SPEC, C'], while including a Neg proper subelement, are not themselves negative.

(1.106) e. [_pp Over niemand] (en) -klaapt ze tegen myn.
about nobody en -talks she against me
'She does not talk about anybody to me.'
f. Niemand zen us (en)-was-ter gereed.
nobody his house en -was-there ready
'Nobody's house was ready.'
g. [The wives of no other men] has John (ever) treated so badly.

However, (1.106e)–(1.106g) crucially contrast with (1.106b) and (1.106d) in that in the former three, but not in the latter two, the negative elements are construed as having wide (clausal) scope. Note that this contrast is essentially parallel to the one between (1.104c) (reproduced below) and (1.104e), where the phrases in [SPEC, C'] properly include a *wh*-element in both cases, but this element is construable as having clausal scope in (1.104c) only, since in (1.104e) the scope of *who* is necessarily limited to the complement of *question*.

(1.104) c. I wonder [_DP which friend's book] they read.
e. *I wonder [_DP the question who did it] they discussed.

The facts in (1.106) strongly suggest that the ((b) subcase of the) Neg-Criterion correlates in English and West Flemish with anticipatory S-Structure requirements analogous to those that were noted above in relation to the ((b) subcase of the) *wh*-Criterion in languages with overt *wh*-Movement. In particular, if we assume a feature [*Neg*] which can be covertly transmitted by the kind of mechanisms that were seen to effect the spread of [*wh*], the S-Structure anticipatory condition seems to be that [*Neg*] should be able to reach [SPEC, C'], and thereby signal that the Neg-Criterion *will* be satisfied at LF. The parallelism between the mechanisms which propagate [*wh*] and [*Neg*] can be appreciated by noting that the latter can 'spread' within a maximal projection (cf. (1.104a) with (1.106c)) or within an Extended Projection (cf. (1.104b) with (1.106e)), and can also be introduced into Extended Projections by Spec-Head agreement (cf. (1.104c) with (1.106f)), as well as by the kind of mechanisms hinted at in n. 19 (p. 233) (cf. (i) and (iii) of n. 19 with (1.106g)). For an additional type of situation where a feature 'penetrates' an Extended Projection and subsequently 'spreads' within it, see n. 3, p. 227.

We have so far illustrated two of the three difficulties with Rizzi's view of the *wh*-Criterion which were noted at the beginning of this section. We now turn to the third problem, namely, that some languages where *wh*-phrases must occur *in situ* at S-Structure none the less exhibit anticipatory requirements at that level. Watanabe (1991) argues, on the basis of certain complex Subjacency effects found in Japanese interrogative clauses, that these constructions involve NO-Movement prior to S-Structure, the launching site of the NO being the Specifier of a *wh*-phrase, or of a DP which properly contains a *wh*-phrase.[21] A reasonable interpretation of this state of affairs is that [*wh*] covertly spreads by mechanisms of the kind we saw above to the NO, which then conveys this feature to [SPEC, C'], thereby signalling at S-Structure that some *wh*-phrase *will* satisfy the ((b) subcase of the) *wh*-Criterion at LF. Under this interpretation, English and Japanese emerge as much less different in respect to the *wh*-Criterion than might appear at first sight. Both languages have essentially the same kind of S-Structure requirements and differ only in the ways in which these requirements are satisfied (movement to [SPEC, C'] of an overt phrase in English and of an NO in Japanese). The anticipatory requirements posited for Japanese cannot be automatically assumed with respect to every language with interrogative phrases *in situ*. For example, Lakhota, which exhibits no Subjacency effects in its interrogative constructions (Williamson 1987), is arguably a language without S-Structure anticipatory requirements.

In the course of our discussion of the *wh*-Criterion, we have proposed that the ability of a *wh*-element to trigger the Pied-Piping of a phrase which properly contains it depends on the possibility of conveying [*wh*] to the 'top' of that phrase. Why then can an NO not trigger Pied-Piping (as noted in Chapter 2)? True, an NO bears no overt [*wh*] feature, but might it not be assumed to bear some abstract operator feature? And if yes, as seems reasonable, then why can it not convey this feature to a containing phrase? The answer to the last question lies, I suggest, in the recognition of the fact that whatever features an NO carries (for example, [+NAOP], [+COIND], [+OP]) need to be identified before they can be transmitted, because NOs are instances of *pro* (Browning 1987). The only element which can plausibly identify such features is a C° that carries them. But now observe that the locality condition on identification of *pro* by an antecedent is satisfied if an NO is in [SPEC, C'], but not if it is properly contained within a phrase in [SPEC, C']. Accordingly, there can be no Pied-Piping in cases of NO-Movement.

Recently, Pollock (1993) offered a different account of the inability of NOs to trigger Pied-Piping. Basically, he proposed that elements which lack specifications for phi-features, in particular, for [PERSON], [NUMBER], and [GENDER], may not trigger Pied-Piping, whether they are null or overt. An overt element which is unable to trigger Pied-Piping is, according to Pollock the French item *dont* 'of whom/which', which is only specified for GEN Case. Observe, however, that the Romanian relative pronoun *care*, which is used in restrictive and appositive relatives (and which bears NOM/ACC Case), has no phi-feature specifications for [PERSON], [NUMBER], or [GENDER] either, but can certainly trigger Pied-Piping (for illustration, see (1.108b) and (1.108d)). Pollock's proposal thus seems to be on the wrong track; presumably, the properties of *dont* need to be analysed in some other way (for example, by assuming, as proposed in Tellier (1988), that *dont* is a lexical complementizer).

3.2.4 Anti-Pied-Piping Effects as a Result of *pro*-Identification Requirements

Having established in the preceding section that Pied-Piping of some phrase depends on the ability of the feature [*wh*] to spread to the root node of that phrase, we now address the issue of the special anti-Pied-Piping effects found in *wh*-FRCs. I submit that these effects are deducible from the assumption that the FR is the necessary identifier of *pro* in conjunction with two independently-motivated assumptions, to which we now turn.

First, observe that the content of *pro* cannot be identified by the [*wh*] feature, or by specifications which define the operator type, such as [+NAOP] or [+COIND]; rather, the identifying features must be phi-features, for example, [NUMBER], [GENDER], [ANIMACY], [PERSON], etc. In principle, we may expect such specifications to be transmissible from the *wh*-element to the phrase in [SPEC, C'] by the kind of mechanisms that transmit [*wh*] (I note in passing that in cases where the *wh*-element is morphologically undifferentiated for phi-features, and also in FRs formed with an NO, a default [3PERSON] specification may be assumed, since FRCs are typically third person; see, however, n. 28, p. 236). In fact, however, phi-feature specifications appear to be transmissible only *within* an Extended Projection, but not *from* one Extended Projection *into* another, a generalization in fact captured by the descriptive statement in (1.71). What can be responsible for this state of affairs, in particular for the more limited propagation ability of phi-features as compared with [*wh*]? The answer to this question is, I submit, that phi-features which migrate into an Extended Projection are rendered syntactically inactive by phi-features inherent to that projection; putting this in a slightly different way, 'native' features have priority over 'immigrant' ones.

There is independent evidence for the correctness of the proposal just made. Thus consider the following Hungarian and Flemish data (cited in Szabolcsi (1983) and Grimshaw (1991: § 3.2.3) respectively).

```
(1.107) a. [_DP az én-∅ vendég -e -m].
              the I -NOM guest -POSS-1.SG.
           'My guest.'
        b. [_DP a te -∅ vendég-e -d].
              the thou-NOM guest -POSS-2.SG.
           'Thy guest.'
```

```
c.  ...[_CP da   Jan noa Gent    goat].
          that Jan to   Ghent   goes
    '...that Jan goes to Gent.'
d.  ...[_CP dan  Jan en  Pol noa Gent   goan].
          that Jan and Pol to   Ghent  go
    '...that Jan and Pol go to Ghent.'
```

In Hungarian, as illustrated in (1.107a, b), the head noun of a DP bears not only its own morphological specifications for number, person, etc., but also those of a (possessive) phrase in [SPEC, D'] (by Spec-Head agreement). Crucially, such specifications do not become syntactically-active properties of the bracketed DPs, since the only phi-feature specifications which play a role in those DPs' interactions with their environment are their inherent ones, never those inherited from the possessor (demonstration omitted). This clearly shows the need for a mechanism assigning priority to 'inherent' specifications over 'immigrant' ones. The same conclusion emerges from a consideration of the Flemish data in (1.107c, d), which illustrate the fact that, in this language, the phi-features of a subject are reflected not only in the verbal inflection, but also in the morphology of the complementizer. None the less, CPs of this type invariably interact with their context as [SING, 3PERSON] phrases, whatever the phi-specifications inherited from the subject (demonstration omitted).

To sum up, the anti-Pied-Piping effects are arguably a consequence of the mechanism which 'deactivates' feature-specifications that must compete against inherent specifications of some Extended Projection.[22] However, this mechanism does not fully explain the effects at issue. To achieve an explanation, it must furthermore be assumed that *pro* identification necessarily takes place at (or no later than) S-Structure; without this assumption, the LF operations which assign operator status to *wh*-phrases properly contained within Pied-Piped phrases (see section 3.2.3) would incorrectly make possible the identification of *pro* by CP. Note that the contemplated assumption is quite natural, since the featural content of *pro* is relevant not only to LF, but also to PF. In the particular case where *pro* is the Head of an FRC, note that the FRC as a whole needs to participate in various agreement processes of a morphological nature, as can be seen, for example, in [*pro* [*whatever books she buys*]] *always please/*pleases her.* Furthermore, the features which take part in such morphological processes may have an arbitrary (that is, semantically unmotivated) character (for illustrations, see Rizzi (1986)), and it seems quite reasonable that such features should be identified at S-Structure, rather than at LF. I thus propose to assume that the identification of *pro in general* takes place at S-Structure.[23]

This proposal is independently needed with respect to two distinct phenomena. First, note that unless S-Structure identification of *pro* is assumed, the analysis of the total absence of Pied-Piping with NOs which

THE SYNTAX OF FREE RELATIVE CONSTRUCTIONS

was put forward in section 3.2.3 does not really go through, since LF manipulation of NOs contained within a larger phrase (analogous to the kind of operations assumed to apply to *wh*-elements; see preceding paragraph) could conceivably place them in a local configuration with respect to C°.

The second phenomenon which supports the assumption that *pro* is identified at S-Structure consists in certain internal-syntax effects found in Japanese Head-Internal relatives. In addition, this phenomenon supports, much like the anti-Pied-Piping effects, the assumption that the *pro*-Head of an amount relative clause needs to be identified by that clause, as well as the assumption that the propagation of phi-features across the boundaries of Extended Projections is blocked by phi-features inherent to the 'host'.

As noted in section 2.4, Japanese Head-Internal relatives, which were illustrated by the reduced version of (1.92b) (reproduced below),

```
(1.92) b.  [John -ga ronbun-o  kaita -no] -ga
           John NOM paper ACC wrote -NM  NOM
           LI-ni   notta.
           LI-LOC  appeared
           'The paper that John wrote appeared in LI.'
```

exhibit Subjacency effects, something which led Watanabe (1991) to assume NO-Movement from the specifier of the internal Head; an illustration of this construction's sensitivity to the Complex NP Constraint is provided in (1.92b').

```
(1.92) b'. *John-ga  subarasii ronbun-o   kaita hito  -o
           John-NOM  excellent paper -ACC wrote person-ACC
           homete -ita-no-ga    shuppan-sareta.
           praised-had-NM-NOM   was published
           'An excellent paper which John had praised
           the person who wrote (it) was published.'
```

In n. 21 (p. 234), it was pointed out that Japanese interrogative constructions also exhibit Subjacency effects, with the exception that non-exclamatory *wh*-phrases are exempt from the Complex NP Constraint (albeit not from the *wh*-island Constraint); the reduced version of (ii) of that note, which is reproduced below as (1.92b"), illustrates the exemption just alluded to.

```
(1.92) b". Mary-wa  [Tom-ni  nani-o    ageta
           Mary-TOP  TOM-DAT what-ACC  gave
           hito  -ni] atta no?
           person-DAT met  Q
           'What is such that Mary met the person
           who gave it to John?'
```

As indicated in note 21, Watanabe proposed to account for the 'surprising' acceptability of (1.92b") by assuming that [*wh*] has more extensive propagation privileges in Japanese than in English, so that in cases like the above, this feature can spread to the specifier of the complex DP, thereby enabling a NO launched from that position to satisfy the anticipatory requirements of the *wh*-Criterion that hold in Japanese; in this way, a Subjacency violation may be avoided.

Why then can the Subjacency violation in (1.92b') not be circumvented in a comparable fashion? Note that NO-Movement evidently serves the same anticipatory function with respect to the *wh*-Criterion in both interrogatives and Head-Internal relatives (that the internal Head bears [*wh*] is the null hypothesis, and is no way contradicted by the homonymy of internal Heads and canonical nominals; note that [*wh*] is by no means necessarily realized in a morphologically uniform way throughout a language, as shown, for example, by the fact that German interrogative pronouns are *w*-marked, while the corresponding relative pronouns are *d*-marked). The reason for the contrast in grammaticality between (1.92b') and (1.92b") is, I submit, that phi-features, unlike [*wh*], are unable to spread across Extended Projection boundaries due to the blocking effect of inherent phi-features. Since the relative must identify *pro*, only the phi-features of the internal Head are appropriate, as those of the complex DP would induce an incorrect interpretation; hence a Subjacency violation is unavoidable.

Observe that, just as in the case of the anti-Pied-Piping effects, the proposed account goes through only if *pro* identification necessarily takes place at S-Structure. If this process could be delayed until LF, whatever mechanisms ensure the correct scope interpretation for the *wh*-phrase in (1.92b") could also operate on the internal Head in (1.92b'), thereby making it possible for CP to identify *pro* at LF and to circumvent a Subjacency violation by NO-Movement.

In conclusion, the view that *pro* needs to be identified at S-Structure seems to rest on firm grounds (see, however, section 3.3.3 for further discussion of this matter).

3.2.5 On the notion 'local domain' for *pro*-Identification

In section 3.1.3, it was proposed that the locality conditions for *pro* identification are better characterized in terms of (a generalization of) Chomsky's notion of 'Minimal Domain' than in terms of a government configuration, as assumed in Rizzi (1986). There arguably exists, however, an additional *pro* construction for which this proposal is (at least *prima facie*) too restrictive.

The kind of construction at issue consists of a determiner and a restrictive modifier, in particular, a restrictive relative clause, such as *those who sing*. If we assume Grimshaw's (1991) theory of phrase structure, which disallows intransitive functional Heads, the example just given ought to have the structure in (1.98a'), where CP is a sister of *pro* (note that (1.98a') is structurally parallel to the full version of (1.98a), except for the fact that the strong/weak status of D and its projections is unspecified and that the lower nominal categories are NPs, rather than weak DPs).

(1.98) a.

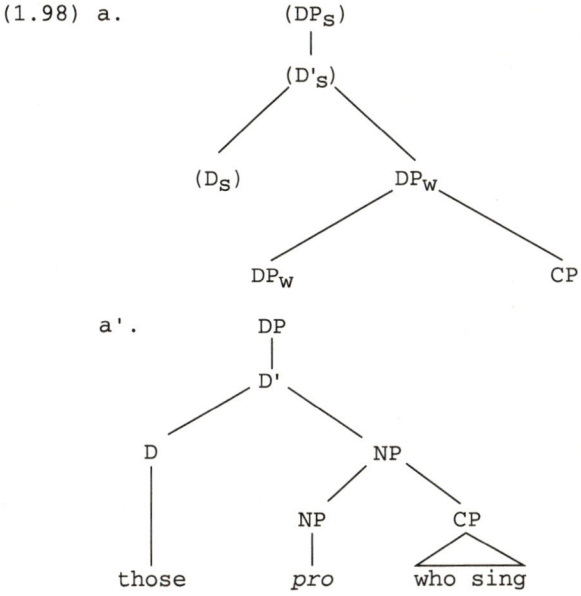

Since the restrictive CP in (1.98a') cannot identify *pro* (see section 3.1.3), the presumed identifier of *pro* is D, the closest element with appropriate (overt) phi-feature specifications. How can we, however, allow identification by an X° *into the Head* of a YP in this case, without allowing it in general (see section 3.1.3)?

There are (at least) two possible answers to this question, both of which exploit the fact that D and *pro* in (1.98a') lie within the same Extended Projection. One possibility is to assume that the upper limit of the locality domain for *pro* identification may be extended to include the lowest Extended Projection that contains *pro*. This will allow the identification of *pro* in the configuration under consideration, without however permitting free restrictive relative constructions (and, more generally, 'free adjunct constructions'; see section 3.1.3). Another possibility would be to assume that *pro* may raise prior to S-Structure and adjoin to the next higher Head, provided that this process does not cross Extended Projection boundaries. This kind of analysis also captures the distinction just noted, and without necessitating an extension of the locality domain.

Whichever of these two approaches is adopted, we are faced with the following interesting question: in an OHRC with the structure in (1.98a) where D_s is overt, the lower DP_w is *pro* and CP is of the amount type, can *pro* be identified by D_s, or must it be identified by CP? The way to answer this question which most immediately come to mind is to check whether CP, under such circumstances, exhibits anti-Pied-Piping effects; note that the absence of such effects would indicate that the relative need not identify *pro*. While this verification procedure is straightforward in principle, its application is sometimes prevented by objective reasons. In particular, it is inapplicable in English, where amount OHRCs are formed with an NO (which, recall, rules out Pied-Piping of any sort).

One language which offers some possibility for verification is Romanian, where amount OHRCs employ the *wh*-form *ce* 'what', in contrast to restrictive relatives, which employ the *wh*-form *care* 'which'. That OHRCs which contrast in the *wh*-forms they use in the way just indicated also correspondingly contrast in respect to amount/restrictive status is shown by the data in (1.108a, b).

(1.108) a. Tot pro la ce   se   uită Maria (*la ce   se
            all pro at what REFL looks Maria   at what REFL
            uită şi Ion) mă intereseaza personal.
            looks and Ion me interests   personally
            'All that Maria is looking at (that Ion is also looking at)
            interests me personally.'
       b. Cei   pro la care se   uită Maria (la care
          those pro at whom REFL looks Maria   at whom
          se   uită şi Ion) mă intereseaza personal.
          REFL looks and Ion me interest   personally
          'Those that Maria is looking at (who Ion also
          looks at) interest me personally.'

Observe that the *ce*-relatives in the (a) subcase do not stack, while the *care*-relatives in the (b) subcase do stack. Now, consider the data in (1.108c, d), where material not contained in an Extended Projection of the *wh*-element has Pied-Piped.

(1.108) c. *Tot pro de raportul   despre ce
            all pro of report-the about   what
            e răspunzătoare Maria ...
            is responsible   Maria
            'Everything for the report about which
            Maria is responsible...'
       d. ?Cei   pro de rapoartele despre care
          those pro of reports-the about   which
          e răspunzătoare Maria ...
          is responsible   Maria
          'Those for the reports about whom
          Maria is responsible ...

For some reason (1.108d) is not perfect; presumably, the propagation of [*wh*] by mechanisms other than percolation and Spec-Head agreement is not entirely free in Romanian. None the less, (1.108d) is distinctly better than (1.108c), which points to the conclusion that the functional Head can identify *pro* in the former example, but not in the latter.

What seems to be needed here is some principle which marks CP as the preferred identifier of *pro* in situations where both CP and D are potentially fit to fulfil this role. Under the analysis of *pro* identification in (1.98a') which assumes an extension of the locality domain from Minimal Domain to lowest Extended Projection, extension may be viewed as a marked option, to be appealed to only when identification within the Minimal Domain is impossible. Under the view which assumes raising of *pro* to D_s prior to S-Structure, such an operation may be viewed as violating the economy principle of 'Last Resort' (Chomsky 1992), and thus as unavailable if identification without raising is possible.

3.2.6 A German Correlative-like Construction

In section 3.2.1, I noted that the locality constraint on *pro* identification disqualifies correlatives of the kind in (1.98b) from functioning as identifiers, and pointed to the prediction that correlatives with overt *wh*-Movement to [SPEC, C'] should be free from anti-Pied-Piping effects. This prediction is not testable with respect to Hindi, where *wh*-phrases do not move to [SPEC, C'] prior to S-Structure. There is, however, a construction of German which arguably confirms this prediction.

In section 1.4.3.3, I noted that German left-dislocated FRCs unexpectedly fail to show anti-Pied-Piping effects, as illustrated by the following data which I have reproduced here.

(1.79) [Wessen Frau du verführst], *dessen* Zorn muss du fürchten.
       whose wife you seduce   his anger must you fear
    '(He) whose wife you seduce, you must fear his anger.'

(1.80) a. (?)[Wessen Frau du verführst], *der* wird dich immer hassen.
          whose wife you seduce   he will you always hate
      '(He) whose wife you seduce, that one will always hate you.'

I now suggest that what we took to be FRCs are in fact a sort of correlative, that is, 'bare' FRs in the position of Left-Dislocation whose corresponding weak DP is the null complement of the italicized demonstrative pronouns. This analysis solves the mystery of the grammaticality of the above examples.[24]

We may, of course, wonder why other languages, for example English and Romanian, do not allow such correlative-like constructions (see section 1.4.3.3). A possible reason may be connected with the fact that German, in contrast to English and Romanian, assigns no invariant (default) Case to the Left-Dislocation position. Thus, while Romanian and English necessarily assign NOM and Objective respectively to the position in question (demonstration omitted), German assigns to it either a default Case (NOM), or the case of the 'resumptive' demonstrative in the ensuing clause, a state of affairs that was already noted in section 1.4.1 and illustrated in (1.42) (reproduced below).

(1.42) Dieser Mann(NOM)/diesen Mann(ACC), den(ACC) würde ich
        this   man   this   man   him   would I
        gern einladen.
        gladly invite
        'This man, I would gladly invite him.'

This state of affairs is amenable to the interpretation that German, in contrast to English or Romanian, does not *automatically* assign *any* Case to left-dislocated elements (overt nominals in that position are, of course, permitted only if they do get *some* Case). Now, if the position in question necessarily has Case, an FR must have a *pro*-Head, because a 'bare' FR would be non-canonical under such circumstances (see section 3.2.1); hence, the anti-Pied-Piping effects found in English and Romanian. But if the position at issue may fail to receive Case, a 'bare' FR ought to be possible; hence, the acceptability of data like (1.79) and (1.80a).

3.2.7 Summary

In the preceding sections we have outlined a unified approach to amount constructions, and have worked out the conditions under which an amount CP may function as identifier of *pro*. It was shown that certain internal-syntax effects found in FRs yield to the view that an FR is the necessary identifier of its *pro*-Head in conjunction with the assumptions that *pro* needs to be identified at S-Structure and that the spread of feature specifications 'into' Extended Projections is blocked by inherent specifications of corresponding types.

3.3 TOWARDS A UNIFIED THEORY OF *pro*

In sections 3.1 and 3.2, I argued – primarily on the basis of constructions where *pro* occurred in Head position – for a theory of *pro* which, while indebted to the theory in Rizzi (1986), differed from the latter in three important respects: (i) the Head-government requirement for formal licensing was given up, retaining Case-assignment only; (ii) the locality domain for identification was redefined as the *Minimal Domain of a Head of any rank*, a natural extension of a locality construct put forward in Chomsky (1992); and (iii) the linkage between formal and content licensing was given up.

In this section, I propose to explore the consequences of my theory of *pro* with respect to a wider variety of *pro* constructions. As we shall see, while certain constructions turn out to fall on neutral ground between Rizzi's theory and mine, there exist (aspects) of specific constructions with respect to which my theory makes better predictions than his.

Before proceeding to this task, it will be useful to make explicit an assumption which has been implicit all along. Thus, I view *pro* as a nominal null pro-form whose hierarchical rank may vary, in particular, between N° and strong DP. To illustrate some of these options, *pro* is a strong DP when functioning as a definite argument, a weak DP when heading an FRC, an NP when heading the complex NP of a restrictive relative construction (1.98a'), and an N° in contexts like [*those* [pro *of the king*]], where *of the king* is presumably a complement of *pro*.[25]

3.3.1 Formal Licensing

In respect to formal licensing, the following constructions are, as far as I can see, neutral between the two theories under consideration: (i) *pro* in various A-positions; and (ii) *pro* in a context like (1.98a'), where CP may be replaced by any kind of modifier (note that in the latter case, D governs and assigns or conveys Case to *pro*).

The following *pro* constructions appear to be inconsistent with Rizzi's theory, but not with mine: (i) FRCs in ungoverned positions, for example, that of Left-Dislocation, to which Case none the less needs to be assigned; (ii) the 'Null (discourse) Topics' (which may serve as antecedents for an NO) proposed in Huang (1984) and Cole (1987b), which are plausible instances of *pro*, and which are presumably ungoverned but need to receive Case in some alternative way (presumably in the way in which overt topics do); (iii) Null Operators, which – as noted in section 3.2.3 – may be analysed as instances of *pro*, and are governed at S-Structure by C°, but do not (in general) receive Case from it: rather, they either belong to a chain whose foot typically receives Case, so that NOs typically 'inherit', if anything, Case from the variable they bind; alternatively, NOs may bind an RP, and presumably inherit Case from it. NOs may thus be analysed as formally licensed by Case, but not by Case-*government*.

3.3.2 Identification

In respect to identification, there exist identifying mechanisms other than antecedence, and the constructions where they apply are irrelevant to both Rizzi's theory and mine. I none the less list two of these in subsections 3.3.2.1 and 3.3.2.2, for the sake of completeness.

3.3.2.1 *Identification by Discourse or Situational Context*

Identification by discourse or by the context of situation appears to be necessary for Null Topics (see section 3.3.1), and also for certain instances of argument *pro*.

Concerning the latter possibility, Cole (1987b) argues that (definite) null objects need to be analysed in certain languages (for example, Thai, Korean and Quechua) as instances of *pro*, rather than as traces of NOs. To the extent that their content is allowed to vary with the (discourse or situational) context, the latter is the most plausible source of identification. A comparable state of affairs seems to be found in Romanian past subjunctive constructions, as illustrated by (1.109), which, in appropriate contexts, can have any of the readings indicated (note that the verbal system exhibits no overt AGR specifications).

(1.109)　E　imposibil *pro* să　　fi spus aşa　ceva.
　　　　　is impossible　　SUBJ be said thus something
　　　　　'It's impossible that I/you/he/she/we/they should have
　　　　　said something like this.

3.3.2.2 *Identification by default*

Situations where *pro*'s content takes on a fixed default value in a local structurally-definable context (where no plausible antecedent exists) are found with null direct objects in Brazilian Portuguese (Farrell 1990), as well as with null P-objects in French (Zribi-Hertz 1984; Farkas 1987). These are invariably construed as [3PERSON], although their overt counterparts are in no way subject to this limitation; illustrations are provided in (1.110a) and (1.110b, c) respectively.

(1.110)　a.　Coitado do　　　João/*de *mim*/*de *você*.
　　　　　　　poor　　of the João　of me　　of you
　　　　　　　O　chefe mandou *pro* embora.
　　　　　　　the boss　sent　　　　away
　　　　　　　'Poor João$_i$/me$_i$/you$_i$. The boss sent him$_i$/*me$_i$/*you$_i$ away.'
　　　　　b.　Jean est venu (?) *la*[26] /*te/ **me* visiter,
　　　　　　　Jean is come　　her　you　me visit
　　　　　　　mais a　refusé　de sortir avec *pro*.
　　　　　　　but has refused of to-go-out　with
　　　　　　　'Jean came to visit her$_i$/you$_i$/me$_i$, but refused to go out
　　　　　　　with (?) her$_i$/*you$_i$/*me$_i$.'
　　　　　c.　Jean a　trouvé *le*　*collier* et　a　　essayé
　　　　　　　Jean has found　the necklace and has tried
　　　　　　　de s'　　enfuir　　　avec *pro*.
　　　　　　　of REFL. to-run-away with
　　　　　　　'Jean found the necklace$_i$ and tried to run away with it$_i$.'

3.3.2.3 *Identification by an antecedent*

Antecedent mechanisms for *pro* identification that have been proposed in the literature fall into two broad categories, depending on whether they are/are not subject to locality requirements.

Appeal to a non-local antecedent was made in Cinque (1990, Ch. 3), where it was argued that certain unbounded base-generated operator-variable dependencies utilize *pro* with variable import. In such constructions, *pro* typically occurs in A-positions, where it receives Case under government. However, identification is not locally effected, because *pro* is not in general allowed in such contexts without a binding operator; accordingly, Cinque proposes to view the operator as identifier. Under this analysis, the sources of formal and content identification do not coincide. This state of affairs is consistent with my theory, which denies the existence of a 'linkage', but is inconsistent with Rizzi's.

In respect to identification by a local antecedent, the major constructions addressed by Rizzi (subject and object *pro*) are neutral between his theory and mine. Also neutral are NO constructions, where the NO is both governed (albeit not Case-governed; see section 3.3.1) and identified by C^{o27}, and the kind of construction illustrated by (1.98a'), where D is both a Case-governor and an identifier.

There exists, however, at least one type of construction, which has already been prominently discussed and for which the linkage hypothesis appears to be too strong. I am referring to *pro*-headed amount relative constructions, in which the relative is the necessary identifier, but not the source of formal licensing (that is, Case). This applies both to FRCs and to OHRCs like those in (1.108a) and (1.108c).

To sum up, the linkage hypothesis cannot be maintained in general either in constructions with non-local or with local antecedents.

There is one additional aspect of identification which I wish to address briefly here. As has often been observed, in cases of local identification by AGR, considerations of 'sufficient richness' appear to be relevant. I should like to suggest – and propose to argue the point in Chapter 4 – that this is to a certain extent true in cases of identification by an amount relative. Recall that an amount relative inherits its identifying features from a phrase in [SPEC, C']. It appears that even when that phrase is an NO and no other sources for feature-specifications exist, the relative still possesses a (default) [3PERSON] specification, which appears to be sufficient for *pro* identification, in view of the existence of constructions like those described in Chapter 2 of this study.[28] When, however, the phrase in [SPEC, C'] is overt, considerations of 'sufficient richness' arguably play a part, in the sense that Kase-matching effects tend to manifest themselves especially when the identifying operator is relatively 'poor' in phi-specifications, compensating, as it were, for such 'poverty' by Kase-specifications. For elaboration of this point, see section 4.4.2.

3.3.3 On the S-Structure Identification of *pro*

In section 3.2.4, I exhibited a number of arguments in favour of effecting *pro* identification at S-Structure. The argumentation was based on constructions where *pro* functioned as either Head or NO, but the proposed view seems to be consistent with all *pro*-constructions, as far as I can tell.

One area where the view at issue has implications of some interest is that of parasitic gap constructions. Chomsky (1982) observed that parasitic gaps must be bound by an operator *at S-Structure*, LF binding being insufficient, as illustrated in (1.111) ('pg' is an *ad hoc* notation for 'parasitic gap').

(1.111) a. *What* did John buy [e] after Mary sold [pg]?
       b. *Who bought *What* after Mary sold [pg]?

(At least) two well-known types of analyses have been proposed for pg constructions. In Chomsky (1986a), it is proposed that pgs arise through NO movement (basically, in order to account for Subjacency effects); in (1.111a), the NO would move to the [SPEC, C'] of the subordinate clause, then adjoin to the PP headed by *after*, and the chain thus created would form a 'composite chain' with the chain of the 'real gap'. In Cinque (1990: Ch. 3), this analysis is rejected, and it is proposed instead that a pg is simply an instance of *pro* which is interpreted as a variable, due to binding (without chain-formation) by an operator at S-Structure (Subjacency effects are accounted for in an alternative independently-motivated way).

The implications alluded to above are two. First, under the assumption that parasitic gaps are operator-identified instances of *pro*, the facts in (1.111) are automatically accounted for. Second, while the assumption just noted can be made under both Cinque's and Chomsky's accounts, the former emerges – under such circumstances – as better motivated than the latter. The reason is that, as argued for in section 3.2.4, NOs (viewed as instances of *pro*) must in general move to [SPEC, C'] prior to S-Structure in order to be identified by C^0. But in parasitic gap constructions like (1.111a), identification by C^0 is impossible, since the subordinate clause is a declarative, with the result that the only conceivable identifier is the capitalized *wh*-phrase. But if so, NO movement is deprived of motivation, since *pro* can be operator-identified *in situ*. In short, the S-Structure identification hypothesis accounts for the contrast in (1.111) and yields a higher rating for the account of parasitic gaps in Cinque (1990) than for the one in Chomsky (1986a).

Having presented a battery of arguments in favour of S-Structure identification of *pro*, it is perhaps appropriate to consider how this proposal can be expressed within a theory that does not recognize S-Structure as a level of representation, in particular, within the Minimalistic Theory of Chomsky (1992), from which the construct 'Minimal Domain' was borrowed. I am addressing this issue primarily for completeness, not because there is any necessary logical connection between the rejection of government and the adoption of Minimal Domain on the one hand and the elimination of S-Structure (and/or D-Structure) on the other (in Chomsky (1992) both steps are taken). Within the pre-minimalistic framework adopted in this study, the assumption of S-Structure identification of *pro* has made it possible to account (among other things) for the anti-Pied-Piping effects in realis *wh*-FRCs and for the Subjacency effects in Japanese Head-Internal relatives. Chomsky proposed a single mechanism for forcing 'early' movement to some [SPEC, X'] in general, and to [SPEC, C'] in particular: 'strong' features on X°, which make the derivation 'crash' at PF if those features are not erased by matching features on some phrase in [SPEC, X']. Chomsky assumes that an [OP] feature, which occurs on C° in interrogative (relative, etc.) clauses and is universally strong, invariably forces the early (in Chomsky's terms, pre-SPELL OUT) movement of either an overt *wh*-phrase or an NO to [SPEC, C'] (the universality assumption may be too strong, in view of the absence of Subjacency effects in Lakhota; see section 3.2.3). Now, observe that this mechanism can force the early raising of *some wh*-phrase or NO, but not of a *wh*-phrase or NO which bears *specific phi-feature specifications*, in particular, those of a *pro*-Head. The minimal assumption that would achieve the desired result is, it seems to me, to stipulate that *pro* universally bears some strong features which are eliminated under identification (alternatively, that *pro*'s *phi-features* are universally strong, but their *values* are invisible until identified, and features without specifications cause a derivation to crash). As far as I can see, this solution, while consistent with the minimality framework, is neither more illuminating nor less stipulative than the one we proposed. Accordingly, in respect to the specific problem of *pro* identification, the solution we have proposed is not conceptually or empirically inferior to the one made available within the more recent theoretical framework.

3.4 ON NON-NOMINAL FRCs

The preceding sections have been concerned with uncontroversially nominal FRCs. In this section, we will address the special problems that arise in relation to FRCs which, at least *prima facie*, belong to other categories, and first and foremost to what we called in Chapter 1 'missing-P FRCs'. These are illustrated by the bracketed structures in the French data in (1.21), of which I reproduce the (b) subcase below; I also provide additional illustrations from Romanian, English, Hebrew and German in (1.21d)–(1.21g) respectively.

(1.21) b. Pierre s'   est battu [avec qui tu voulais qu' il
         Pierre self is beaten with who you wanted that he
         sorte].
         go-out
         'Pierre fought (with the one) with whom you wanted him to go out.'
      d. Vorbesc [despre ce   vorbeşti şi tu].
         speak-I about   what speak-you and you
         'I'm talking (about that) about which you, too, are talking.'

e. I will live [in whatever town you live].
f. ani oved [im   mi še   ata oved].
   I work with who that you work
   'I work with (the one) with whom you work.'
g. Sie stürzten sich [auf wen   sie sich
   they threw   REFL on who.ACC they REFL
   nur stürzen konnten].
   only throw could
   'They grabbed who(m)ever they could.'

The reason for this special interest in such data is that they raise, in addition to the issue that confronts all *wh*-FRCs, that is, whether the *wh*-phrase is in Head-position or in [SPEC, C'], an additional issue, namely, whether the *wh*-phrase and the adjacent P are or are not sisters; for ease of reference, I shall refer to these two orthogonal binary distinctions in terms of specifications on the *wh*-phrase of the form [+/−H(eadness)] and [+/−S(isterhood)] (I do not, of course, mean that such specifications are part of the formal representation of the *wh*-phrase).

The four possible combinations of values of [H] and [S] yield the four possible surface representations in (1.112a)–(1.112d), in which all irrelevant details are omitted, and which can be characterized as, respectively, [+H, +S], [+H, −S], [−H, −S] and [−H, +S]. Further variants of [−H, +S] are conceivable if, instead of the undifferentiated null PP in Head position in (1.112d), we assume separate prepositional and nominal null categories, in which case, we get either (1.112e) or (1.112f) (where 'p' stands for a null P).

Example (1.112a) (IP version) is the analysis put forward in Bresnan and Grimshaw (1978); (1.112b) (IP version) was proposed and argued for in Larson (1987); (1.112c) was envisaged as a possibility in Hirschbühler (1976a); and finally, an [−H, +S] analysis has not, to the best of my knowledge, been argued for in print before, but constitutes the analysis I shall defend in this study.

My defence of [−H, +S] will consist of two major steps: first, I shall argue for [+S], second for [−H]. A third step will consist in examining the three variants of [−H, +S], namely, (1.112d), (1.112e) and (1.112f), and in arguing that the last is superior to the first two. In developing the first two steps of my defence, I shall also argue against various conceptual and empirical arguments for [+H] and [−S] put forward in Larson (1987). To the extent that my arguments are successful, they will, of course, also refute (1.112a) and (1.112c).

3.4.1 Larson's proposals

As noted in section 1.1, Bresnan and Grimshaw (1978) dealt with not only nominal and prepositional FRCs, but also with (*prima facie*) adjectival and adverbial ones. For completeness, I reproduce the following (from Larson

THE SYNTAX OF FREE RELATIVE CONSTRUCTIONS

(1.112)

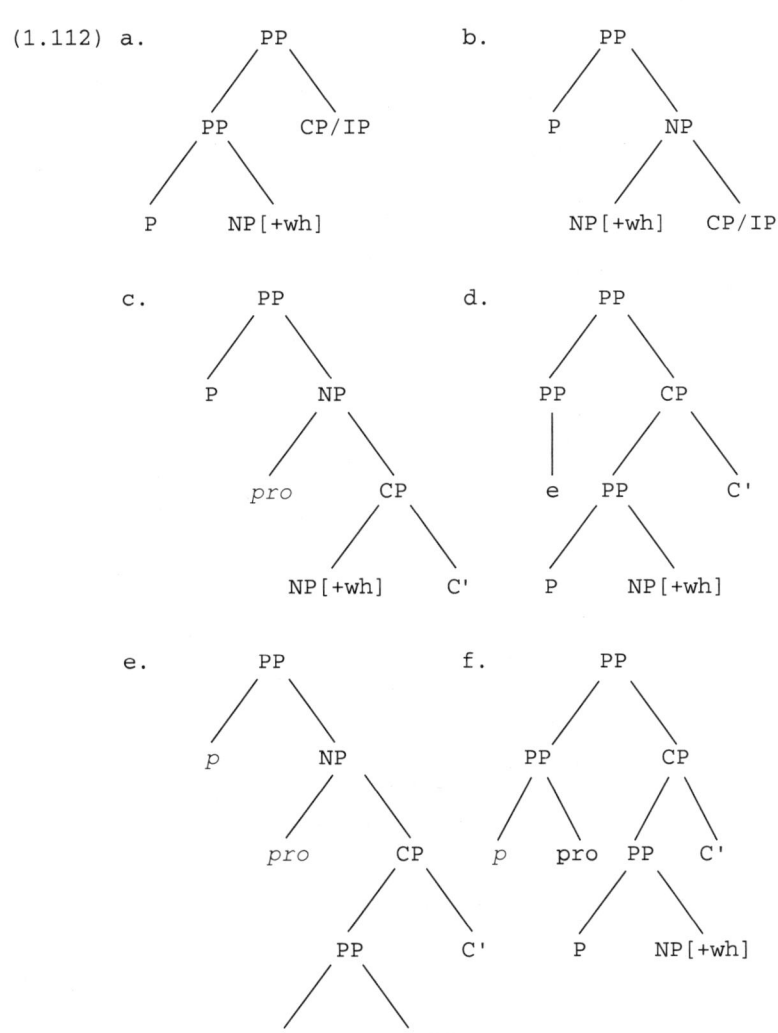

(1987)) data, which illustrate the main FRC-types considered by Bresnan and Grimshaw, as well as the gross structural analyses they assigned to them. Observe that the [+H] analysis assigned to nominal FRCs is extended to prepositional, adjectival and adverbial FRCs.

(1.113) a. I'll buy [$_{NP}$ [$_{NP}$ what(ever)] you want to sell].
b. John will leave [$_{PP}$ [$_{PP}$ when(ever)] Mary leaves].
c. I'll put my books [$_{PP}$ [$_{PP}$ where(ever)] you put yours].
d. I will live [$_{PP}$ [$_{PP}$ in whatever town] you live].
e. I'll word my letter [$_{AdvP}$ [$_{AdvP}$ however carefully] you word yours].
f. John will grow [$_{AP}$ [$_{AP}$ however tall] his father grew].

Bresnan and Grimshaw's data illustrated in (1.113b) and (1.113c) were reanalysed in Larson (1985) as headed by nouns of a special sort, rather than by PPs. I have nothing of interest to say about this analysis, beyond the rather obvious point that if the [–H] analysis is vindicated for nominal constructions like (1.113a), it ought also to generalize to those reanalysed as nominal by Larson.

Of primary interest to us is Larson's (1987) reaction to Bresnan and Grimshaw's analysis of (1.113d). While accepting, and in fact arguing for the [+H] feature (see below), Larson objected to the [+S] feature on the grounds that 'full' relative clause constructions, in particular, restrictive ones, are never PP-headed, and that (1.112a) thus rests on *ad hoc* structural assumptions. To avoid this perceived problem, he proposed to analyse missing-P FRCs as in (1.112b) (IP version). Note that under (1.112b), the relative-internal PP-gap no longer has an obvious antecedent at S-Structure, since the only PP that includes a suitable overt P also includes the null PP, and copying the containing PP onto the null one automatically creates another token of the latter, thereby triggering an infinite regress. Example (1.112b) constitutes an instance of the phenomenon known as 'antecedent-contained deletion', and Larson proposes to adopt the type of approach to this phenomenon put forward in May (1985), which basically relies on QR(aising) to create a *derived* 'non-containing' antecedent for the null PP. Specifically, Larson proposes that a construction like (1.113d) has the representation in (1.113d') at (D- and) S-Structure, the one in (1.113d") in the output to QR, and the one in (1.113''') in the output to the process that 'reconstructs' the content of the null PP.

(1.113) d'. I will live [$_{PP}$ in [$_{NP}$ [$_{NP}$ whatever town] [$_{IP}$ you live [$_{PP}$ e]]]]

d". [$_{IP}$ [$_{NP}$ [$_{NP}$ whatever town] [$_{IP}$ you live [$_{PP}$ e]]] [$_{IP}$ I will live [$_{PP}$ in e]]]

d'''. [$_{IP}$ [$_{NP}$ [$_{NP}$ whatever town] [$_{IP}$ you live [$_{PP}$ in e]]] [$_{IP}$ I will live [$_{PP}$ in e]]]

Larson also offered an argument in support of his decision to adopt a [+H] analysis. Noting that English missing-P FRCs are acceptable only when they exhibit *wh-ever* forms, but not simple *wh-*forms, he proposed to account for this distinction by assuming that only FRCs of the former type have the status of quantified NPs; with respect to FRCs of the latter type, he viewed them as 'typically equivalent to definite NPs . . . [which] are understood as referring expressions (that is, as nonquantificational)' (1987: 249). On the assumption that only *quantified NPs* undergo QR (which, recall, is viewed by Larson as a necessary condition for coherent interpretability), the contrast between *I'll work with whoever you work* and **I'll work with whom you work*, or between *I will live in whatever town you live* and **I will work in what town you live*, is accounted for under the assumption that the *wh-*phrase is the Head of a complex NP, but not under the assumption that it occupies the position [SPEC, C'], since it is hard to see how, in the latter type of configuration, it could determine the (non)quantificational properties of the complex NP.

I hope to be able to show in what follows that neither Larson's objections to PP-headed FRCs nor his argument for a [+H] analysis of missing-P FRCs go through.

Before proceeding to this task, it is appropriate to indicate how Larson envisages the analysis of (1.113e) and (1.113f). By and large, he assigns to adjectival and adverbial FRCs structural analyses parallel to those he assigns to nominal and prepositional ones, the adverbial suffix *-ly* having a function partly analogous to that of a P. Thus, he proposes that APs, just like NPs, must bear Case, and that *-ly*, just like P, is a Case assigner. For the sake of explicitness, I provide in (1.113e') the (D- and) S-Structure assigned to (1.113e) (I omit representing the results of applying QR and 'reconstruction' to (1.113'), which can easily be deduced on the basis of (1.113d") and (1.113''')).

(1.113) e'. I'll word my letter [$_{AdvP}$ -ly [$_{AP}$ *however careful*]
[$_{IP}$ you word yours [$_{AdvP}$ e]]]

I find the proposal that APs must bear Case appealing, and I will integrate it into my own analysis of (1.113f). As for Larson's analysis of data like (1.113e), I will not address it directly, but the results achieved with respect to data like (1.113d) may be taken to generalize to constructions of the former type.

3.4.2 Arguments for the [+S] property in missing-P FRCs

I propose to show in this section that Larson's conceptual objections to PP-headed FRCs are unfounded, and that there are empirical arguments based on data from English, French and German which indicate that the *wh*-phrase and the adjacent P form a PP constituent.

As indicated above, Larson objected to PP-headed FRCs on the grounds that there are no 'full' PP-headed relative constructions, and that (1.113a) would thus have an *ad hoc* character. This objection fails to go through for two reasons. First, as we shall see in section 3.4.6, there do seem to exist certain (admittedly somewhat marginal) 'full' PP-headed relative constructions in English. But, far more importantly, within the very framework of assumptions Larson espouses, not *all* FRCs derive their 'configurational legitimacy' from a corresponding 'full' *relative* construction. In particular, adjectival FRCs like (1.113f) are taken by Larson to derive their legitimacy from the existence of adjectival *comparative* constructions, such as (1.114a). But observe that this step voids his objection to PP-headed FRCs of any force, since comparative constructions come not just in adjectival, but also in nominal, adverbial and, crucially, prepositional varieties, as illustrated by the (b)–(d) subcases of (1.114).

(1.114) a. John is [$_{AP}$ [$_{AP}$ more successful]
than his father ever was].
b. I have [$_{NP}$ [$_{NP}$ more books] than Bill has].
c. John writes [$_{AdvP}$ [$_{AdvP}$ more quickly] than Mary ever did].
d. John is [$_{PP}$ [$_{PP}$ more in control of the situation]
than anybody else in the office ever was].

Accordingly, the structure in (1.113a) is no more *ad hoc* than the one in (1.113f), which Larson accepts.

In fact, as long as one insists on independent legitimization of structural analyses, it makes at least as much sense to view nominal FRCs as legitimized by nominal comparatives like (1.114b) than by restrictive OHRCs, in view of the fact that the subordinate clauses in both constructions are formed with an 'amount' operator (for comparatives, this is brought out by data like *there is at least as much gold in Peru as there is in Guatemala*).

Having shown that PP-headed FRCs are not objectionable, I now proceed to present three empirical arguments for the [+S] property, which, if successful, will rule out analyses like (1.112b) or (1.112c).

Consider first the English data in (1.115 and (1.115').

(1.115) a. I'll eat with [what(ever) you eat with].
b. It's [what(ever) you eat with] that I will eat with.
c. What I will eat with is [what(ever) you eat with].
d. [What(ever) you eat with], I will also eat with.

(1.115') a. I'll eat with [whatever you eat].
b. *It's [whatever you eat] that I will eat with.
c. *What I will eat with is [whatever you eat].
d. *[What(ever) you eat], I will also eat with.

In (1.115a), the bracketed string is an uncontroversial nominal FRC, whose constituent status is brought out by its ability to occur in the focus position of cleft and pseudo-cleft constructions and in a topicalized position, as shown in (1.115b)–(1.115d). In (1.115'a) on the other hand, the bracketed string is a constituent only according to the analyses in (1.112b) and (1.112c), but not according to those in (1.112a) or (1.112d)–(1.112f). Its inability to occur in the focus position of cleft and pseudo-cleft constructions or in a topicalized position (see (1.115'b)–(1.115'd)) argues against Larson's [−S] analysis in (1.112b).

Now, unacceptable data like (1.115'd) were in fact put forward by Bresnan and Grimshaw in support of their own analysis in (1.112a). Larson argued *contra* Bresnan and Grimshaw that such data can also be ruled out within the analysis in (1.112b), and this because uncontroversial 'antecedent-contained deletion' constructions also disallow the topicalization NPs that contain the deletion site, for example, **everyone that Mary did, John suspected*. My feeling is that such data can be substantially improved by slight intonational and lexical changes, as in *everyone that MARY did, John ALSO* *suspected* (where capitalization indicates contrastive stress); similarly, the pseudo-clefting of such constituents is also, it seems to me, basically acceptable, for example, *what John wants to achieve is EVERY goal that Mary ever did*. In contrast, comparable intonational and lexical manipulation of data like (1.115'c) and (1.115'd) does not lead to any substantive improvement, as can be seen by comparing the preceding data with **what I will eat with is whatever YOU eat* and **whatever YOU eat, I will ALSO eat with*. I thus do not see that Larson has successfuly deflected the thrust of arguments that data like (1.115') provide against (1.112b), and I consider that the arguments in question stand.

Next, consider the following interrogative constructions from French.

(1.116) a.   **Quoi te plaît?*
          what you pleases
          'What do you like?'
     b.   De quelle situation/*de *quoi* qui intéresse le fisc
          of which situation of what that interests the IRS
          a -t-il été question?
          has it been question
          'Which situation/what that most especially interests
          the IRS was talked about?'
     c.   De quoi parles-tu?
          of what talk -you
          'What are you talking about?'

Example (1.116a) illustrates the generalization that *quoi* 'what' may not appear in [SPEC, C'] of a finite clause without an adjacent P. (1.116b) shows that a *non-sister* adjacent P does not succeed in licensing *quoi*, and (1.116c) shows that a *sister* P does. The entire set of data in (1.116) thus jointly shows that fronted *quoi* in finite interrogative clauses must exhibit the [+S] property.

Now consider the FRCs in (1.116'), whose subcases are entirely parallel to the corresponding subcases of (1.116).

(1.116') a.   *[Quoi tu fais] me deplaît.
           what you do   me displeases
           'I dislike that what you do.'
      b.   *Pierre parle de [quoi t' intéresse].
           Pierre speaks of   what you interests
           'Pierre is talking of what interests you.'
      c.   Je parle [de quoi toi-même tu parles].
           I talk   of what yourself you talk
           'I am talking about what you yourself are talking about.'

Example (1.116'a) exhibits a nominal FRC where *quoi* has no adjacent P, and (1.116'b) exhibits a nominal FRC where *quoi* is immediately preceded by a non-sister P. The deviance of these two examples suggests that *quoi* is subject to the same constraints as in interrogative contexts. (1.116'c) is a missing-P FRC in which *quoi* occurs adjacent to a P. The fact that this example is grammatical indicates that P and *quoi* must be sisters. The data in (1.116') thus provide a second strong argument for the thesis that missing-P FRCs are [+S].

Finally, consider the German data in (1.117).

(1.117) a. Er kämpft gegen   uns/da- gegen.
           he fights against us /that-against
           'He fights against us/against that.'
       b. Er hat sich gegen   alles/*da- gegen, was uns
          he has REFL against all   / that-against what us
          heilig ist, geäussert.
          holy   is   expressed
          'He has declared himself against everything/that which
          is holy to us.'
       c. Er hat sich gegen   alles/da- gegen   geäussert,
          he has REFL against all   /that-against expressed
          was uns heilig ist.
          what us holy   is
          'He has declared himself against everything/that
          which is holy to us.'
       d. Gegen wen /wo- gegen   bist du?
          against whom/what-against are you
          'Who/What are you against?'
       e. *Wo- gegen, was uns heilig ist, hat er sich geäussert?
           what-against what us holy   is has he REFL expressed
       f. Wo- gegen   hat er sich geäussert, was uns heilig ist?
          what-against has he REFL expressed   what us holy   is
          'What has he declared himself against which is holy to us?'
       g. Die armen Hausfrauen stürzen sich auf was /*worauf
          the poor housewives throw   REFL on what/*what-on
          sie nur   kaufen können.
          they only buy   can
          'The poor housewives grab whatever they can buy.'

Examples (1.117a) and (1.117d) show that a P and an adjacent inanimate demonstrative or *w*-pronoun metathesize and contract. (1.117b) and (1.117e) show that this process is blocked when P and the adjacent pronoun fail to be sisters; non-sisterhood is due to the fact that the (sister) object of P is a complex NP, which *properly* includes both the adjacent pronoun and the relative clause. Contraction is, however, possible in (1.117c) and (1.117f), which are 'extraposed' versions of (1.117b) and (1.117e) respectively. All this indicates that contraction is possible only in sisterhood configurations, where 'sisterhood' ignores branching with null terminals, such as the (possible) traces of Extraposition in (1.117c) and (1.117f); note that the latter qualification makes good sense if contraction is a PF process. This conclusion is reinforced by the contrast in (1.117g). The non-contracted version exhibits a nominal FRC which is a sister of a P. The ungrammaticality of the contracted version is a result of the fact that there is no Extraposition process that can separate the *w*-pronoun of an FR from its remainder; this is clearly brought out by the fact that data like (1.23d) (reproduced below), where Extraposition would be non-vacuous, do not have counterparts like (1.23f).

(1.23) d. Hans hat, [wen   Gretchen ihm geschickt hat], empfangen.
           Hans has whom Gretchen him sent   has   received
           'Hans has received whom Gretchen sent him.'
       f. *Hans hat wen empfangen Gretchen ihm geschickt hat.

Now, consider the data in (1.117').

(1.117') a. Achte,   [worauf   ich dich aufmerksam mache].
            pay-attention what-to I   you attentive make
            'Pay attention (to that) which I draw your attention to.'
         b. Schneide das Brot, [womit   ich es
            cut   the bread what-with I   it
            geschnitten habe]!
            cut   have
            'Cut the bread (with that) which I cut it with!'
         c. Ich spreche [wovon   auch du   sprichst].
            I   talk   what-from also you speak
            'I am talking (about that) which you, too,
            are talking about.'
         d. Ich habe (mehrere Male) nachgedacht,
            I   have several times reflected
            [worüber   du gesprochen hast].
            what-about you spoken   have
            'I have reflected (several times)
            (about that) which you spoke about.'

All these data exhibit missing-P FRCs in which contraction has operated. Since the data in question are grammatical, they yield, in conjunction with the ungrammaticality of the contracted version of (1.117g), a third argument for the view that missing-P FRCs exhibit the [+S] property.

To summarize, it has been shown that Larson's only argument against PP-headed amount relatives is without force, and that the [+S] hypothesis is supported by three distinct sets of facts from three different languages. I propose, until presented with evidence to the contrary, to make the strongest assumption consistent with the data, that is, to assume that the [+S] hypothesis is correct with respect to missing-P FRCs in all the languages in which they occur.

3.4.3 Missing-P FRCs are [–H]

In this section, it will be shown that Larson's argument for a [+H] analysis of missing-P FRCs does not go through, and a positive argument based on data from German will be adduced in support of the [–H] property.

3.4.3.1 *Critique of Larson's argument for [+H]*

Larson's argument, which attempted to account for the impossibility of removing *-ever* from (1.113d) (as illustrated by his example (21), reproduced as (1.113d'''') below) in terms of a quantificational/nonquantificational contrast between FRCs whose *wh*-forms do/do not exhibit *-ever*, fails to go through for a number of reasons.

(1.113) d''''. I will live in whatever/*what town you live.

First, as was shown in section 1.1 (see discussion of (1.19) and (1.20)), there is direct evidence that nominal FRCs with *wh+ever* forms are [–H]. This argues against accounting for (1.113d'''') by assuming a [+H] analysis for nominal FRCs, as Larson does.

Second, as pointed out in earlier sections, *all* nominal (realis) FRCs are definite, even when they appear to have universal quantificational force, and whether they exhibit *-ever* or not. One environment which seems to allow definite, but not universally quantified nominals, is the focus position of a cleft, as illustrated by the contrast in *it's the/*any necklace you buy that I shall wear at the party*. The acceptability of *it's whatever necklace you buy that I shall wear at the party* supports the thesis that an FRC with *-ever* is a definite nominal.

Third, as Larson himself admits in his note 9, FRCs with 'plain' *wh*-forms may also have (universal) quantificational force when 'the main and the subordinate clause are placed in the future tense. Thus, *I'll visit who you visit* seems to be synonymous with *I'll visit whoever you visit.*' But if so, the deviance of the version without *-ever* in his own example reproduced in (1.113d'''') fails to be accounted for under the proposals he puts forward because the combination of tenses in the two clauses of (1.113d'''') is exactly the same as in the example he provides in his note.

In sum, whatever the reason why *wh+ever* forms are, as it seems, a necessary condition for the well-formedness of missing-P FRCs *in English*, this state of affairs in no way yields an argument for the [+H] hypothesis. This conclusion is strongly supported by the observation that the use of (counterparts to English) *wh+ever* forms is by no means a *universal* necessary condition for missing-P FRCs. As shown by the (b), (d), (f) and (g) subcases of (1.21), the missing-P FRCs of French, Romanian, Hebrew and German do not require *wh+ever*-type forms, even though all these languages have means of conveying the import of English *wh+ever* expressions, as illustrated in terms of nominal FRCs in (1.118a)–(1.118d) respectively.

(1.118) a. Mă interesează [orice   spune Maria].
            me interests   whatever says Maria
            'Whatever Maria says interests me.'
       b. [Quiconque m' insulte] est un scélérat.
            whoever   me insults   is a scoundrel
            'Whoever insults me is a scoundrel.'
       c. ani e?ese [ma   še   lo tagid].
            I   will-do what that not you-say
            'I will do whatever you say.'
       d. Ich tue [was immer du willst].
            I   do   what always you want
            'I (will) do whatever you want.'

I have argued so far that Larson's argument for the [+H] property fails to go through *within his framework of assumptions*, in particular, under the view that missing-P FRCs *may* have the structure in (1.112b). In the preceding section, however, it was shown that (1.112b) is not a possible representation for missing-P FRCs. Specifically, arguments were provided to the effect that these constructions are [+S], so that only (1.112a) is in fact open to a proponent of the [+H] hypothesis. But if so, QR becomes irrelevant to data like (1.113d'''') because, under (1.112a), missing-P FRCs are *not* antecedent-contained deletion constructions. Thus, the putative contrast in quantificational properties between *wh*-forms with and without *-ever* cannot in any obvious way be brought to bear on data like (1.113d'''') (at least, in the manner envisaged by Larson).

In short, there is no known positive argument for viewing missing-P FRCs as [+H].

3.4.3.2 An empirical argument for [−H]

In the preceding section, we eliminated the only argument provided by Larson in favour of a [+H] analysis of missing-P FRCs. If so, generally assumed methodological principles require that the conclusions reached in earlier sections with respect to *nominal* FRCs, in particular, to their [−H] status, be extended, in the absence of evidence to the contrary, to all other FRCs, and thus to missing-P FRCs. We do not, however, need to rely exclusively on such methodological considerations, because at least one language, German, yields an empirical argument for this conclusion, as will be seen directly.

In section 3.4.2, it was shown that German Ps may not contract with the Heads of their overtly-modified objects, except when the Head and the modifier do not superficially form a constituent (see (1.117) and comments thereon). The same point is brought out by the contrasts between the corresponding subcases of (1.119) and (1.119'); the deviance of the various subcases of (1.119') also shows that the strings consisting of the capitalized and bracketed sequences may not be base-generated as PP-headed (restrictive) relative constructions.

(1.119) a. Du solltest DARAUF achten,
  you should that-on pay-attention
  [*worauf* ich dich aufmerksam mache].
  what-on I you attentive make
  'You ought to pay attention to that
  to which I draw your attention.'
 b. Versuche, das Brot DAMIT zu schneiden,
  try the bread that-with to cut
  [*womit* ich es geschnitten habe].
  what-with I it cut have
  'Try to cut the bread with that with which I cut it.'
 c. Er hat sich DAGEGEN geäussert,
  he has REFL that-against expressed
  [*wogegen* auch du dich geäussert hast]
  what-against also you REFL expressed have
  'He has spoken out against that against which
  you also spoke out.'
 d. Ich habe mehrere Male DARÜBER nachgedacht,
  I have several times that-about reflected
  [*worüber* du gesprochen hast].
  what-about you spoken have
  'I thought several times about that
  about which you spoke.'

(1.119') a. *Du solltest DARAUF, [*worauf* ich dich
   aufmerksam mache], achten.
 b. *Versuche, das Brot DAMIT, [*womit* ich es
   geschnitten habe], zu schneiden.
 c. *Er hat sich DAGEGEN, [*wogegen* auch du
   dich geäussert hast], geäussert.
 d. *Ich habe mehrere Male DARÜBER,
   [*worüber* du gesprochen hast] nachgedacht.

Contraction is also possible when the modifier is 'vacuously' extraposed, as shown by the acceptability of the following data.

(1.120) a. Achte DARAUF, [*worauf* ich dich aufmerksam mache].
   pay-attention that-to what-to I you attentive make
   'Pay attention to that to which I draw your attention.'
 b. Schneide das Brot DAMIT, [*womit* ich es
   cut the bread that-with what-with I it
   geschnitten habe]!
   cut have
   'Cut the bread with that with which I cut it!'
 c. Ich spreche DAVON, [*wovon* auch du sprichst].
   I talk that-of what-from also you speak

'I am talking about that about which you are also talking.'

Next, consider the following versions of the data in (1.119), where both the capitalized and the bracketed sequences occur after the embedded verb.

(1.119") a. *Du solltest achten DARAUF, [worauf ich dich
   aufmerksam mache].
b. *Versuche, das Brot zu schneiden DAMIT, [womit ich es
   geschnitten habe].
c. *Er hat sich geäussert DAGEGEN, [wogegen auch du
   dich geäussert hast].
d. *Ich habe mehrere Male nachgedacht DARÜBER,
   [worüber du gesprochen hast].

The high degree of unacceptability of these data cannot plausibly be attributed to an impossibility for the relative clause to 'separate' from its Head following an embedded verb (a state of affairs which would reduce (1.119") to (1.119')), since a verb can in principle be followed by *two* constituents, the second of which is a CP, as illustrated below.

(1.121)   Ich habe mindestens so viele Offiziere gekannt
           I   have at-least   so many officers   known
           [wie du], [die am   Krieg teilgenommen haben].
           as you   who at-the war   taken-part   have'
           'I have known at least as many officers
           who took part in the war as you   (have).'
        b. Ich habe alle Kinder   gefragt, [die da   waren],
           I   have all children asked   who there   were
           [ob   sie nicht etwa   mitkommen wollten].
           whether they not perhaps come-along want
           'I asked all the children who were there
           whether they wouldn't like to come along.'

Rather, the deviance of the data in (1.119") seems to be due to two factors. First, while PPs are, unlike NPs, not *absolutely* excluded after an embedded verb, their occurrence in this position is clearly a marked option, to be used especially when the VP would otherwise be exceedingly long and complex. Thus, (1.122b) was felt by my informants to be distinctly less acceptable than (1.122a), while (1.122d) was felt to be appreciably better, although perhaps not quite as (normatively) impeccable as (1.122c).

(1.122) a. Man wird sich noch   ausführlich
           one will REFL still thoroughly
           mit   diesem Problem beschäftigen.
           with   this   problem occupy
           'We will thoroughly tackle this problem.'

b. (??)Man wird sich noch ausführlich beschäftigen
   mit diesem Problem.
c. Man wird sich noch ausführlich *mit dem Problem*
   one will REFL still thoroughly with the problem
   beschäftigen, *das erwähnt wurde.*
   occupy   which mentioned was
d. (?)Man wird sich noch ausführlich beschäftigen
   mit dem Problem, das erwähnt wurde.

The fact that the data in (1.119″) are vastly more deviant than (1.122d) is arguably due to a second factor, namely, to the fact that the post-verbal PP branches in the 'wrong' direction. Longobardi (1991: § 9) proposes a *Consistency Principle*, which says that 'an XP immediately expanding a lexical category on the non-recursive side is directionally consistent in every projection'. As Longobardi observes, a 'prediction of our formulation of the Consistency Principle is that left-branching phrases should not occur on the right side of basically left recursive XPs, like VPs in German or Dutch'; he then shows this prediction to be confirmed by certain Dutch data. Since the various subcases of (1.119″), in contrast to (1.122d), exhibit a left-branching PP complement on the right side of VP, their deviance is straightforwardly predicted by the Consistency Principle.

Finally, consider the following variants of the data (1.119), which exhibit missing-P FRCs on the right side of an embedded verb.

(1.119‴) a. Du solltest achten,
             you should   pay-attention
             [*worauf* ich dich aufmerksam mache].
             what-on I   you attentive   make
             'You ought to pay attention (to that) to which
             I draw your attention.'
         b. Versuche, das Brot zu schneiden,
             try   the bread to cut
             [*womit* ich es geschnitten habe].
             what-with I it cut   have
             'Try to cut the bread (with that) with which I cut it.'
         c. Er hat sich geäussert,
             he has REFL expressed
             [*wogegen*   auch du dich geäussert hast]
             what-against also you REFL expressed have
             'He has spoken out (against that) against which
             you also spoke out.'
         d. Ich habe (mehrere Male) nachgedacht,
             I   have several times reflected
             [*worüber*   du gesprochen hast].
             what-about you spoken   have
             'I thought (several times) (about that)
             about which you spoke.'

THE SYNTAX OF FREE RELATIVE CONSTRUCTIONS

Under the analysis in (1.112a), the bracketed phrases are complements of the embedded verb and the italicized constituents violate the Consistency Principle, just like the capitalized ones in (1.119"); the full acceptability of the data in (1.119''') is thus unexpected. Under the analysis in (1.112d), however, the bracketed sequences are analysable as extraposed CPs, comparable to those in (1.119). Such CPs do not fall under the Consistency Principle, because they are not complements of the verb; their acceptability is thus unsurprising.

To sum up, the German data considered in this section yield a positive argument for a [–H] analysis of missing-P FRCs in German, and, until proof to the contrary arises, of missing-P FRCs in general.

3.4.4 The syntax of null categories in missing-P FRCs

It now remains to make a principled choice between the three options consistent with a [+S, –H] analysis, namely, (1.112d), (1.112e) and (1.112f) (reproduced below for convenience).

(1.112) d.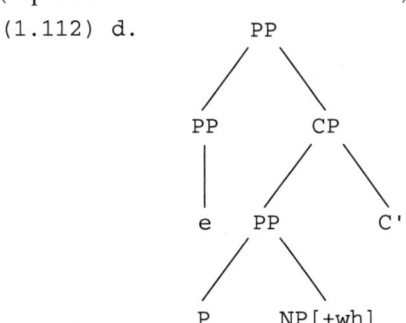

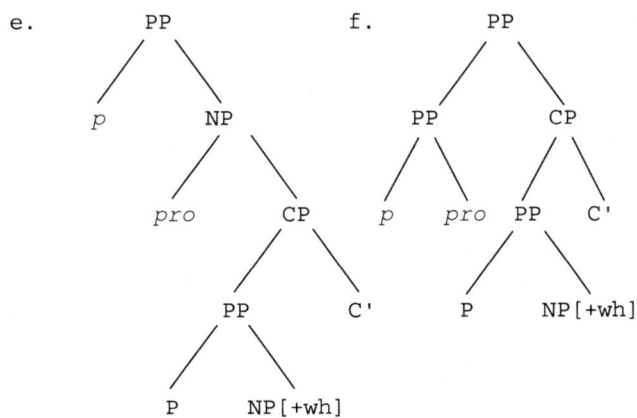

Example (1.112e) is objectionable on (at least) two grounds. First, the

103

prepositions occurring in such constructions may well have semantic content (as is the case, for example, in the various subcases of (1.21) provided at the beginning of section 3.4), in which case we appear to be faced with an instance of 'identity-of-sense anaphora' in which the 'anaphor' asymmetrically c-commands its antecedent at S-Structure, something that is in general not possible (Ross 1967). Second, the object of the null P is a *non-matching* nominal FRC, and this leads us to expect that languages which do not tolerate non-matching nominal FRCs disallow missing-P FRCs as well, a prediction which is falsified by a number of languages, in particular by French and Italian. For these reasons, I do not view (1.112e) as a possible representation for missing-P FRCs.

Turning now to (1.112d), note that it avoids the two objections just raised against (1.112e). The construction is clearly matching (in P-Kase), and the problem of an asymmetric c-command configuration for the content-reconstruction of the null PP does not arise, since the features of the *wh-*phrase, including its Kase features, may be conveyed to the null PP via CP, which does c-command it. Nevertheless, there are other objections one may raise against (1.112d). First, it would seem that the null category in Head position needs to be viewed as a sort of *pro*. But Cinque (1990: Ch. 3) argued on the basis of a different set of constructions that *pro* can be a nominal, but not a prepositional category; it would thus seem desirable to avoid positing a prepositional *pro*. Second, it is not obvious, under such a view, why missing-P FRCs should have – as they seem to have – a more 'marked' status than nominal FRCs (Bresnan and Grimshaw (1978) proposed to make the existence of subtypes of PP-*pro* dependent on that of corresponding overt *pro*-PPs, but Groos and van Riemsdijk (1981) showed that such a solution does not work in general – for example, it fails to work for French and Hebrew). It thus seems that (1.112d) is not quite an optimal representation for missing-P FRCs, either.

Finally, let us consider (1.112f), which differs crucially from (1.112d) in assuming, instead of a PP-*pro*, a nominal *pro* which bears null P-Kase. Note that (1.112f) avoids the problems which confront (1.112e) in the same way in which (1.112d) does, and this without positing a PP-*pro*. At the same time, the identification of *pro* by CP is less straightforward in (1.112f) than in (1.112d), because *pro* is not a Head in the former and thus does not have a Minimal Domain; rather, it is a complement of P, and thus, according to the proposals in section 3.1.3, ought to be identified within the Minimal Domain of the latter by some appropriate antecedent, but none seems to be available (note that CP, which carries appropriate phi-feature specifications, bears no significant structural relation to *pro*, and is thus hard to view as the latter's antecedent). The way out of this quandary is suggested, I submit, by the fact that *pro*'s PP-parent (i) is structurally related to CP just as *pro* is in (1.98a); (ii) is itself null, and thus a plausible target for identification operations; and (iii) is an Extended Projection of *pro*. One may thus propose that, when *pro* is not identifiable in one of the ways put forward in section 3.1.3, that is, *by* a Head or *as* a Head, it may be identified via its Extended Projection, provided that the latter is itself in need of identification (as a whole). That is to say, CP may convey the phi-features it has inherited from NP[+wh] to the null PP, from where they reach *pro* by percolation through an Extended Projection. As for the null P, it may be semantically identified by the overt P (which does not c-command it), and also morphologically identified at PF under Kase-matching (concerning the need for both forms of identification, see section 4.1).

The identification procedure we have just proposed also makes possible an account of the relatively marked status of missing-P FRCs. Note that NP[+wh]'s phi-features have to 'go through' two PP nodes in order to reach *pro*, and PP is not a usual carrier of phi-features. The marked status of the construction is thus attributable to the markedness of the procedure. Furthermore, we also arguably get an account of the fact that some languages, for example, French and Hebrew, allow missing-P FRCs without also allowing non-matching nominal FRCs. Thus, while both types of construction involve the assignment of phi-features to a PP-node, non-matching constructions also deprive *pro* of (morphologically) unambiguous Kase-identification[29] (for elaboration of this point, see Chapter 4).

This completes our argumentation for (1.112f) as the analysis of missing-P FRCs.

3.4.5 Adjectival and Adverbial FRCs

The results achieved in respect to nominal and prepositional FRCs generalize naturally to adjectival and adverbial FRCs, if we accept Larson's proposals that A(P)s bear Case and that (at least certain) adverbs are decomposable into an Adv⁰ and an adjectival complement (the former being, we may assume, a functional category comparable to P). Specifically, we may assume that constructions like (1.113f) and (1.113e) have representations like (1.123a) and (1.123b) respectively.

(1.123) a. [$_{AP}$ [$_{AP}$ pro] [[$_{AP}$ wh-phr] C']]
  b. [$_{AdvP}$ [$_{AdvP}$ adv⁰ pro] [$_{AdvP}$ Adv⁰ wh-phr] C']

Given the assumption that APs must receive Case, pro^{30} is formally licensed by the Case it inherits from the 'complex AP'; in constructions like (1.123b), Case is assigned by (the null) adv^0 (which is identified by the overt Adv^0, much like the null P in (1.112f) is identified by the overt P). Content identification takes place by coindexation at S-Structure in precisely the manner indicated with respect to nominal and prepositional FRCs.

3.5 SUMMARY AND CONCLUSIONS

To summarize the results of this section, it has been argued (i) that *wh*-FRCs may be nominal, adjectival, prepositional or adverbial; (ii) that the *wh*-phrases of *all wh*-FRCs occur in [SPEC, C']; (iii) that *all* FRCs exhibit an instance of *pro* in Head position; (iv) that the additional 'missing' elements of prepositional or adverbial FRCs occur as null sisters to *pro*; and (v) that the overt antecedents to such 'missing' elements occur as sisters to the *wh*-phrase.

At the beginning of section 3.4.2, I hinted at the existence of a somewhat marginal relative clause construction which is headed by an overt PP. The construction in question is brought up in Larson (1987), who notes that certain speakers of English accept the reduced version of (1.124a).[31]

(1.124) a. By 1999, I will have lived [$_{PP}$ in every city
that John has lived (in)].
b. What I will have lived in (by 1999) is
every city that John has lived *(in).
c. Every city that John has lived *(in),
I have also lived in.

Larson assigns to the bracketed PP in the reduced version of (1.124a) essentially the same kind of structure he assigns to missing-P FRCs, specifically, (1.112b) with the relative clause a CP (and, of course, without the specification [+wh] on the NP in Head position). However, the deviance of the reduced versions of (1.124b) and (1.124c) yields an argument against this analysis which is parallel to the argument furnished by the data in (1.115') against (1.112b) as an analysis of missing-P FRCs. (1.124) thus points to a conclusion comparable to the one we reached on the basis of (1.115') – the overt preposition and the adjacent overt NP are *sisters*. Accordingly, the bracketed PP in the version of (1.124a) is headed by an overt PP.

The conclusion we have just reached implies that the NO in [SPEC, C'] must be interpretable as carrying a 'missing' P, just like the data in (1.21); that is to say, that [SPEC, C'] contains at S-Structure a phrase of the form [$_{PP}$ *p pro*]. This, however, would appear to conflict with the otherwise exceptionless generalization that NOs do not trigger Pied-Piping of any sort, and, of course, with the account of this phenomenon that was proposed in section 3.2.4. The solution to this apparent paradox is provided, I submit, by the special procedure for *pro* identification that was put forward in section 3.4.4 (recall that NOs are, according to our account, instances of *pro*). Observe that the PP which immediately dominates *pro* is null, and thus in need of identification as a whole. If so, we may assume that the operator features which *pro* needs to receive from C° are conveyed to it indirectly, that is via PP (as for the null P, it can be identified by the overt P in Head position). We thus correctly predict that P-Pied-Piping is after all possible, but *only if P is null*. The apparently marked character of the construction is predicted on the same grounds as for missing-P FRCs (see section 3.4.4).

4

Coindexation-dependent PF processes

4.1 THE TYPOLOGY OF PROCESSES

4.1.1 Preliminary Remarks

In Chapter 3 of this study, we have been concerned – among other things – with universal effects that occur in *pro*-headed amount constructions (that is, realis FRCs) in particular with constraints on Pied-Piping. In this chapter, we will address certain Kase-interaction effects which occur in headed [+COIND] constructions, and which are subject to systematic cross-linguistic variation. Our primary concern will be with Kase-matching phenomena in FRCs, especially with the characterization of their systematic cross-linguistic variation. For the sake of completeness, however, we will also address, albeit less thoroughly, other Kase-interaction processes which share a number of important properties with Kase-matching.

As noted in section 3.2, coindexation of the operator of a [+COIND] clause with the latter's Head can in principle arise at S-Structure, provided that Pied-Piping does not prevent the index of the operator from reaching [SPEC, C']. The possibility of such coindexation is in fact a general property of headed [+COIND] constructions, not just of FRCs; that is to say, coindexation may occur in overtly or covertly headed constructions, which may moreover be of the restrictive or amount type. Now, given the 'T property' of the model assumed here, the kind of coindexation at issue is in principle relevant not only to LF, but also to PF. In particular, it can form the basis for Kase-interaction between the two coindexed elements under consideration, that is, the *wh*-phrase in [SPEC, C'] and the Head.

The kind of Kase-interaction that can involve the two elements referred to above depends to some extent on their overt/null status. We may distinguish the following combinatorial possibilities: (i) both elements are overt; (ii) the Head alone is overt; (iii) the operator alone is overt; and (iv) both elements are null. Since the phenomena we will address are morphological in nature, (iv) is irrelevant to them. In respect to cases (i)–(iii), two types of processes may be distinguished. When the 'expected' Kase of one element 'unexpectedly' shows up *overtly* on the other, we speak of 'attraction'; observe that, while the 'target' of attraction can only be an overt element, its 'source' may be either overt or null. When the Kase that an overt may bear is restricted as a function of the Kase *covertly* borne by the other element, which is therefore null, we speak of 'matching'. Both attraction and matching may operate either 'upwards' or 'downwards'.

I will not attempt to speculate on the function of attraction in situations of type (i). I do wish to propose, however, that the function of Kase-matching is to contribute to the (partial) identification of the Kase of a null element. A comparable function is fulfilled, in a different way, by attraction in cases of type (ii) and (iii), where the null Kase of one element finds overt expression on the other.

Attraction and matching processes share two important properties. First, both types of Kase-interaction processes make prominent use of a (possibly universal) Hierarchy of Kase-obliqueness/markedness, which regulates Kase-interaction effects of other types as well.[32] For example, a number of Indo-European languages appeal, subject to language-specific limitations, to the Hierarchy in (1.125). The way in which this hierarchy may affect attraction and/or matching is that a more marked Kase may identify (in part) or undergo attraction to a less marked Kase, but not conversely.

(1.125) NOM < ACC < DAT < GEN < ... < P-Kase

One apparently correct prediction made by this Hierarchy is that P-Kases may not be the target of attraction or identification by other P-Kases, since all P-Kases are maximally marked. Note that missing-P FRCs of the kind discussed in section 3.4 are always matching.

The second common feature of the two Kase-interaction effects, which in fact constitutes one of the reasons for concluding that they operate in PF, is that Kase-sameness is defined in terms of *morphological*, rather than *abstract* sameness. This point was already noted in section 1.1 in relation to Kase-matching in situations of type (iii), and will be further illustrated in relation to processes of other types in ensuing sections.

A central thesis of this chapter is that the 'intermediate' language type referred to in section 1.1, which allows non-matching under restricted circumstances, is *in general* reducible to Hierarchy-controlled non-matching. While earlier work has certainly recognized the role of the Hierarchy in restricting non-matching, it has also envisaged restricted non-matching controlled by other factors. I propose to argue in what follows that the latter type of situation does not exist. Before proceeding to this task in particular and to a discussion of Kase-interaction processes in general, a few remarks are in order.

A first point is that the two main types of Kase-interaction and their various subcases do not necessarily occur as a block in specific languages.

For example, while Modern German has Hierarchy-controlled Kase-matching in constructions of type (iii) (see section 4.3.3), it does not have attraction (at least, not of the 'downwards' variety). Another illustration is furnished by Gothic, which did exhibit attraction in cases of type (iii), that is, identification-driven attraction, without, as far as one can tell, exhibiting attraction in situations of type (i) (Harbert 1983, 1990).

A second remark is that the Hierarchy may control only some of the Kase-interaction processes found in some languages. For example, while attraction processes in Classical Greek were apparently always Hierarchy-controlled, certain kinds of non-matching constructions which went beyond the limits allowed by the Hierarchy were permitted.

A third point is that not every language which exhibits the Kases in (1.125) necessarily allows attraction to or identification of every less than maximally marked Kase. For example, Modern Romanian possesses all the Kases in (1.125), but only the NOM can serve as 'target' of Kase-identification or Kase-attraction (see section 4.3.2.1).

A fourth point which bears special stressing is that the correctness of predictions made by appeal to the Hierarchy is sometimes superficially obscured by interfering factors. One such state of affairs is discussed in Harbert (1983), who notes that Classical Greek, which allowed attraction to ACC, surprisingly seems not to have allowed attraction to NOM when this Case was morphologically distinct from ACC (Harbert's account of this state of affairs will not be reproduced here). In what follows, we will invoke two types of interfering factors: (a) the imposition of matching constraints stricter than those imposed by the Hierarchy in some structural position, in particular, in the P-object position; and (b) the availability of a less marked option, which rules out a more marked option that none the less stays within the bounds permitted by the Hierarchy.

For the sake of completeness, I note a third type of interfering factor. The claim that Kase-sameness is defined in *morphological* terms alone appears to be contradicted in situations where Kases are relatively rich in content and abstract differences may imply semantic differences. This is easiest to demonstrate in relation to P-Kase (comparable situations ought to arise in languages with semantically-loaded Cases, but I have no actual examples). Thus, consider (1.40a, b), (reproduced below for convenience).

```
(1.40) a.  Soñaba     [con  quien tú   saliste  ayer].
           I-dreamed   with  who   you  went-out yesterday
           'I dreamed (about the one) with whom you went out
           yesterday.'
       b.  Escribí [a    quien viste     ayer].
           I-wrote  ACC  who   you-saw   yesterday
           'I wrote (to the one) whom you saw yesterday.'
```

Example (1.40b), in which both P-Kases are essentially empty of content (they correspond to ACC and DAT in languages richer in morphological Case), was readily accepted by all my informants. In contrast, (1.40a) (from Suñer (1984), who rates it as fully acceptable), was judged marginal by some of my informants; note that while *pro*'s Kase has no semantic content (it is idiosyncratically selected by the matrix verb), the Kase of the relative pronoun definitely has content. Worse violations seem to arise when both Kases have (distinct) content. One situation of this type is signalled in Hirschbühler (1976a: n. 3) and reproduced as (1.40c) below. Thus, Hirschbühler points out that missing-P FRCs can be formed in French on the basis of the preposition *de* both when the latter means roughly 'about' and when it indicates possession, but not when the overt and null P purport to convey different meanings. I offer an additional illustration of this state of affairs in (1.40d).

(1.40) c. *Le frère   de qui tu parlais   vient d'arriver.
          the brother of who you were-speaking comes of-to-arrive
         'The brother (of the person) of whom you were speaking has just
          arrived.'
       d. *Ne me prends pas pour qui tu travailles!
           not me take   not for who you work
          'Do not take me (for the person) for whom you work!'

This concludes our preliminary remarks on Kase-interaction processes. We now proceed to illustrate their various types and subtypes, noting their exclusion of specific Pied-Piping configurations and their appeal to markedness-hierarchies, as well as the effects of superficially obscuring factors. As pointed out above, an innovative aspect of this section consists in a demonstration that such hierarchies are responsible for certain instances of restrictive non-matching which had been attributed to other factors in earlier literature.

4.2 ATTRACTION PROCESSES

4.2.1 'Downward' Attraction

Downward Kase-attraction is attested in a number of Indo-European languages, in particular Classical Greek, Latin, Gothic, Old and Middle High German and Modern Romanian. Various traditional reference works describe attraction as an optional process, but optionality seems to have been a feature of constructions of type (i), but not of type (iii). That is to say, when attraction has a Kase-identifying function, it seems to be obligatory (on this point, see also section 4.3.3). This conclusion is suggested by the following examples from Classical Greek, which are provided in Groos and van Riemsdijk (1981) and which I have adapted in inconsequential ways.

(1.126) a. Pro [tōn kakōn(GEN) [hōn(GEN) oida e(ACC)]]...
  (from: ha (ACC) oida).
  'Instead of the evils which I know...'
 b. Phoboimen an tōi hegemoni (DAT) hōi(DAT)
  doiē hepesthai e(ACC).
  (from: hōn (ACC) doie)
  'I should fear the leader whom he might give
  to follow.'

(1.127) a. Naumachiā palaitatē [pro(GEN) [hōn(GEN) ismen e(ACC)]]
  (cf. tōn naumachiōn(GEN) has(ACC) ismen)
  'Sea-fight the most ancient (of the sea-fights) that we know...'
 b. ... ekpiein sun [pro(DAT) [hois(DAT)
  malista phileis e(ACC)]].
  '... to drink with whom you best love.'
  (cf. sun toutois(DAT) hous(ACC))
 c. Par' [pro(GEN) [hōn(GEN) boētheis e(DAT)]]
  ouch' apoleipsei charin.
  'From whom you help, you do not get thanks.'
  (cf. par' ekeinōn(GEN) hois(DAT)).

Examples (1.126) and (1.127) illustrate attraction in constructions of type (i) and (iii) respectively; note that attraction is Hierarchy-controlled.

Several conclusions of theoretical interest emerge from a consideration of downward attraction constructions. First, as pointed out in Harbert (1983), attraction must be viewed as a PF process if it is assumed that the Ā-chain formed by the phrase in [SPEC, C'] and its trace needs to bear a single Case at LF. Note that attraction assigns to the former a Case inconsistent with the one it inherits from the latter, and it is only through PF application that Case inconsistency at LF can be avoided. Another reason for viewing attraction as a PF process is its insensitivity to abstract Case distinctions. For example, as noted above, attraction operated on NOM 'targets' in Classical Greek just where NOM was morphologically indistinct from ACC.

Second, a number of conclusions can be drawn from the fact that Pied-Piping configurations were excluded. Harbert (1983) writes that attraction occurred just in case the relative pronoun was adjacent to the Head; note that the data in (1.126)–(1.127) are consistent with this generalization.

A first conclusion is that attraction is, as stated in section 4.1.1, dependent on S-Structure coindexation between its source and target. A second conclusion emerges from the fact that even P-Pied-Piping appears to be excluded, even though such a configuration does not prevent S-Structure coindexation, as implied by the existence of non-matching FRCs (see section 3.2.4). Anticipating a more elaborate discussion of this point in section 4.3.3, I note an important difference between downward attraction and non-matching in a P-Pied-Piping configuration: in the former type of situation, the target of the process occurs in P-object position, while in the latter, the target of Kase-identification (that is, *pro*, and ultimately the FRC) does not necessarily occur in such a position. When, however, an FRC occurs in P-object position, hierarchically-controlled Kase-identification is not possible, as will be seen below. It thus appears that P-objects are unsuitable targets for Kase-interaction in general, a point to which, as already stated, I return in section 4.3.3.

The last point just made, namely, that non-matching is more strongly disfavoured in P-object position than elsewhere is also suggested by the choice of non-attracted data which Groos and van Riemsdijk provide in brackets in (1.127b, c) for purposes of comparison. These data are not FRCs, but OHRCs, which suggests that attraction was in effect obligatory in P-object FRCs.

4.2.2 Inverse 'Upward' Attraction

The attraction of the Kase of the phrase in [SPEC, C'] to the Head (usually called 'inverse attraction') is also attested in a number of Indo-European languages. In principle, one may expect this process to take place in constructions of type (i) and (iii), but all the examples known to me involve data of type (i) (that is, with an overt phrase in [SPEC, C']). Schwyzer (1950: II, 641) lists a variety of examples from Classical Greek, Latin and archaic German; I reproduce some data from the last two languages below.

(1.128) [*Naucratem*(ACC) quem(ACC) convenire volui],
        Naucratem   whom   join   I-wanted
        in navi non erat.
        in ship not was
        'Naucrate, whom I wanted to join, was not on the ship.'

(1.129) a. [*Meinen Tod*(ACC), den(ACC) sie beklagen], ist für
           my   death   whom   they mourn   is   for
           sie gerechter Schmerz.
           them deserved pain
           'My death, which they regret, is a rightful
           punishment for them.'
      b. [*Den liebsten Buhlen*(ACC), den(ACC) ich han],
           the dearest   lover   whom   I   had
           der(NOM) liegt beim   Wirt im   Keller.
           that-one lies   near-the host in-the cellar
           'The most dearly beloved lover that I had, that one
           lies next to the host in the cellar.'

Note that in each of these examples, the Head bears ACC Case (in agreement with the relative pronoun), instead of the expected NOM Case.

Data illustrating upwards attraction in Middle High German were earlier brought up in (1.41), and are reproduced below.

THE SYNTAX OF FREE RELATIVE CONSTRUCTIONS

(1.41) a. [Den(ACC) schatz   den(ACC) sin vater lie],
           the   treasure whom   his father left
           der(NOM) wart mit ir geteilt.
           that   was with her shared
           'The treasure that his father left, *that* was shared with her.'

   b. [Dem(DAT) gote dem(DAT) ich da   dienen soll], den(ACC)
       the   god whom   I   there   serve should that-one
       enhelfent si mir so nicht loben.
       NEG-help they me so not praise
       'The god whom I must serve, they do not thus help me worship him.'

   c. [Fuer alle die si   komen], die(NOM) muosen in
       for all who they come   those   must   them
       des   jehen.
       of-that tell
       'All those for whom they come, those must tell them about it.'

Note that these data exhibit OHRCs in left-dislocated position, which, as pointed out in section 3.2.6, allows for simplex nominals of either NOM Case (by default) or of the Case of the resumptive pronoun (see (1.42)). Neither of these two possibilities is exploited in the various subcases of (1.41); instead, the FRCs evince the Kase of the relative pronoun. (1.41) is of special interest in demonstrating the possibility of P-Kase attraction.

Example (1.129a), which has an ACC OHRC in subject position, where only NOM Case is normally allowed, indicates that upward matching must also be viewed as a PF process; if it were an S-Structure process, the LF rules which interpret subjects would need to be complicated.

Finally, observe that all the above examples are consistent with the assumptions that attraction is Hierarchy controlled and that Pied-Piping of a kind that blocks S-Structure coindexation is disallowed.

4.3 MATCHING REQUIREMENTS

4.3.1 'Downward' Matching

Matching effects are best known in connection with constructions of type (iii), where they operate upwards. None the less, downward matching effects are also attested. Bayer ((1984), cited in Fanselow (1991)) signals the existence of such constructions in Bavarian. It is observed there that the Case of the Head must be either morphologically indistinct from or more marked than the Case the NO inherits from its trace, as illustrated by the reduced versions of the following data.

(1.130) a. Der Mo [NOM], (der[NOM]) wo   uns g'hoifa hot...
         the man   who   where us helped has
         'The man who helped us ... '
      b. Den Mantl [ACC], (den[ACC]) wo   i kaffd hob...
         the coat   which   where I bought have
         'The coat which I bought ...'
      c. Dem Mo [DAT], (dem[DAT]) wo   mir g'hoifa hom...
         the man   whom   where we helped have
         'To the man that we helped ...'
      d. Die Lampn [NOM], (die [ACC(=NOM)]) wo   i gsen'g hob
         the lamps   which   where I seen have
         wor greisslich.
         were dreadful
         'The lamps which we saw were dreadful.'
      e. Des Audo (NOM) (des[ACC(=NOM)]) wo   i mecht
         the car   which   where I want
         is z'teia.
         is too-expensive
         'The car which I want is too expensive.'
      f. Die Mantl [NOM] (die[ACC(=NOM)]) wo   i
         the coats   which   where I
         kaffd hob worn z'rissn.
         bought have were torn
         'The coats which I bought were torn.'
      g. I sog's dem Mo [DAT] (der[NOM]) wo   im
         I said-it the man   who   where in-the
         Gartn arwat.
         garden works
         'I said it to the man who works in the garden.'
      h. Der Mantl [NOM], *(den[ACC]) wo   i kaffd
         the coat   which   where I bought
         hob, wor z'rissen.
         have was torn
         'The coat which I bought was torn.'
      i. Des Kind [NOM], *(dem[DAT]) wo   mir an Apfe schenka...
         the child   whom   where we an apple gave
         'The child (to) whom we gave an apple...'

Note that the Case of the Head is identical to the Case of the NO in the (a)–(c) subcases, abstractly distinct but morphologically indistinct from it in the (d)–(f) subcases, morphologically distinct from it but more marked than it in the (g) subcase, and morphologically distinct from it and less marked than it in the ungrammatical (h)–(i) subcases. It is quite plain that non-matching options are here Hierarchy-controlled.

4.3.2 'Upward' Matching

We now finally turn to the phenomenon which interests us most, namely, upward matching in FRCs.

As noted in section 1.1, a first approximate descriptive characterization of the kind of variation found in natural languages in respect to this phenomenon seems to be that languages fall into three broad groups, namely, (i) languages in which matching is required everywhere; (ii) languages in which matching is required only under certain circumstances; and (iii) languages in which matching is not required under any circumstances. This characterization is approximate at least in that type (iii) is probably a non-existent species (see subsection 4.3.3). Furthermore, it says little of interest concerning type (ii). In fact, earlier literature has envisaged at least two distinct ways in which restricted non-matching can arise, in particular, (a) through some mechanism which is controlled by a hierarchy of the kind provided in (1.125) (see Bresnan and Grimshaw (1978) on Finnish), and (b) through some mechanism that applies to specific structural positions, in particular, to Left-Dislocation and Subject positions (see Hirschbühler and Rivero (1981, 1983) on Catalan, Suñer (1984) on Spanish, and Horvath and Grosu (1987) on Romanian).

I should like to propose a somewhat different tripartite classification of languages, which, as I will endeavour to show, is both empirically more accurate and theoretically more elegant. While the fully-matching type may be left unchanged, I suggest that the languages which permit some non-matching should be distinguished according as to whether non-matching constructions are or are not Hierarchy-controlled. In other words, the typology (i)–(iii) above should be replaced, I submit, with one which distinguishes languages as the Kase of *pro*: (i') needs to be identified by *full* morphological matching with the phrase in [SPEC, C']; (ii') needs to be (partially) identified as a member of the set of Kases which are *at most as marked as* the Kase of the phrase in [SPEC, C']; or (iii') may bear a Kase which is *more marked than* that of the phrase in [SPEC, C'].

Observe that (i')–(iii') differ from (i)–(iii) in offering a *unitary* characterization of the intermediate type. In essence, this typology proposes that the (b) mechanism mentioned above does not exist and that the (a) mechanism is sufficient to characterize 'intermediately lax' languages. In section 4.3.2.1.1, I shall show that the Romance languages for which the (b) mechanism was devised are more adequately characterized in terms of (ii') above than in terms of the various mechanisms proposed in Hirschbühler and Rivero (1981, 1983), Suñer (1984) or Horvath and Grosu (1987). Additional support for (ii') will be provided in section 4.3.2.1.2, where it will be shown that Modern German, which had been viewed as fully-matching in some of the earlier generative literature, is in fact also of type (ii').

THREE STUDIES IN LOCALITY AND CASE

It is important to stress that the typology (i')–(iii') does not purport to account for all non-matching options in the languages of the world. In the two ensuing sections, we will see that non-matching in Romance and German does not occur under all the circumstances permitted by (ii'), and this is due to interaction with some of the interfering factors alluded to in section 4.1.1. In subsection 4.3.3, the effect of such factors will be noted in respect to languages of type (iii'), thereby accounting for the fact, hinted at above, that pure type (iii) languages appear not to exist.

4.3.2.1 Hierarchically controlled non-matching

4.3.2.1.1 Non-matching in Romance languages

The view that certain Romance languages display non-matching options just in Subject and Left-Dislocation positions has relied on data like the following (adapted from Suñer (1984) and Horvath and Grosu (1987) respectively).

(1.29) a. [Con quien me quiero casar] vive a la vuelta.
          with whom me want to-marry lives at the corner
       '(The one) who I want to marry lives around the corner.'
     b. [Con quien me quiero casar,
          ése ni me da la hora.
          that not-even me gives the time
       '(The one) who I want to marry, that one doesn't even
       give me the time of day.'
     c. *Andrea tiene [de quien María tanto se burlaba]
          Andrea has of whom Maria so-much self mocked
          en su clase.
          in her class
       'Andrea has (the one) who Maria was making so much fun of
       in her class.'
     d. *Andrea salió con [de quien María tanto se burlaba].
          Andrea went-out with of whom Maria so-much self mocked
       'Andrea went out with (the one) Maria was making so much fun
       of.'

(1.131) a. [pro(NOM) Cui(DAT) i se dă de mîncare] trebuie
                     who him self give of food must
           să muncească.
           SUBJ. work
         '(He) who gets food must work.'
      b. [pro(NOM) cui(DAT) i se dă de mîncare],
           ăla să muncească.
           that-one SUBJ work
         '(He) who gets food, let him work!'

THE SYNTAX OF FREE RELATIVE CONSTRUCTIONS

    c. *Andrea are [cui   îi   făceai   tu ochi dulci]
       Andrea has who.DAT him made.2.SG. you eyes sweet
       în clasa ei.
       in class her
       'Andrea has (the one) you were courting in her class.'
    d. ?*Nu voi   vota pentru [cui   i   se
       not will-I vote for   who.DAT him SELF.3.
       pare că   sînt   un prost].
       seems that am.SG. a stupid
       'I won't vote for (the one) to whom
       it seems that I am stupid.'

(1.132) a. [Cu   cine iese   Maria] e deobicei un om de nimic.
       with whom goes-out Maria is usually a man of nothing
       '(He) with whom Maria goes out is usually a no-good.'
    b. [Cu cine iese Maria], ăla   e de obicei un om de nimic.
       that-one
       '(He) with whom Maria goes out, that one is usually a no-good.'
    c. *Andrea are [de cine îşi rîdea   Maria] în clasa ei.
       Andrea has of whom self laughed Maria in class her
       'Andrea has (the one) that Maria was making fun of
       in her class.'
    d. *Nu voi   vota pentru [cu   cine vorbea   Maria].
       not will-I vote for   with whom was-speaking Maria
       'I won't vote for (the one) with whom Maria was speaking.'

Closer observation of the above sets of data reveals, however, that the (c) subcases do not really show what they are intended to show, because their deviance is attributable to an independent reason. Thus the FRCs in these subcases are all animate, and animate NPs in Spanish and Romanian typically require certain prepositional markers, in particular, *a* and *pe* respectively; in any event, such prepositions are necessary with animate FRCs, as illustrated in terms of matching FRCs in the (a) subcases of (1.133) and (1.134).

(1.133) a. María no encontró *(a)[pro [quien e(NOM)
       Maria not met   who
       la ayudó   ayer]].
       her helped yesterday
       'Maria didn't meet (the one) who helped her yesterday.'
    b. María vindió hoy (*a) [pro [lo que e(NOM)
       Maria sold   today   it that
       compró ayer]].[33]
       bought yesterday
       'Maria sold today (that) which she bought yesterday.'

(1.134) a. Maria nu a   întîlnit *(pe) [pro [cine e(NOM)
       Maria not has met   who

```
         a  ajutat-o      ieri].
         has helped-her yesterday
         (same meaning as (1.133a))
     b.  Maria a   vîndut azi (*pe) [pro [ce e(NOM)
         Maria has sold  today           what
         a   cumpărat ieri].
         has bought  yesterday
         (same meaning as (1.133b))
```

The (c) subcases of (1.29), (1.131) and (1.132) are thus ill-formed because an obligatory element is missing, and do not show that non-matching in direct object position is not permitted. These data, incidentally, remain ill-formed if the appropriate preposition is added, but this illustrates no more than what the corresponding (d) subcases do, namely, that non-matching FRCs are excluded as objects of prepositions.

To check whether non-matching constructions are or are not possible as direct objects of verbs it is necessary to consider data with inanimate FRCs, since these do not require (in fact, do not allow) the prepositions in question, as illustrated in terms of matching FRCs in the (b) subcases of (1.133) and (1.134). Appropriate data are provided in the (b) subcases of (1.135)–(1.137). These data exhibit essentially the same (somewhat marginal) acceptability as the corresponding (a) subcases, in which identical FRCs appear in subject position, rather than the much more severe unacceptability of (1.29d), (1.131d) and (1.132d), where non-matching FRCs appear as objects of prepositions (I note that data like those in (1.135)–(1.137) are easier to accept when the inanimate *pro* refers to something abstract; for example, in (1.136), to bank credits, rather than to a bunch of bank notes). It thus emerges that, contrary to what was thought before, the set of (marginally) permissible non-matching FRCs in these languages includes those that function as objects of verbs.

```
(1.135) a.  [Con lo que  soñe        la otra noche] me espanta todavía.[34]
            with it that dreamt-I the other night  me scares   still
            '(That) of which I dreamt last night scares me still.'
        b.  No quiero revivir [con lo que  soñe      la otra noche]
            not will-I relive  with it that dreamt-I the other night
            'I don't want to relive (that) of which I dreamt the
            other night.'

(1.136) a.  [Cu  ce   plănuiam    să    ne construim o nouă casă]
            with what planned-we  SUBJ  us build     a new  house
            va   fi greu de obținut.
            will be hard of obtained
            '(That) with which we were planning to buy a new house
            will be hard to obtain.'
        b.  Nu  vom       putea obține
            not will-we   can   obtain
```

THE SYNTAX OF FREE RELATIVE CONSTRUCTIONS

```
       [cu   ce   plănuiam    să    ne construim o nouă casă].
       with what planned-we SUBJ us build       a new house
       'We will not be able to get (that) with which we
       were planning to buy a new house.'
```

(1.137) a.
```
       [La ce    s   -a    făcut aluzie   mai înainte]
       at what REFL-has made allusion more before
       ar     îngrozi pe   oricine.
       would terrify ACC anyone
       'What was hinted at before would terrify anyone.'
```
   b.
```
       Nu aş     dori   să   retrăiesc
       not would-I wish SUBJ relive
       [la ce    s   -a    făcut aluzie   mai înainte].
       at what REFL-has made allusion more before
       'I would not like to relive (that) which was
       hinted at a few moments ago.'
```

The data in (1.135)–(1.137) show quite clearly that the distribution of non-matching FRs in certain Romance languages cannot be characterized in terms of non-subcategorized positions, as Hirschbühler and Rivero (1983) thought, and this quite independently of the objections to 'Head bypass' analyses that have already been noted (see section 1.2.2). On the other hand, it is *not* the case that non-matching is freely allowed outside of the P-Object position, because data like the following are crashingly unacceptable.

(1.138) a.
```
       **M -am    ADRESAT [pro(DAT) [cu   cine vorbeai]].
          me-have-I addressed         with whom were-speaking-you
       'I addressed (the one) with whom you were speaking.'
```
   b.
```
       **Ion e  FRATELE [ pro(GEN) [cu   cine vorbeai]].
         Ion is brother-the         with whom were-speaking-you
       'Ion is the brother of (the one) with whom you were speaking.'
```

Putting aside for the moment the impossibility of non-matching in prepositional object position (illustrated by (1.29d), (1.131d) and (1.132d)) and restricting the discussion to Romanian, I submit that there is a property which neatly distinguishes between acceptable constructions like the (a) and (b) subcases of (1.131) and (1.132) and the (b) subcases of (1.136)–(1.137) on the one hand, and unacceptable constructions like those in (1.138) on the other. This property is the fact that in all the acceptable constructions, the FRC, and thus *pro*, have either NOM Case or inanimate ACC Case, which is non-distinct from NOM (in so far as *wh*-pronouns are concerned), while in the unacceptable constructions, the FRC has DAT or GEN (as in (1.138)) or *pe*-Kase (as in (1.131c) and (1.132c)), all of which are distinct from NOM. The contrasts at issue can be straightforwardly explained by assuming that non-matching in Romanian is controlled by a 'reduced' version of (1.125), namely, (1.139).

(1.139) NOM < Other

In Romanian, the Kase Hierarchy which constrains Kase-identification, that is, (1.139), also constrains downward attraction, as shown below. Thus, a non-NOM Kase (the DAT/GEN) may be attracted to a NOM position (see (1.140a)–(1.140c)), but not to a *pe*-Kase position (see (1.140d)–(1.140f)). Note that attraction in (1.140a)–(1.140c) has the effect of salvaging constructions that would otherwise be ungrammatical, because the non-attracted versions are non-matching in a way that exceeds the options allowed by (1.139) (attracted versions are, of course, fully matching).

```
(1.140) a.   Mă voi     adresa [pro(DAT) [cui(DAT)/*cine(NOM)
             me will-I address          who       who
             [t(NOM) mă poate înțelege]]].
                     me can   understand
             'I shall turn to who can understand me.'
        b.   Ne vom    ridica contra [pro(GEN) [cui(GEN)/*cine(NOM)
             us will-we raise against           who       who
             [t(NOM) ne asuprește]]].
                     us oppresses
             'We will rise against who oppresses us.'
        c.   Ion e fratele [pro(GEN) [cui(GEN)/*cine(NOM)
             Ion is brother-the      who       who
             [t(NOM) ne asuprește]]].
                     us oppresses
             'Ion is the brother of (the person) who
             oppresses us.'
        d.   *Mă voi adresa [pro(DAT) [cui(DAT)/pe cine
             [(îl) pot   înțelege t(pe-Kase)]]].
              him can-I understand
             'I will turn to who I can understand.'
        e.   *Ne vom ridica contra [pro(GEN) [cui(GEN)/pe cine
             [l-) am       susținut t(pe-Kase)]]].
              him have-we supported
             'We will rise against who we supported.'
        f.   *Ion e fratele [pro(GEN) [cui(GEN)/pe cine
             [l-) am       susținut t(pe-Kase)]]].
              him have-we supported
             'Ion is the brother of (the person) who we supported.'
```

The Kase-hierarchy in (1.139) can also be used to characterize the non-matching options found in Spanish (again, momentarily putting aside data with non-matching FRCs in prepositional object position, such as (1.29d)). Spanish has no inflectional Kase (which means that data like (1.138) cannot be constructed), but it does have prepositional Kase. The acceptability of (1.29a, b) and (1.135a, b) versus the unacceptability of (1.29c) indicates that, just as in Romanian, non-matching is allowed in the positions of subject, Left-Dislocation, and inanimate direct object, all of which exhibit a Kase morphologically indistinct from NOM, but not in the position of animate direct object, which has *a*-Kase. It emerges that, much as in Romanian, non-matching is permitted just in Kase *pro* has non-oblique Kase.

Hirschbühler and Rivero (1981, 1983) write that Catalan data parallel to those in (1.29) have the same acceptability values as their Spanish counterparts. If data parallel to (1.135) or (1.136)–(1.137) also have comparable acceptability values (I have been unable to check whether this is in fact so), then the conclusion just reached in relation to Spanish can be extended to Catalan as well.

We have so far ignored the data in the (d) subcases of (1.29), (1.131) and (1.132). Clearly, their deviance is not predicted by (1.139), since the Case required by the preposition which governs the FRC is morphologically indistinct from NOM (for example, *pentru* 'for' in the Romanian examples assigns to an animate *wh*-pronoun the form *cine*, which is appropriate for NOM/ACC, rather than the form *cui*, which is appropriate for DAT/GEN). It seems we have here one of the additional constraining factors to which I alluded in section 4.1.1. Apparently, non-matching is disallowed, or at least distinctly more constrained, in P-object position, possibly because P and its object, but not other X⁰-s and their objects, form an Extended Projection (in the sense of Grimshaw (1991)), and violations of the Kase-requirements of some X⁰ are plausibly more constrained within a local domain than across such domains. That we are dealing here with a separate constraining factor emerges from (at least) two considerations. First, hierarchically-controlled non-matching in P-object position yields less crashingly unacceptable results than counter-hierarchical non-matching, as can be seen by contrasting (1.131d)[35] with (1.138) (repeated below for convenience).

```
(1.131) d. ?*Nu  voi      vota pentru [cui      i     se
           not will-I vote for       who.DAT him SELF.3.
           pare   că   sînt    un prost].
           seems that am.SG. a  stupid
           'I won't vote for (the one) to whom
           it seems that I am stupid.'

(1.138) a. **M -am     ADRESAT [pro(DAT) [cu    cine vorbeai]].
           me-have-I addressed              with whom were-speaking-you
           'I addressed (the one) with whom you were speaking.'
        b. **Ion e  FRATELE [ pro(GEN) [cu    cine vorbeai]].
           Ion is brother-the            with whom were-speaking-you
           'Ion is the brother of (the one) with whom you were speaking.'
```

Second, P-Object effects are detectable even in languages in which (some) counter-hierarchical non-matching is allowed, as will be seen in section 4.3.3.

4.3.2.1.2 Non-matching in Modern German.

As noted in Chapter 1, Groos and van Riemsdijk (1981) claimed that Modern German is a fully-matching language. This view was furthermore assumed by a number of subsequent writers, at least in respect to positions other than that of Left-Dislocation (for example, Harbert (1983), and also Grosu (1989)). It emerges, however, that this characterization of Modern German is too restrictive. Thus, Engel (1988: 249) cites sentences like (1.141) and marks them as basically acceptable.

(1.141) (?) Wen   sie mir empfohlen   hatte,
             who.ACC she me   recommended   had
             erwies sich als ungeeignet.
             proved REFL as unsuitable.
         '(The person) whom she had recommended to me
          turned out to be unsuitable.'

Pittner (MS.) cites a number of examples from written texts on the basis of which she proposes that non-matching is possible in Modern German within the limits allowed by the Hierarchy in (1.142) (which needs to be construed in terms of morphological non-distinctness, so that inanimate ACC belongs with 'NOM').

(1.142)   NOM <ACC <Other

Recent work of mine with informants, as well as examination of written texts, fully confirm Pittner's findings. I provide below some of the data I have personally checked.

(1.143) a.   Wonach   man eifrig   strebt,
              what-after one eagerly aspires
              bleibt oft   unerreicht.
              remains often unattained
           '(That) towards which one eagerly aspires
            remains often beyond reach.'
        b.   Womit   er sich auch immer beschaeftigt hat,
             what-with he REFL ever ever busied   has
             hat ihm nie   Spaß   gemacht.
             has him never pleasure made
           'Whatever he occupied himself with has never
            given him pleasure.'
        c.   [pro(NOM) [auf was ich aus bin]], ist, mich und meine
                         for what I   out am   is   me   and my
               Kinder   mit dem Wagen durchbringen.
               children with the cart see through
             'What I am out to achieve is see my children and
              myself through [the war] with the cart.'

(Bertold Brecht, *Mutter Courage*, 1939)

(1.144) a. Ich werde nie *pro*(ACC=NOM) veräussern,
        I will never   sell off
        worauf meine Familie so stolz ist.
        what-of my   family   so proud is
        'I will never alienate (that) which my family is so proud of.'
    b. Er berichtet, wie er ... kennenlernte, *pro*(ACC=NOM)
        he reports   how he   learned
        [*wovon* er früher keinen Begriff gehabt hatte].
        what-of he earlier no   idea   had   had
        'He reports how he ... came to know (that) about which he had had no idea earlier.'

                                                    (Tewarson 1988: 66)

(1.145) a. Ich bin bereit, *pro*(ACC) zu treffen, [*mit wem* du
        I am ready   to meet   with whom you
        auch mitarbeiten   willst].
        also work-together want
        'I am prepared to meet with whomever you want to work together.'
    b. Ich nehme, *pro*(ACC) [*wem*(DAT) immer
        I accept   who   ever
        du auch vertraust.
        you also trust
        'I take whoever you trust.'

In (1.143), *pro* has NOM Case, in (1.144) it has inanimate ACC Case (indistinct from NOM), and in (1.145), it has animate ACC Case (distinct from NOM); in each instance, the Case of the relative pronoun is more marked than that of *pro*. All my informants accepted these data, with the proviso that some of them felt them to be slightly less natural than matching constructions, or than non-matching ones in Left-Dislocation position.[36] In contrast, none of them accepted non-matching FRCs that did not conform to (1.142), such as the following. (Examples (1.146a, b) are from Pittner (1991).)

(1.146) a. *Er zerstört, *pro*(ACC) [*wer*(NOM) ihm
        he destroys   who   him
        in die Quere kommt].
        in the cross comes
        'He destroys (those) who cross his way.'
    b. *Er vertraut, *pro*(DAT) [*wen*(ACC) er kennt].
        He trusts   who   he knows
        'He trusts (those) whom he knows.'
    c. *Er vertraut, *pro*(DAT) [*mit wem* er arbeitet].
        he trusts   with whom he works
        'He trusts (those) with whom he works.'

In short, Modern German permits, just like the Romance languages discussed in section 4.3.2.1.1, non-matching FRCs which conform to language-specific Kase-hierarchical restrictions.

In the preceding section, it was noted that non-matching is excluded in Romance in P-object position even when it does not violate Kase-hierarchical restrictions. The same is true of Modern German. Thus, the version of (1.147) with *pro* is completely impossible.

```
(1.147)    Ich erinnere mich noch an dasjenige/*an pro(ACC)
           I   remember  me   yet at that        at
           worauf  meine Familie so stolz war.
           what-of my    family  so proud was
           'I still remember (that) which my family was so proud of.'
```

4.3.3 Non-matching in maximally-liberal languages

In subsection 4.3.2.1, we looked at languages in which non-matching was restricted by language-specific Kase-Hierarchies. In this final section of the chapter, we shall look at languages in which non-matching is freer, but not entirely unrestricted. In particular, we shall examine older stages of German and Classical Greek.

The greater liberality of these languages lies in the following fact: although a distinction between oblique and non-oblique Kases is as motivated as elsewhere and although Kase-Hierarchies based on this distinction were in most instances demonstrably exploited by those languages (for attraction processes, for example), non-matching did not always operate within the limits imposed by such hierarchies. Thus, Paul (1920: IV, par. 411) explicitly points to the fact, which he also abundantly illustrates, that in archaic Modern German, FRCs are attested in which the *w*-pronoun has NOM (and thus, least marked) Case and the FRC (and thus, *pro*) has a more marked Case; the latter could be ACC, DAT or GEN, as illustrated by the following examples (adapted with inconsequential modifications from Paul).

```
(1.148) a.  Ich liebe, [pro(ACC) wer(NOM) Gutes tut], und hasse,
            I   love               who    good  does and hate
            [pro(ACC) wer(NOM) mich verletzt].
                      who      me   offends
            'I love whoever does good and hate whoever offends me.'
        b.  [pro(DAT) Was(NOM) ein Mädchen ist von gutem Gefuehl],
                      what     a   girl    is  of  good  feeling
            müssen dergleichen Sachen zuwider    sein.
            must   such        things  repugnant be
            '(To anyone) who is a girl of good sense such
            things must be repugnant.'
        c.  Er fiel um      den Hals,
            he fell around  the neck
```

124

```
            [pro(GEN) wer(NOM) ihm in den Weg trat].
                     who      him in the way stepped
            'He embraced whoever crossed his path.'
```

In the work just mentioned, Paul makes no mention of other types of counter-hierarchical non-matching FRCs. In Paul (1904: par. 344), however, where he addresses non-matching options in Middle High German FRCs formed with a *d*-pronoun (a form which, to this day, also serves as restrictive and appositive relative pronoun, as well as demonstrative), he cites both instances in which *pro* and the *d*-pronoun had DAT and GEN Case respectively and instances in which they had GEN and DAT Case respectively; illustrations of these two possibilities are provided in (1.149).

```
(1.149) a.  ... daz  wir durch  dîne hulde vergeben
                that we  through your grace forgive
            [pro(DAT) dër(GEN) wir ie    genâmen dekeinen schaden
                      whose    we  ever  taken   whatever damage
            '... that we forgive, through your grace, (those)
            from whom we suffered damage'
        b.  ... daz  ich mich underwunden hân
            ... that I   me   care-taken  have
            [pro(GEN) dem(DAT) alle liute sprechent wol
                      whom     all  people speak    well
            '... that I took care (of those)
            to whom everybody speaks kindly'
```

Paul provides no evidence for assuming that DAT and GEN differed in rank in the Hierarchy which operated at that stage of the language. In fact, he states explicitly that only *d*-pronouns in the NOM or ACC could be targets of attraction to a more marked Case. Accordingly, two possibilities may be envisaged. Either DAT and GEN were both maximally (and thus, *equally*) marked Cases, in which case both subcases of (1.149) illustrate *counter-*, or, more exactly, *non*-hierarchically controlled non-matching; or one of these was *more* marked than the other, in which case counter-hierarchically controlled non-matching occurs in one of the two subcases of (1.149). In either case, Middle High German tolerated some non-hierarchically controlled non-matching and was thus more liberal than the languages discussed in section 4.3.2.1.

Despite this greater liberality, non-matching appears to have been constrained at older stages of German by at least two independent factors.

First, neither in Paul (1920) nor in Paul (1904) is there any mention of non-matching FRCs *in P-object position*. This omission is probably significant, given the thoroughness of the research and the abundance of illustrative citations, and strongly suggests that such constructions were ungrammatical at the relevant stages in the development of German, just as in contemporary Modern German (see section 4.3.2.1.2) or in the Romance languages discussed in section 4.3.2.1.1. More generally, it points to the possibility that the greater restrictiveness of the position at issue may be a general property of languages. At the very least, it shows that this property is independent of whether non-matching in general is or is not hierarchically controlled.

Second, Paul (1904: par. 344) states that in FRCs, but not in OHRCs, (downward) attraction was *obligatory* wherever it could occur. As pointed out earlier in section 4.1, such attraction has the effect of rendering non-matching FRCs matching. More exactly, FRCs which would otherwise be maximally 'marked', in that Kase-identification would need to operate counter-hierarchically, are turned by attraction into minimally-marked FRCs. It seems that we are dealing with a kind of situation that has been claimed in earlier work to exist elsewhere, and which can informally be characterized as follows: 'Avoid a particular type of construction when a less marked minimally different and semantically equivalent one is available' (an earlier proposal of this type is the 'Avoid Pronoun Principle' of Chomsky (1981)).[37]

In sum, it emerges that even the very liberal earlier stages of German 'balked at' particular types of highly marked situations, either in general (in P-object position) or when markedness could be circumvented (in attraction contexts).

Turning now to Classical Greek, another highly liberal language in respect to non-matching options, there are well-attested instances of counter-hierarchical non-matching FRCs comparable to the data in (1.148), as illustrated by (1.150a) (adapted from Groos and van Riemsdijk (1981)) and (1.150b) (kindly provided to me by J. Auberger).

(1.150) a. Stugōn [*pro*(ACC) hē(NOM) m'etikten].
hating   who   me-engendered
'Hating who gave me birth.'
b. Kratō   [*pro*(GEN) hoi(NOM) se   philousi.
command-I   who   you love
'I command (those) who love you.'

At the same time, non-matching is not completely unrestricted; rather, it seems to obey restrictions analogous to those found in relation to older stages of German.

For one thing, it seems that downward attraction was, just like in Middle High German, optional in OHRCs, but (see below) obligatory in FRCs (Hirschbühler 1976b). (1.150) is not an exception to this generalization, because the non-neuter NOM forms of Classical Greek were not possible targets of downward attraction (see Harbert (1983) for some discussion of this fact). Thus the tendency to avoid maximally-marked non-matching constructions when minimally-marked variants existed seems to have been operative here, too.

A second parallelism with Middle High German is the fact that the P-object position seems to impose tighter restrictions on non-matching than other positions. Thus it appears that, despite what was said in the preceding paragraph, attraction in FRCs may not have invariably applied wherever it could, *except for the P-object position*; this possibility is suggested by certain remarks in Schwyzer (1950: II, 640), who writes that downward attraction in FRCs occurs *insbesondere wenn der Kasus von einer Präposition abhängt* ('when the Case is dependent on a preposition').[38] Another distinguishing property of the P-object position in Classical Greek is that counter-hierarchical non-matching was apparently disallowed in this position even when attraction could not apply, that is, in constructions parallel to (1.150). Thus according to Auberger (personal communication), data like (1.151) do not seem to be attested.

```
(1.151) *ekpiein  meta [pro(GEN) hoi(NOM) se   philousi
        to-drink  with             who      you  love
        'to drink with (those) who love you'
```

4.3.4 Summary

The various facts considered and discussed in section 4.3.2 yield the following overall picture.

A basic parametric[39] distinction between languages (enunciated at the beginning of section 4.3.2) falls along the following lines: Kase-identification of *pro* by a coindexed overt phrase in [SPEC, C'] (i') requires full morphological matching, or (ii') may operate without matching, provided that the identifier stands higher than the element to be identified on a hierarchy of Kase-markedness, or (iii') may operate even without the benefit of the mechanisms in (i') or (ii'). The added options allowed by (ii') and (iii') are increasingly marked in that they correspondingly augment the indeterminacy of *pro*'s Kase, something which, in some languages, results in comparatively marginal status.

Languages typically limit the amount of indeterminacy which is in principle allowed under (ii') or (iii') by restricting the Case of *pro* and of the *wh*-phrase in, respectively, hierarchically-controlled and counter-hierarchical non-matching constructions to some initial *proper* sub-segment of a fully articulated Kase-Hierarchy. Illustrations of this state of affairs in (ii')-type languages are provided by Romanian, where *pro*'s Kase in (hierarchically-controlled) non-matching FRCs is restricted to NOM; by Modern German, where it is restricted to NOM or ACC; and by Finnish, where it is restricted to NOM, ACC or PART; significantly, the total set of non-prepositional Kases in these languages is, respectively, two, four and thirteen. Illustrations of the state of affairs at issue in type (iii') languages are provided by archaic Modern German, where the Kase of the *wh*-phrase in counter-hierarchical non-matching FRCs was restricted to NOM, and by

Classical Greek, where it was restricted to NOM and ACC; both languages had four non-prepositional Kases. Note that a type-(iii') language may in principle restrict the Kase of both *pro* and the *wh*-phrase in hierarchically-controlled and counter-hierarchical non-matching constructions. A case in point seems to have been archaic Modern German, where *pro*'s Kase could be only NOM or ACC under hierarchically-controlled non-matching, and the Kase of the *wh*-phrase could be only NOM under counter-hierarchical non-matching.

Further reduction in indeterminacy concerning the Kase of *pro* results from interference with certain factors which also have the effect of partly blurring the typology (i')–(iii'). Thus, Kase-mismatches are more drastically constrained in P-object position than in other positions, and counter-hierarchical non-matching is often disallowed if an unmarked alternative option is made available by attraction processes.

Are there interfering factors which blur the typology (i')–(iii') not by restricting, but by increasing non-matching options? A possible case in point was pointed out to me by A. Culioli (personal communication). Thus in French, which we have so far viewed as being of type (i'), data like (1.152a) are none the less possible.

(1.152) a. [pro à qui je donne l'ordre de partir]
              to who I give the-order to leave
           doit m'obéïr à l'instant.
           must me-obey at the-moment
           'He whom I order to leave must instantly obey me.'
       b. *[pro à qui je donne l'ordre de partir]
              to who I give the-order to go
           doit embrasser Marie.
           must kiss
           'He whom I order to leave must kiss Marie.'
       c. Celui à qui je donne l'ordre de partir
          the-one
          doit embrasser Marie.
          'The one whom I order to leave must kiss Marie.'

Note that mismatches in subject position are not automatically tolerated in French, as shown by the deviance of (1.152b), which furthermore cannot be attributed to semantic incongruity, since its 'OHRC counterpart' (1.152c) is well-formed. A clear distinction between (1.152a) and (1.152b) is that in the former, but not in the latter, the main clause expresses a 'logical' sequence to the subordinate clause. This invites the conjecture that the semanto-pragmatic connection between the two clauses of (1.152a) facilitates the recognition of the thematic role played by the FRC and ultimately (via rules which link such roles to Kases) of the Kase of *pro*; that is to say, (1.152a), but not (1.152b), has at its disposal an alternative way of identifying the Kase of *pro*. It would be highly interesting to explore the implications of this hypothesis in relation to a wider range of data; for practical reasons, this must be left for future research.

4.4 THE THEORETICAL STATUS OF MATCHING EFFECTS: BASIC OR DERIVED?

4.4.1 Preliminaries

From the summary of typological variation in respect to Kase-matching which was provided in section 4.3.3, it emerges that languages differ significantly in respect to how much they restrict non-matching options. A natural question at this point is whether this typology needs to be fully stipulative, or is to some extent derivable from independent properties of individual languages. The answer I wish to propose in this section is that, while the degree of laxity/restrictiveness of a language is not, as far as one can tell at the moment, derivable in the *strict* sense of the term, it does none the less exhibit an *approximate* sensitivity to the richness/poorness of *wh*-phrases in respect to their phi-features. This sensitivity seems to me similar in nature and degree to the one found between the existence of a *pro*-subject/object option and the 'richness' of (the corresponding) verbal agreement (see section 3.1.1). While neither type of correlation is obviously amenable to rigorous quantification, both seem hard to dismiss as entirely accidental.

The correlation I have proposed in respect to FRCs resembles the one found in AGR-antecedence constructions in another respect as well: both are manifested just in case an *overt* (potential) identifying source exists. Thus, in languages or constructions without any overt agreement between verbs and their subjects/objects, the *pro*-subject/object option is not automatically ruled out; rather, a mechanism other than AGR-antecedence may be appealed to, for example, identification by the contextual setting (see section 3.3.2.1). Similarly, in languages where FRs exhibit no overt element in [SPEC, C'], headed FRCs are by no means ruled out (see Chapter 2); rather, the language 'contents itself', as it were, with the abstract Kase assigned to *pro* at S-Structure.

It should be noted that richness/poverty in the morphological diversification of phi-features (such as [NUMBER], [GENDER], [ANIMACY], [PERSON]) does not result in identical states of affairs in the two types of construction, arguably for objective reasons. Thus while in cases of subject–verb/object agreement, insufficient richness in phi-features results in the elimination of the *pro* option, in FRCs, it typically induces 'compensatory' tighter constraints on non-matching options. The objective difference between the two types of construction is that the Kase-agreement option exists only in FRCs; the verb/verbal inflection typically *assigns* Case to arguments, without however *agreeing* with them in Case, so that a comparable compensatory mechanism is unavailable. Note that, *modulo* this objective difference, the two types of situation are similar in that identification is typically successful if some 'sufficiently large' proper subset of the total set of potentially applicable features has morphologically diversified members. Thus, in subject-*pro* constructions, the verb may fail to exhibit [GENDER] specifications (for example, in Spanish or Romanian); conversely, in FRCs, the *wh*-phrase may fail to exhibit (overt) [NUMBER] and/or [GENDER] specifications, provided that non-matching is sufficiently restricted, or non-matching may be (virtually) unconstrained, provided that the phi-features are richly diversified.

The remainder of this section is organized as follows. In section 4.4.2, I illustrate the proposed 'trade-off' between phi-feature diversification and restrictions on non-matching. In 4.4.3, I discuss a number of situations which are in *prima facie* conflict with the proposed correlation, and suggest ways to resolve the conflict. Section 4.4.4 offers some thoughts on diachronic processes relevant to the problems discussed in section 4.4.3.

4.4.2 The trade-off between 'richness' and Kase-restrictions

Of the type-(iii') languages noted in section 4.3.3, Classical Greek and Middle High German possessed relative pronouns that were richly inflected for [NUMBER], [GENDER] and [ANIMACY]; a third language of this type, Latin, which tolerated at least counter-hierarchical FRCs with a NOM *wh*-phrase (as illustrated in (1.153)), had a comparably rich relative pronoun system. The (free) relative pronoun paradigms in these three languages are given in (1.154)–(1.156).[40]

Of the languages of type (ii') touched on above, Finnish is inflected for [NUMBER] and [ANIMACY], but not for Gender, as can be seen in (1.157).

```
(1.153)  Praemium prōposuit [pro(DAT) qui(NOM) invēnisset
         prize    offered              who     should-invent
         novam voluptātem.
         new   pleasure
         'A prize offered (to the one) who should invent
         a new pleasure.'
```

(1.154) C l a s s i c a l   G r e e k

	Singular			Dual	Plural		
	M	F	N		M	F	N
Nom.	hos	hē	ho	hō	hoi	hai	ha
Acc.	hon	hēn	ho	hō	hous	hās	ha
Gen.	hoy	hēs	hoy	hoin	hōn	hōn	hōn
Dat.	hō	hē	hō	hoin	hois	hais	hois

130

(1.155) *Middle High German*

	Singular			Plural	
	M	F	N	M & F	N
Nom.	der	diu	daz	die	diu
Acc.	den	die	daz	die	diu
Gen.	des	der	des	der	der
Dat.	dem	der	dem	den	den

(1.156) *Latin*

	Singular			Plural		
	M	F	N	M	F	N
Nom.	qui	quae	quod	qui	quae	quae
Acc.	quem	quam	quod	quos	quas	quae
Gen.	cuius	cuius	cuius	quorum	quarum	quorum
Dat.	cui	cui	cui	quibus	quibus	quibus
Abl.	quo	qua	quo	quibus	quibus	quibus

(1.157)[41]

	Animate	Inanimate
Sg.		
Nominative	kuka	mikä
Accusative	kenet	----
Genitive	kenen	minkä
Partitive	ketä	mitä
Essive	kenenä	minä
Illative	keneen	mihin
Inessive	kenessä	missä
Elative	kenestä	mistä
Adessive	kenellä	millä
etc.		
Pl.		
Nominative	ketkä	mitkä
Genitive	keitten	minkä
Partitive	keitä	mitä
Essive	keinä	minä
Illative	keihin	mihin
Inessive	keissä	missä
etc.		

Finally, the languages of type (i') that were brought up above, in particular, Modern English, Modern French, Modern Hebrew and Russian,[42] all exhibit no more than a distinction in [ANIMACY]; for illustration, I provide the English paradigm in (1.158).

(1.158)   Animate   Inanimate
    Nominative   who   what
    Accusative/Dative   whom   what
    Genitive   whose   whose

It thus emerges that for a number of languages (Classical Greek, Middle High German, Latin, Finnish, English, French, Russian and Hebrew), increased morphological richness in *pro*'s antecedent does indeed correlate with increased liberality in respect to non-matching options.

4.4.3 Some 'unexpected' states of affairs

While, as was shown in the preceding section, FRCs in a number of languages support the hypothesis of a connection between richness and liberality, other FRCs raise (at least *prima facie*) puzzles for such a hypothesis. These occur in a number of Germanic and Romance languages.

A first problem is raised by Middle High German and (archaic and contemporary) Modern German. Middle High German had, in addition to FRCs introduced by *d*-pronouns, FRCs introduced by *w*-pronouns (it seems to have been a general feature of older West Germanic languages that FRCs could be formed with pronouns derived either from the demonstrative or from the interrogative set). Now, while *d*-pronouns were richly inflected (see (1.155)), *w*-pronouns were inflected for [ANIMACY] alone; none the less, the two kinds of FRCs were comparably liberal in that both permitted counter-hierarchical non-matching. This is unexpected in that other languages with FR pronouns inflected for [ANIMACY] alone (that is, the modern versions of English, French, Russian and Hebrew) are strictly matching (see preceding section). During the subsequent evolution of German, *d*-FRCs fell out of use (in the contemporary language, they occasionally occur in written elevated style, but are no longer part of the colloquial language), so that (colloquial) Modern German has only *w*-FRCs. Since these, too, are inflected only for [ANIMACY] and since Modern German tolerates non-matching FRCs, it also contrasts in liberality with the type (i') languages noted above without a corresponding contrast in the richness of FR pronouns.

The converse type of problem is raised by Old English. This language had, just like Middle High German, both demonstrative- and interrogative-based FR pronouns, which moreover had comparable morphological properties (the former were richly inflected, the latter exhibited only a distinction in [ANIMACY]). According to Allen (1980), both types of FRCs had to be matching in A-positions, but not in Left-Dislocation position. I shall ignore the Left-Dislocation context here, on the plausible assumption that whatever is responsible for the exceptional liberality of this position in Modern German (see section 3.2.6) is also responsible for its liberality in

Old English. Concentrating then on A-positions, Old English and Middle High German unexpectedly contrast in that, despite their comparable FR pronoun systems, the former was of type (i') and the latter of type (iii').

Finally, we find an unexpected contrast within the Romance family. While French, Spanish and Romanian all have FR pronouns distinguished for [ANIMACY] alone, French is of type (i') and the remaining two are of type (ii').

Unless there are independent synchronic properties of the languages brought up above which can explain the unexpected contrasts we have just noted (and I do not know of any at the moment), the conclusion seems inescapable that the correlation noted in the preceding section does not have the status of a principle of synchronic grammars, but reflects only a general tendency, much like the correlation between the richness of AGR and its ability to identify *pro*. For the time being, I accept this conclusion. None the less, I should like to suggest that the various 'unexpected' contrasts which were pointed out above become less mysterious when we (also) examine them from a diachronic perspective.

To begin with, recall that both Old English and Middle High German had two distinct types of FRCs, one of which behaved 'expectedly', while the other behaved 'unexpectedly'; in Old English, it was the type with 'poor' interrogative-based pronouns that behaved in an expected fashion, while in Middle High German, it was the type with 'rich' demonstrative-based pronouns that showed such behaviour. This state of affairs points to the possibility that one FRC-type may have 'forced' its (characteristic) behaviour on the other. This hypothesis raises two expectations: (i) that the 'winning' pronoun set may demonstrate greater 'strength' in additional forms; and (ii) that the set which shows 'parasitic' behaviour may tend to adopt an 'expected' form of behaviour in case the construction on which it is parasitic loses ground. Both expectations find some confirmation.

Concerning (i), I note that the 'stronger' status of the demonstrative-based set in German is reflected in the fact that *d*-FRCs have survived, albeit as a non-preferred and limited option, up to the contemporary stage of the language; in contemporary English, on the other hand, demonstrative-based FRCs are completely unknown. Furthermore, demonstrative-based relative pronouns are the most common option in the restrictive and appositive relative clauses of contemporary German, while they fail to occur anywhere in contemporary English.[43]

Concerning (ii), it seems clear that the liberality of *w*-FRCs has gradually diminished in the course of the subsequent development of German. Thus, as pointed out in section 4.4.2, archaic Modern German still tolerated counter-hierarchical non-matching FRCs, while contemporary German no longer allows them. In addition, as also noted in section 4.3.2.1.2, non-matching FRCs have marginal status for some speakers of German.

Finally, let us consider the situation found within contemporary Romance languages, in particular, the fact that Romanian and Spanish show greater liberality than French, although all three languages have equally 'poor' FR pronouns. In contrast to Germanic, the Romance languages do not have, and have never had, relative pronouns morphologically related to demonstratives; rather, Latin and its daughter languages exhibit only relative pronouns (in FRs and elsewhere) that are morphologically related to interrogatives. In so far as we consider Latin and contemporary Romance languages, we find an expected state of affairs: Latin had a rich relative pronoun system and was a language of type (iii'), while the various contemporary Romance languages have a comparatively poor pronoun system and are either of type (i') or of type (ii'). What needs to be explained is the difference between the two sets of contemporary languages.

An examination of the evolution of Romance shows that the various languages were all more liberal at earlier stages than at the present time. For example, as noted and illustrated by Hirschbühler (1976a: § 4), sixteenth-century French still allowed such non-matching constructions as the one in (1.159), which are no longer possible today; similarly, sixteenth-century Spanish even permitted the extremely rare option of non-matching in P-object position (see (1.160)), which is definitely excluded today.

```
(1.159)  Dieu gard    [sans    qui gardé    je ne  puis être].
         God  protect without  who protected I  not can  be
         'May God protect (the one) without whom
         I can't be protected.'

(1.160)  No  quería ver mas  a  [con    quien estava].
         not wanted see more ACC with   who   was
         'He no longer wanted to see (the one) with whom he was.'
```

It thus seems fairly clear that the impoverishment of the pronoun system has led to a gradual reduction in liberality, with the only difference that this reduction has been more pronounced in French than in Spanish or Romanian. But this is hardly surprising in view of the fact that there are numerous other domains in which French emerges as more 'revolutionary' than its two sisters, Romanian in particular. For example, Romanian still retains some of the Case distinctions of Latin, while French lost them many centuries ago. More generally, it seems to be a typical property of geographical linguistic continua that the peripheral languages tend to be more conservative than the central ones. The hypothesized comparatively slower loss of liberality by the peripheral Romance languages is thus an expected state of affairs.

4.4.4 Some thoughts on diachronical evolution

The discussion in the preceding section has shown that even an approximately definable amount of richness is not synchronically necessary for the licensing of a specific degree of liberality, and this, because the disappearance of licensing factors does not seem to have led to an *immediate* reduction in liberality in the languages we have examined. All the same, the process in question does seem to have led to a *gradual* reduction in liberality. That is to say, it appears that linguistic systems react gradually to change that introduces imbalance, a conclusion which converges with those that emerge from a number of earlier studies that addressed distinct types of data. Thus, one can deduce from Bever and Langendoen (1971, 1972) and Adams (1987), who examined, respectively, the disappearance from English of constructions like *I know a man *(who) likes his beer cold* and the disappearance from French of finite clauses with a *pro* subject, that these evolutionary processes were completed many centuries after the disappearance of what the respective writers viewed as licensing factors.

It is interesting to compare this view of linguistic change with the one apparently assumed by Harbert (1983); note that this issue is independent of Harbert's arguably incorrect identification of licensing factors (see section 1.2.3). Recall that, according to Harbert, one presumed licensing factor for non-matching was the morphological diversity of the Cases assignable by X^o elements to FRCs functioning as their complements or specifiers. In confronting the (from his point of view) unexpected fact that Old English and contemporary German are far less liberal than Middle High German in spite of the fact that all three languages have the same Kase system (that is, NOM, ACC, DAT, GEN), he suggested that certain incipient tendencies towards an eventual elimination of the Case system were already detectable at the point where these languages became of type (i') (an assumption which, as shown in section 4.3.2.1.2, is incorrect for Modern German); in Harbert's view, such tendencies were reflected, for example, in the fact that some German X^o's which, at an earlier stage, assigned only the most marked Case, GEN, began to also assign less marked Cases, in particular, DAT or ACC, and in some instances eliminated the GEN option entirely. The proposed view of linguistic evolution assumes that languages 'give up' at the first sign of potential future 'trouble', in other words, that they practice 'profilaxis', rather than 'repair'.

While I cannot now test the two distinct views formulated up above against a large number of past evolutionary processes, I do wish to stress that the view which underlies Harbert's suggestion strikes me as far less plausible psychologically than its alternative. Neither in acquisition nor in comprehension do humans give up when confronted with 'marked' states of affairs; rather, they typically do their best to cope with them. These psychological considerations apart, Harbert's view fares far worse than mine on empirical grounds, particularly when certain incorrect assumptions are set straight (specifically, the assumptions that Russian is a very liberal language and that contemporary German is strictly matching in A-positions). While my account above provides plausible and independently supportable reasons for the various instances of correlation failure, there is no obvious explanation, within Harbert's account, for the fact that Russian, which has five Cases, and Old English, which had four, are less liberal than Spanish (which has none), nor for the fact that Finnish, which has thirteen Cases, is less liberal than Latin, Classical Greek, Middle High German and archaic Modern German, which have no more than five Cases.

5

The analysis of non-indicative/irrealis FRCs

At a number of earlier points in this study, in particular, in the Introduction and section 3.2.1, it was pointed out that amount relative CPs are semantically equivalent to weak DPs and thus ought in principle to constitute, *at least under some circumstances,* an alternative realization of what weak DPs are interpreted as (that is, sets of sets of entities satisfying some cardinality condition); it was also pointed out that such an alternative cannot be expected to be available *in general,* in view of its non-canonical status. In this final part of this study, we will exhibit a type of construction which instantiates the predicted alternative. As will be seen, the construction in question is of interest not just as a curiosity, but first and foremost because it provides especially strong support for a variety of analytical proposals that were made in earlier sections. Specifically, the lack of a nominal which plays a resumptive role with respect to CP demonstrably turns out to correlate with the absence of precisely those properties of canonical amount constructions which have been argued to be consequences of the existence of resumptive nominals of various sorts. This construction thus provides, as I hope to show, a complementary type of argument for the conclusions which were reached on entirely independent grounds and strengthens our confidence in the correctness of those conclusions.

The construction at issue has the following easily observable characteristics: (i) it superficially consists of no more than a CP, and is thus a sort of FRC; (ii) the verb of this CP occurs in an irrealis form (for example, infinitival or subjunctive); and (iii) the entire FRC receives an interpretation comparable to that of indefinite non-specific nominals. Properties (ii) and (iii) distinguish such FRCs from those discussed in earlier sections. Illustrations from Spanish (where irrealis FRs are infinitival) were provided in (1.37), and are reproduced below; illustrations from Romanian (where irrealis FRs may be either infinitival or subjunctive) are provided in (1.161) and (1.162); I also provide an illustration from Modern Hebrew (where such FRs are infinitival) in (1.163).

(1.37) a. Briana no encuentra [*con quien* salir].
       Briana not finds   with whom to-go-out
       'Briana does not find (anyone) with whom to go out.'
   b. Briana no encuentra [*de quien* fiarse].
      Briana not finds   of whom to-trust-self
      'Briana does not find (anyone) whom to trust.'
   c. Andrea tiene [*de quien* burlarse]   en su clase.
      Andrea has   of whom to-mock-self in her class
      'Andrea has (someone) of whom to make fun in her class.'
   d. Andrea tiene [*con quien* votar].
      Andrea has   with whom to-vote
      'Andrea has (someone) for whom to vote.'

(1.161) a. Maria nu găseşte [*cu cine* ieşi].
           Maria not finds   with whom go-out
           'Maria doesn't find (anyone) with whom to go out.'
    b. Maria nu găseşte [*în cine* avea încredere].
                         in whom have confidence
       'Maria does not find (anyone) in whom to trust.'
    c. Maria are [*de cine*-şi râde].
       Maria has of whom REFL laugh
       'Maria has (someone) of whom to make fun.'
    d. Maria are [*cu cine* vota].
                  with whom vote
       'Maria has (someone) for whom to vote.'

(1.162) a. Maria nu găseşte [*cu cine* să iasă(SUBJ)].
           Maria not finds   with whom SUBJ go-out
           'Maria doesn't find (anyone) with whom to go out.'
    b. Maria nu găseşte [*în cine* să aibe(SUBJ) încredere].
                         in whom SUBJ have   confidence
       'Maria can't find (anyone) in whom to trust.'
    c. Maria are [*de cine* să -şi râdă(SUBJ)].
       Maria has of whom SUBJ REFL laugh
       'Maria has (someone) of whom to make fun.'
    d. Maria are [*cu cine* să voteze(SUBJ)].
                  with whom SUBJ vote
       'Maria has (someone) for whom to vote.'

(1.163) Eyn li   [*im mi* le-daber].
        not-is to-me with whom to-talk
        'I do not have (anyone) with whom to talk.'

I begin by providing two pieces of evidence that irrealis FRCs are amount constructions.

First, such FRCs arguably exhibit the defining property of amount constructions, namely, a *weak* internal nominal coindexed with CP (and taking scope within the latter). This is suggested by the fact that the constructions at issue employ only *wh*-pronouns which belong to the *non-D-*

linked interrogative set; thus, if the *wh*-pronouns in, for example, (1.162a) or (1.163) are replaced by their D-linked counterparts, unacceptability results, as can be seen in (1.164a) and (1.164b) respectively.

(1.164) a. *Maria nu găseşte [cu   care   să   iasă(SUBJ)].
            Maria not finds   with which one SUBJ go-out
        b. *Eyn   li   [im   eyze   le-daber].
            not-is to-me with   which one   to-talk

Since D-linked interrogative pronouns behave like strong nominals with respect to the 'there be ——' test, as can be seen in (1.165), the exclusion of such pronouns from irrealis FRs strongly suggests that the CP-internal coindexed nominal must be weak.

(1.165) a. Who was there at the party?
        b. *Which one was there at the party?

A second piece of evidence is that irrealis FRCs do not stack, as the Romanian data in (1.166) show. Observe the striking contrast between (1.166a) and (1.166b), whose reduced versions are virtually synonymous and which contrast minimally in that the former exhibits an irrealis FRC where the latter exhibits a restrictive irrealis construction. The restrictive status of the construction in (1.166b) is brought out not only by its tolerance for stacking, but also by the fact that the *wh*-pronoun belongs to the D-linked interrogative set, which is moreover homonymous with the realis restrictive relative set.

(1.166) a.   Maria nu   are   cu   cine să   iasă
              Maria not have with who SUBJ go-out.3.SG.
             (*de cine să   se   poată ataşa).
              of who SUBJ   REFL   can   attach.
              'Maria does not have (anyone) with whom to go out
              (to whom to be able to get close).'
        b.   Maria nu   are   pe   nimeni cu   care   să   iasă
              Maria not have   ACC nobody with which SUBJ go-out.3.SG.
             (de care să   se   poată ataşa).
              of who SUBJ   REFL   can   attach.
              'Maria does not have anyone with whom to go out
              (to whom to be able to get close).'

Having established the amount status of irrealis FRCs, we now proceed to justify an analysis of them as 'bare' CPs, and to show how such an analysis in conjunction with the assumption that realis FRCs are *pro*-headed can shed light on a number of differences between irrealis and realis FRCs.

A first difference is that irrealis FRCs in Spanish and Romanian *may not* exhibit the prepositional Kase-markers *a* and *pe*, while realis FRCs *must* exhibit such markers, as shown in (1.167) and (1.168) respectively.

(1.167) a. María no encuentra (*a) [quien la ayude].
         Maria not finds   who   her help(SUBJ)
         'Maria doesn't find (anyone) who would help her.'
     b. Maria nu are (*pe) [cine s   -o ajute].
         Maria not has   who SUBJ-her help
         'Maria doesn't have (anyone) who would help her.'

(1.168) a. María no encontró *(a) [quien la ayudó   ayer].
         Maria not met   whom   her helped(IND) yesterday
         'Maria didn't meet (the one) who helped her yesterday.'
     b. Maria nu a întîlnit *(pe) [cine a ajutat-o(IND)
         Maria not has met   who has helped-her
         ieri].
         yesterday
         (same meaning as (1.168a))

These Kase markers typically occur with animate nominals that function as direct objects. Their distribution is also sensitive to (in)definiteness and (non-)specificity in rather complex ways, but what matters for current purposes is that the deviance of the full versions of the two subcases of (1.167) certainly cannot be blamed on the non-specific construal of the FRCs, and this, because the essentially synonymous (non-specific) bracketed constituents in (1.169) do require object Kase-markers of the kind at issue.

(1.169) a. María no encuentra *(a) [nadie quien la ayude].
         Maria not finds   nobody who   her help(SUBJ)
         'Maria doesn't find anyone who would help her.'
     b. Maria nu are *(pe) [nimeni care s   -o ajute].
         Maria not has   nobody who SUBJ-her help
         'Maria doesn't have anyone who would help her.'

Now the essentially synonymous bracketed constituents in (1.167) and (1.169) contrast none the less in the following respect: the latter are uncontroversially headed by (overt) nominals and the former are not obviously headed by nominals at all. If we assume that irrealis FRCs are in fact 'bare' clauses, the impossibility of Kase-markers can be accounted for by appealing to the fact that uncontroversial 'bare' CPs never bear such Kase-markers, not even when they have a D-linked and/or animate *wh*-phrase in their specifier, as illustrated by (1.170).

(1.170) a. No sé (*a) [quien vino con quien].
         not I-know who came with who
         'I don't know who came with whom.'
     b. Nu ştiu (*pe) [cine a venit cu cine].
         not I-know who has come with whom
         'I don't know who came with whom.'

As for the contrast between (1.167) and (1.168), it follows straightforwardly from the proposal just made in conjunction with the assumption, defended in earlier sections, that realis FRCs do have (null) Heads.

A second difference between realis and irrealis FRCs is that, while the former have the essential distribution of DPs (cf. (1.2) with (1.3)), the latter have a far more restricted, and, as far as I can tell, not fully predictable distribution. Thus (i) they are not found in all the languages which allow realis FRCs (Modern Standard English being a case in point); (ii) in the languages where they do occur, they are allowed in some positions only (typically, in direct object position); and (iii) their distribution is furthermore controlled by idiosyncratic properties of selecting verbs. Such a state of affairs is found in Romanian, where the verb *a cunoaşte* 'to know (a person)', disallows irrealis FRC objects, although it does allow essentially synonymous objects consisting of a non-specific indefinite pronoun modified by an irrealis (restrictive) relative, as illustrated in (1.171).

(171) a. Nu cunosc pe nimeni [cu   care să vorbesc].
         not know ACC nobody with whom SP talk
         'I don't know anyone *with whom* to talk.'
      b. *Nu cunosc [cu cine să vorbesc].

This difference in distributional privileges comes as no surprise if realis FRCs have a *pro*-Head (and are thus canonical constructions), while irrealis FRCs have no Head (and are thus non-canonical constructions).

A third difference between realis and irrealis FRCs is that the former are construed as definite while the latter are construed as indefinite and non-specific (as pointed out at the beginning of this section). Recall that the definite status of realis FRCs was attributed to the 'resumptive' status of the external nominal. But in irrealis FRCs, under the 'bare' CP analysis, there is no resumptive element. Accordingly, CP – which, as proposed in the Introduction, has the logical status of a weak DP – serves as input to the LF rule of Existential Closure, and thus receives an indefinite construal. Concerning the fact that it is also construed as non-specific, I suggest this is a consequence of a semantic property which characterizes the class of selecting verbs, that is, 'future orientation'. Presumably, this feature is also responsible for the irrealis form of the verb.

A fourth difference between realis and irrealis FRCs is that the latter, in contrast to the former, seem to be entirely free from Kase-matching effects. This state of affairs is revealed by the full acceptability (for everyone, as far as I was able to check) of all the data in (1.37), (1.161) and (1.162), something which contrasts with the marginality (for at least some speakers) of non-matching realis FRCs, such as those in (1.65b), (1.135b), (1.136b) and (1.137b). An additional illustration of the point at issue is provided by the contrast between (i) and (ii) of n. 42 (see p. 240), which brings out the fact that in Russian, non-matching realis FRCs are usually impossible, while non-matching irrealis FRCs are fine.

Fifth, realis FRCs, in contrast to irrealis FRCs, fail to exhibit anti-Pied-

Piping effects. This point is brought out by the contrast between the Spanish and Romanian irrealis FRCs in (1.172a) and (1.172b) on the one hand, and the comparable realis FRCs in (1.66b) and (1.67b) on the other.

(1.172) a. María no tiene [la foto   de quien mirar].
             Maria not has   the picture of whom to-look-at
       b. Maria nu are [la fotografia cui   să se   uite].
             Maria not has at picture-the whose SP self look
          'Maria doesn't have (anyone) at whose picture to look.'

In Chapters 3 and 4 of this study, I argued that constraints on Pied-Piping and non-matching in realis FRCs are due to the fact that their violation interferes with the identification of a Head-*pro*. Under the assumption that, in irrealis FRCs, there is no Head-*pro* to identify, the lack of comparable constraints follows straightforwardly.

In conclusion, five differences between realis and irrealis FRCs have been pointed out, and it has been shown that each of these five differences can be derived from the assumption that realis FRCs exhibit a *pro*-Head and irrealis FRCs are truly headless. To the extent that my argumentation has been successful, it has provided the strengthening of earlier analyses that was promised at the beginning of this section.[44]

5.1 SUMMARY OF RESULTS

This study has dealt with a number of interrelated issues of some complexity. In concluding it, I should to indicate what seem to me to be its most significant results.

First, a unified approach to a variety of types of amount relative constructions has been outlined. It has been proposed that all amount constructions crucially differ from restrictive relatives in that CP is co-indexed with an internal *weak DP that is construed as taking CP-scope*; an important consequence of this proposal is that CP is interpreted not as a predicate, but as a logically primary 'mention' of an entity-set.

Second, it has been shown that earlier theories of *pro*, which only attempted to deal with argumental uses of *pro*, can be reformulated in a way which makes it possible to account for uses of *pro* as Head of an amount relative construction. A crucial way in which the proposed alternative theory of *pro* differs from some prominent earlier ones in that it defines the locality conditions on *pro*'s antecedent not in terms of Head-government, but in terms of a natural extension of Chomsky's (1992) notion of 'Minimal Domain'.

Third, it has been shown how the characterization of 'amount relative' in conjunction with the novel theory of *pro* can provide a convincing account of a number of syntactic differences between restrictive and amount relative constructions on the one hand, and between *pro*-headed amount relative constructions and other kinds of relative constructions on the other hand.

Fourth, the proposed theory of *pro* has been used to account for a number of properties of Null Operator constructions.

Fifth, a novel analysis of free relative constructions with a 'missing' preposition has been argued for.

Sixth, it has been shown that 'Head-Internal Relative' is a pre-theoretical term which does not entail a uniform analysis. In particular, it was demonstrated that some Head-Internal relative constructions are restrictive constructions and others are amount constructions.

Study II

Romanian determiners as functional categories

INTRODUCTION

The last few years have seen a blooming of various approaches to the theory of *functional* categories. One of the topics of interest within this field of research has been the approach to the internal syntax of 'nominal phrases' which, since Abney (1987), has come to be known as the 'D(eterminer) P(hrase) Hypothesis'. The central goal of this chapter is to emphasize the relevance of certain facts of Romanian to the theory of functional categories in general and to the DP Hypothesis in particular.

In an earlier study in which some of the facts discussed in this study were addressed (Grosu 1988a), it was proposed that a particular morpheme of Romanian, that is, -*L*, which in *some* contexts functions as a determiner, is the sole assigner of GEN(itive) Case in Romanian, and this, *regardless of whether or not it has Determiner status*. In this study, the stronger and theoretically more interesting view will be defended that the morpheme in question, while sole assigner of GEN Case in Romanian, possesses this ability *only when it has the status of a functional Head of a special kind*; in particular, the functional Head in question may select an NP complement, in which case it is a 'prototypical' Determiner, or lexical categories of other sorts, in which case it is a Determiner whose categorial and semantic featural content has been (partly) neutralized. The basis for this proposed refinement is that uncontroversial instances of the morpheme at issue do not possess GEN-assigning ability when serving a purely phonological euphonic role.

On a more general theoretical plane, this study will explore and compare the analyses of certain locality effects that are made available by the theory of Government and Binding, which assumes Case (i) assignment (ii) at S-Structure, (iii) under government, (iv) subject to directionality constraints, and (v) subject to adjacency conditions, and by the Minimalistic Program for linguistic theory outlined in Chomsky (1992), which assumes Case (i) checking (ii) at either LF or PF, and (iii) in a Spec-Head configuration. Directionality stipulations specific to Case checking, that is, independent of the linear order of Heads and Specifiers, have no place within the latter framework. The locality effects at issue are found in relation to the distribution of adnominal 'possessors' in Romanian, English, German and Hebrew, as well as of GEN phrases in Romanian in general. Among other things, the two theories differ in respect to the mechanisms that they make available for the analysis of the adjacency effects found in the four languages under consideration. Thus, while the Government and Binding framework permits in principle a treatment in terms of an adjacency stipulation on Case assignment, the Minimalistic Programme does not allow such a treatment. As will be seen, however, none of the mechanisms mentioned above adequately deals with the full range of locality effects found in the constructions at issue. It will be suggested that such mechanisms need to be supplemented with processes that appear to belong in PF.

The remainder of this study is broken down as follows. Chapter 6 highlights relevant aspects of the theory of functional categories and reviews the major results achieved in a number of earlier studies which applied the DP Hypothesis to (aspects of) the syntax of nominal phrases in English, German and Hebrew, and which assumed the framework of the theory of Government and Binding. Section 6.1 brings up certain facts concerning the Romanian Case and Determiner systems and points to their implications for the theory of functional categories; a feature of some importance, which will play a central role in our subsequent explorations, is that -L, which does not need to function as D at the level of syntax in order to be able to assign GEN Case (as noted above), does need to be a syntactic determiner in order to serve as host to morphological Case. Sections 6.2–6.5 explore the relevance to the DP Hypothesis of the distribution of GEN phrases in Romanian, by investigating the (im)possibility of cooccurrence of such phrases with the enclitic morpheme -L when the latter is hosted by Nouns, Prepositions, Adjectives and Determiners respectively. Throughout sections 6.1–6.5, the Government and Binding framework is assumed, primarily for expository purposes. Chapter 7 investigates the theoretical analyses that the two theoretical frameworks mentioned above make available in respect to certain phenomena that concern genitive phrases and their licensing elements in Romanian and in the other three languages discussed in Chapter 6. The phenomena in question are (i) the manner in which -L and comparable elements in other languages combine with their hosts; (ii) cross-linguistic contrasts in the linear order of 'possessor' DPs and 'possessed' Ns; and (iii) adjacency effects involving 'possessor' phrases and adnominal APs. Section 7.3 summarizes the results of the chapter.

6

Theoretical background and earlier results

In earlier versions of X̄-theory, the current 'functional categories' were either analysed as specifiers of some lexical category (see, for example, the treatment of determiners in Jackendoff (1977)), or not integrated into X̄-theory at all (see, for example, the treatment of INFL and COMP in Chomsky (1981)). A first important change was brought about when Chomsky (1986a) reanalysed clausal structure as exhibiting two functional Heads, INFL and COMP, and the lexical Head V, all of which were assumed to be regular from the point of view of X̄-theory; more exactly, V^2 was taken to be a complement of $INFL^0$, and $INFL^2$, of $COMP^0$. The reanalysis of phrases into a 'subordinate' lexical nucleus and one or more 'super-ordinate' functional categories was subsequently extended to nominal expressions (Abney 1987, Fukui and Speas 1986), and more recently to prepositional phrases (van Riemsdijk 1990, Rouveret 1991). A major integrative effort was made in Grimshaw (1991), aspects of which were brought up and put to use in Study 1.

The reanalysis of functional categories as Heads recognizes the fact that these elements often exhibit properties that are typically associated with Heads. For example, complementizers and/or certain components of the verbal inflection, in particular mood, often determine the (in)appropriateness of complement clauses in specific environments. At the same time, they also clearly differ from lexical Heads in being comparatively 'thin' in content, in not assigning theta-roles to their complements, and in typically (although not invariably) allowing a single type of category as complement. By and large, the functional categories, despite their ability to head their own projections, none the less appear to be dependent on specific lexical categories in a way in which lexical categories are not. Two attempts to come to grips with this state of affairs seem to me to be especially worthy of mention.

One approach is found in Abney (1987), where it is proposed that a lexical maximal projection and the various functional maximal projections that dominate it without 'intervening' lexical projections form a single *Semantic Projection*. A Semantic Projection has a *semantic* Head (the *lexical* Head of the 'lowest' maximal projection), as well as a *categorial* Head (the *functional* Head of the 'highest' maximal projection). The (near-)uniqueness of cooccurrence restrictions between specific functional and lexical categories is accounted for by imposing (stipulated) constraints on categorial selection by functional Heads.

Another approach, which is clearly indebted to the preceding one, but none the less differs from it in important respects, is found in Grimshaw (1991). According to Grimshaw, lexical and immediately containing functional categories form an Extended, rather than merely a Semantic, Projection. A crucial difference between these two notions is that in an Extended Projection, the categorial features of the lexical categories are *shared* by the containing functional categories; accordingly, a 'non-extended' projection can no longer be distinctively characterized as 'categorial', as Abney did (the term used by Grimshaw is 'perfect projection'). This definitional property of Extended Projections ensures the cooccurrence effects without added stipulations on categorial selection. Furthermore, the features projected from the lexical level to 'higher' functional levels need not be strictly semantic; for example, non-semantic phi-features that are inherent to the lexical Head alone, for example, arbitrary gender and/or number, may – and, as Grimshaw shows, sometimes must – be projected to 'higher' functional members of an Extended Projection. All in all, Extended Projections form the domains within which certain syntactic operations, in particular, feature transmission and Head-to-Head movement, may operate.

There are certain additional distinctions between Abney's and Grimshaw's models. For one thing, Abney proposes that definite pronouns are Ds, on the grounds that definite pronouns and definite determiners are often morphologically related (or even identical) in the languages of the world, and that the two kinds of elements are in general mutually exclusive. This view seems reasonable enough, and is moreover consistent with Grimshaw's theory, as far as I can see. However, Abney also proposes that definite pronouns are *intransitive* Ds. This position is inconsistent with Grimshaw's theory, where intransitive functional categories are ruled out by the definition of 'Maximal Projection'. Another distinction is that Grimshaw's model incorporates a proposal argued for in earlier work (for example, Fukui and Speas (1986)) to the effect that *all* thematic arguments, including the subject, originate within the (non-extended) *lexical* projection, thereby ensuring the locality of theta-role assignment. A related feature of the model, which we have already made use of in Study 1, section 3.2, is that the specifiers of functional projections do not belong to the Extended Projection of the lexical Head. In my opinion, Grimshaw's position on these various points could easily be incorporated into Abney's model.

The distinctions between Abney's and Grimshaw's models are immaterial with respect to some of the facts addressed in ensuing sections. In certain instances, however, the distinctions become important, and they usually favour Grimshaw's model, as will be seen.

I now proceed to outline the results achieved in Abney (1987), Haider (1987) and Ritter (1988, 1991) with respect to the nominal phrases of English, German and Hebrew; as indicated in the Introduction to this study, these results will form the basis for a comparison with corresponding facts of Romanian in ensuing sections.

6.0.1 English nominal constructions

The following are well-known properties of English nominal phrases: (i) they may exhibit a pre-nominal genitive phrase, typically recognizable by the ending *'s*; (ii) they may exhibit a post-nominal phrase introduced by the prepositional marker *of*; (iii) *'s* is a phrasal affix, not a Case-affix realized on individual words; (iv) prenominal genitive phrases do not cooccur with other determiners, in particular, with the definite article *the*; and (v) *of*-phrases need not be adjacent to the Head Noun. The properties (i)–(iii) are illustrated in (2.1a, b), property (iv) in (2.1c), and property (v) in (2.2).

(2.1) a. [The king of England's] description of the facts
b. *[The king's of England]/[the's king of England]
   description of the facts
c. John's (*the) book

(2.2) a. the famous portrait *of our great king* by Picasso
b. the famous portrait by Picasso *of our great king*

Chomsky (1986b) proposed to account for properties (i) and (ii) by assuming that N assigns *inherent* Case *twice* at D-Structure, once to its complement and once to its specifier, the assigned Case subsequently finding morphological expression as *of* and *'s* respectively. This analysis has, in Abney's view, a number of objectionable features. First, the proposed alternative realizations of the same Case are dependent on the structural position in which Case is realized; in contrast, inherent Case typically retains its realization under syntactic displacement (see, for example, Sigursson (1991) on inherent Case in Icelandic). Second, as Abney (1987) and Ritter (1988) point out, no other *lexical* Head of English assigns Case twice, or into its Specifier position. These difficulties can be avoided if, as Abney proposes, *of* is viewed as assigned by the N (if P-Kase is indeed 'assigned'), and *'s* is analysed not as a manifestation of Case, but rather as a D which assigns abstract Case to the element in [SPEC, D'] (which, under the view that arguments originate within the lexical projection, has raised to that position from [SPEC, N']). Note that Case assignment by D is automatically structural, since the notion of inherent Case (that is, Case associated with a specific thematic 'slot') is inapplicable to functional Heads, which assign no theta roles. Note also that, in contrast to the behaviour of *lexical* Heads in English, *functional* Heads, in particular, INFL, do assign Case into their specifier position, so that the proposal in question is rather natural. Furthermore, the assumption that *'s* is a D, rather than a form of Case, accounts for property (iv), that is, for the fact that prenominal genitives do not cooccur with the definite article *the*, even though the entire nominal construction is in general construed as definite (for argumentation of this point and an explanatory analysis, see Woisetschläger (1983)). The fact that *'s* is analysed as originating under the node D° also makes it in principle possible to account for property (iii) above, that is, for the fact that it is hosted by phrases, rather than by words; such an account is especially straightforward within Grimshaw's model. Thus, since [SPEC, D'] is not part of the Extended Projection which includes D°, and Head to Head movement occurs only within Extended Projections, D° cannot move to either the functional or the lexical Head of the Extended Projection in [SPEC, D']; all it can do is cliticize to that Extended Projection. On the other hand, if *'s* is viewed as a concrete realization of (abstract) Case assigned to an Extended Maximal Projection, its failure to be realized on one or both of the Heads of this projection is unexpected. As for property (v), it seems to be a general feature of PPs in English (and in other languages) that their surface position is not rigidly determined in relation to Heads with respect to which they function as arguments or modifiers. This is in contrast to NPs, whose position *is* sometimes rigidly determined in relation to certain Heads; for example, non-'heavy' direct object NPs need to be adjacent to their verbs in English, and prepositional objects typically need to be adjacent to their prepositions. This state of affairs has usually been accounted for within the theory of Government and Binding by assuming that the assignment of Case (but not the realization of 'Kase' in prepositional form) is sometimes subject to an adjacency requirement (see Chomsky (1981); for a proposal to derive the adjacency effects exhibited by English direct objects from other principles, see Johnson (1991)). In this connection, I wish to note that, under an assignment view of Case distribution, *'s* is arguably subject to an adjacency requirement in respect to its Case-assignee. Without such a requirement, it is not obvious why (2.3a), which is derived from (2.3c) by raising the subject from [SPEC, N'] to [SPEC, D'], does not have an alternative realization as in (2.3b), which could in principle be obtained from (2.3c) by also raising the Head noun from N° to D°.

(2.3) a. John's initiative
b. *John initiative's
c. $[_D{}^2 \ [_D{}^1 \ [_D{}^0 \ 's] \ [_N{}^2 \ John \ [_N{}^1 \ [_N{}^0 \ initiative]]]]]$

To summarize, all five properties of English nominal constructions that were noted at the beginning of this subsection receive a natural account in terms of the DP Hypothesis in conjunction with the theory of Extended Projection and with other well-established assumptions.

6.0.2 German nominal constructions

German nominal constructions (discussed in some detail in Haider (1987)) share with English nominal constructions the property of exhibiting prenominal 'subjects' and postnominal 'objects', as well as the property that prenominal subjects do not cooccur with determiners, in particular, with the definite determiner *der* 'the' (cf. (2.1c) with its German counterpart *Johns* (**das*) *Buch*). There are, however, a number of differences, namely: (i) the post-nominal argument bears no preposition but instead exhibits GEN affixal morphology, just like the pre-nominal argument; (ii) GEN morphology is realized on specific words of the nominal construction, in particular on determiners, adjectives and the Head N, in contrast to English *'s*, which is a phrasal affix; and (iii) the post-nominal phrase must be adjacent to the Head N. These three points are illustrated in (2.4)–(2.6) respectively. Note, in (2.5) the italicized realizations of GEN Case on the first three words of this phrase (which belong, respectively, to the categories D, A and N), and the absence of GEN Case markings on the ensuing PP complement of N.

```
(2.4) Schrödingers  Beschreibung  Napoleons
      Schrödinger's  description   Napoleon's
      'Schrödinger's description of Napoleon'

(2.5) der bittere Nachgeschmack [seiner schmerzlichen
      the bitter aftertaste      his    painful
      Erinnerungen an Milena].
      memories(GEN) at Milena
      'the bitter aftertaste of his painful memories of Milena'

(2.6) a. der Stolz unseres Lehrers      auf unsere Errungenschaften
         the pride our   teacher(GEN) on  our    achievements
         'our teacher's pride in our achievements'
      b. *der Stolz auf unsere Errungenschaften unseres Lehrers
      c. Das Schicken eines  Briefes      all deinen   Freunden
         the sending  a      letter(GEN) all your     friends(DAT)
         'the sending of a letter to all your friends'
      d. *das Schicken all deinen Freunden eines Briefes
```

As Haider (1987) points out, a natural way to account for the ungrammaticality of (2.6b, d) within his framework of assumptions is to propose that GEN Case assignment by N is subject to an adjacency requirement[1].

Chomsky's proposal to view GEN Case assignment in English as an *inherent* property of the Head N, and one which can be appealed to *twice*, remains equally problematic if applied to German data for essentially the same reasons. This type of proposal faces in fact an additional problem in German: in contrast to post-nominal genitives, which need to be adjacent to N (as just noted), pre-nominal genitives are subject to no such requirement, as illustrated by (2.7).

(2.7) Edisons   fantastische Erfindung
      Edison's   fantastic   invention

The proposal in question thus requires the strange assumption that Case assignment by N is subject to an adjacency condition when applying to a complement, but not when applying to a specifier.

The problems just noted can be avoided by appealing to the DP Hypothesis, as does Haider (1987). Haider's proposal is, essentially, that N assigns GEN Case to a postnominal phrase under adjacency, and that some element under D° assigns GEN Case to the prenominal phrase. Since German exhibits morphological Case with multiple realization, it would seem necessary to posit a *null* D, which is sufficient to account for the inability of prenominal genitives to cooccur with definite articles, and which need not in principle move to combine with some host. Haider, however, takes the view that the Case assigner is a clitic, much like English *'s*, with the difference that it requires a lexical, rather than a phrasal host. The reason for this proposal is that prenominal genitive phrases are subject to an adjacency condition stronger than the usual adjacency constraint on Case assignment. Thus, it is not sufficient for genitive DPs to be adjacent to the (presumed) D° position; rather, they must also end in a word capable of bearing morphological Case, as illustrated in (2.8).

(2.8) seiner schmerzlichen Erinnerungen (*an Milena)
      his   painful   memories   of Milena
      bitterer Nachgeschmack
      bitter   aftertaste
      'the bitter aftertaste of his painful memories (of Milena)'

Haider's proposed analysis of this phenomenon is that the morphological Case on *Erinnerungen* is in reality the result of the cliticization of D on it. Observe, however, that clitics do not usually participate in agreement processes; it is thus mysterious why the D and A of the 'possessor' DP exhibit the same GEN morphology that they do whenever a DP receives GEN Case. I thus do not find Haider's proposal particularly convincing. I return to the problem raised by (2.8) in section 7.4.

Before concluding this section, I wish to point to a fact of German that provides some suggestive support for the DP Hypothesis in general and against Haider's conjecture in particular. The fact in question is that Case inflection is more diversified on Ds than on Ns, as illustrated in (2.9).

(2.9)   Singular   Plural
         Nom.   der Freund   die Freunde
         Gen.   des Freundes   der Freunde
         Dat.   dem Freund   den Freunden
         Acc.   den Freund   die Freunde

This state of affairs makes good sense if (i) determined nominal phrases are headed by D, rather than by N, and (ii) Case is primarily assigned to DP, rather than to N (as Haider assumes); the reason is that under the assumptions (i)–(ii), D is the element to which Case most immediately spreads (by percolation). The situation at issue makes less sense if determined nominal phrases are assumed to be headed by N, or if Case is viewed as triggered by cliticization of D to N.

6.0.3 Hebrew nominal constructions

Unlike English and German, Hebrew nominal constructions exhibit only post-nominal complements. Accordingly, the kind of problem which was seen to arise with respect to the former two languages under a strict NP analysis of such constructions – in particular, the apparent need to assume that N can assign Case (in the case of English, Kase) twice and in opposite directions – does not arise in Hebrew. None the less, as Ritter (1988, 1991) points out, Hebrew also exhibits some data which are hard to reconcile with the assumption that non-prepositional complements of N necessarily receive Case from N.

Hebrew has two major types of nominal constructions with 'genitive' phrases. In one type (called the *F(ree) S(tate)* construction in Ritter (1991), and illustrated in (2.10a)), the 'genitive' phrase is marked with the preposition *šel* 'of'. In the other type (known as the *C(onstruct) S(tate)* construction, and illustrated in (2.10b)), the 'genitive' phrase bears no Kase marking, and must moreover be strictly adjacent to the Head N (as illustrated by the ungrammaticality of the full version of (2.10b)).

(2.10) a. Ha -tmuna   (ha -yafa)   šel ha -yalda
          the-picture the-beautiful   of the-girl
          'the beautiful picture of the girl'
       b. Tmunat[2] (*ha -yafa)   ha -yalda
          picture   the-beautiful   the-girl
          'the (beautiful) picture of the girl'

The FS construction is unproblematic. Nominal phrases introduced by *šel* receive Case from the latter, and there can in principle be more than one *šel*-phrase per construction (Shlonsky 1988). In CSs, however, not only must the (abstract) genitive phrase be adjacent to N (which implies that only one such phrase per CS is possible), but the Head N is unable to exhibit the definite determiner *-ha*, and this, even when the entire CS construction is construed as definite; to illustrate, note that the reduced version of (2.10b), which is construed as definite[3], disallows the definite article, as illustrated in (2.11).

(2.11) *Ha -tmunat   ha -yalda
        the-picture the-girl

As Ritter points out, the ungrammaticality of (2.11) is unexpected, if it is assumed that *ha-yalda* receives Case from the Head N. On the other hand, this fact can be made sense of within the DP Hypothesis in the following way: suppose that the reduced version of (2.10b) has an intermediate syntactic representation with the essential properties of (2.12); in particular, the 'possessor' DP occurs in [SPEC, N'], that is, in Specifier position within the phrase which serves as complement to the element under D°, either through direct base-generation or through movement from the complement-of-N position. I note in passing that Ritter (1991) argues for an additional functional category between D and N – NUM(ber) – and proposes that the possessor must raise to [SPEC, NUM']; this refinement has no crucial bearing on the way in which the possessor receives Case, so I choose to ignore it in the present context for the sake of simplicity (see, however, section 7.4. for discussion of additional facts to which it is potentially relevant).

(2.12)

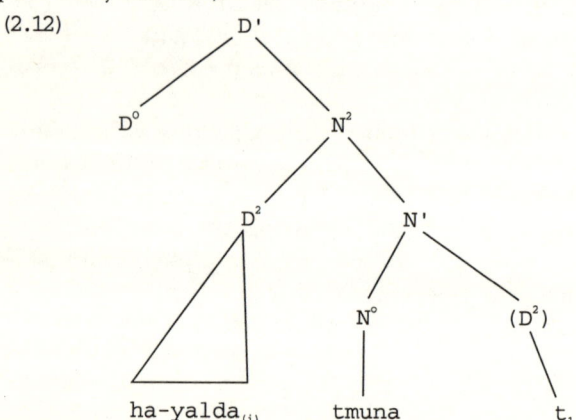

In contrast to the underlying representation of FS constructions like (2.10a), where the D° position is occupied by the definite proclitic article *ha-* (which subsequently cliticizes on the Head N), the D° position in (2.12) may be assumed to be occupied by an abstract element which has the ability to assign (abstract) Case to the right, under adjacency and under government (it is generally assumed that a Head governs the Specifier of its complement). Now, if the Head N *tmuna* is raised to D°, it will adjoin to the left of the abstract D, occasionally showing morphological reflections of this combinatory process. This move leaves D adjacent to the phrase that needs to receive Case; *ha-yalda* thus receives Case from D, and (2.10b) is therefore grammatical. Note that both the necessary adjacency of the 'genitive' phrase to the Head N and the inability of the latter to cooccur with overt determiners is accounted for under the proposed analysis. In contrast, (2.11) is ungrammatical because the D° is initially occupied by *ha-*, so that there can be no abstract D that can assign Case to *ha-yalda*.

The DP-Hypothesis thus succeeds in shedding light on facts of Hebrew which do not have an obvious explanation under a strict NP analysis.

6.1 SOME FACTS OF ROMANIAN AND THEIR THEORETICAL SIGNIFICANCE

In the preceding section, we reviewed a number of earlier proposals which, on the basis of data from English, German and Hebrew, put forward the view that (overt or null) elements of category D can assign (overt or null) Case into their own Specifier, or into the Specifier of their complement[4]. Positing such elements was seen to account not only for the Case properties of the phrases in question, but also for the inability of such phrases to cooccur with other determiners, in particular, with the definite article. A notable feature of the proposed Case-assigners is that they are only found in 'possessor' contexts, that is, in contexts where they need to assign Case.

In Romanian, the picture is partly different. 'Possessor' constituents by no means exclude a token of the definite article because, as I hope to show in ensuing sections, the morpheme which assigns GEN Case to such constituents – and which, abstracting away from its various morphological realizations, I shall represent by the symbol *-L* – is precisely the definite article. More precisely, this morpheme occurs as definite article in non-possessor contexts, but also serves as GEN Case assigner in contexts where it also functions as definite article. In addition, this morpheme also serves as GEN Case assigner in contexts where it no longer functions as definite article in the synchronic grammar of Modern Romanian; none the less, *-L* arguably retains its D status even in such contexts. Crucially, in contexts in which it arguably does not have D (and, more generally, functional Head) status, *-L* may not function as Case assigner. Finally, Romanian has no other assigner of GEN Case. The conclusion which emerges from the facts just noted and which constitutes the central object of argumentation in what follows is that Romanian provides especially strong support for the DP Hypothesis, and more generally for the theory of functional categories, in that the decisive property of the (sole) GEN Case assigner is its *functional* Head status.

Before arguing for the conclusion just indicated, I wish to note one further fact of Romanian which provides some support for the DP Hypothesis.

In section 6.0.2, it was observed that the German *nominal* declensional paradigm is 'degenerate' compared to the declensional paradigm of *determiners*, and noted that this makes good sense under the DP Hypothesis, according to which D – as Head of DP – is the 'primary target' of Case percolation. The facts of overt Case realization in Romanian point in the same direction. Thus, Romanian has five morphologically distinct Cases, one of which (the Vocative) need not concern us here. The remaining four (NOM, ACC, DAT and GEN) are all distinct in certain definite personal pronouns (for example, the forms of the 2.SG. personal pronoun are, respectively, *tu, tine, ţie* and *tău*). In non-pronominal expressions, there is only a bi-partite morphological contrast between NOM and ACC on the one hand and DAT and GEN on the other; NOM/ACC have zero realization, but DAT/GEN have an overt affixal realization, specifically, as *-ui, -ei,* and *-or* for M.SG., F.SG. and Pl. respectively. Now, these affixes can only be realized on determiners, and, more generally, on functional Heads, as illustrated in (2.13), where the non-primed subcases are in the NOM/ACC and the primed ones, in the DAT/GEN.

(2.13) a. Acest băiat deștept
           this boy   clever
           'this clever boy'
      a'. Acest*ui* băiat deștept
           this   boy   clever
           'to/of this clever boy'
      b. Această fată deșteaptă
           this   girl clever
           'this clever girl'
      b'. Acest*ei* fete deștepte
           this   girl clever
           'to/of this clever girl'
      c. (Toţi) acești băieţi deștepţi
           all   these boys   clever
           '(all) these clever boys'
      c'. (Tutur*or*) acest*or* băieţi deștepţi
           all   these   boys   clever
           'to/of (all) these clever boys'
      d. (Toate) aceste fete deștepte
           all   these girls clever
           '(all) these clever girls'
      d'. (Tutur*or*) acest*or* fete deștepte
           all   these   girls clever
           'to/of (all) these clever girls'

Note that nouns and adjectives do not bear affixal Case, and in fact show (stem) distinctions from NOM/ACC only in the F.SG. What is more, nouns and adjectives may not bear affixal Case even when no overt functional Heads are present; as shown by the full version of (2.14b), attaching affixal Case directly to the noun stem results in ungrammaticality; failure to attach affixal Case to the noun stem does not improve acceptability, as shown by the reduced version of (2.14b), because oblique Case must be affixally

ROMANIAN DETERMINERS AS FUNCTIONAL CATEGORIES

realized. To convey the intended meaning of (2.14b), a determiner must be used, as in (2.14c).

(2.14) a. Caut   prieteni puternici.
           Look-for.a.SG. friends powerful
           'I am looking for powerful friends.'
       b. *Datorită prieteni(or) puternici.
           thanks-to friends   powerful
           'thanks to powerful friends' (purported reading)
       c. Datorită un -or prieteni puternici
           thanks-to some-GEN friends   powerful
           'thanks to powerful friends'

The roles of functional Heads as primary loci for overt Case realization is clearly demonstrated by the facts just considered.

Before concluding this section, I wish to note that the inability of lexical Heads to bear affixal Case may be used as a test of functional/lexical status in uncertain cases. As shown in (2.15), Romanian cardinal numerals may not bear affixal Case; the only way to convey the purport of (2.15a) and (2.15c) is to use a preposition which does not require affixal Case, as shown in (2.15b) and (2.15d).

(2.15) a. *Voi   scrie trei -or donatori.
           will-I   write three-DAT donors
       b. Voi   scrie la trei   donatori.
           will-I   write to three donors
           'I will write to three donors.'
       c. *Ofertele   trei -or donatori
           offers-the   three-GEN donors
       d. Ofertele   a trei   donatori
           offers-the of three   donors
           'the offers of three donors'

Apparently, Romanian numerals are adjectives of some sort, rather than determiners (a comparable behaviour of numerals is reported in Gil (1987) in relation to Japanese).

6.2 THE N-BORNE ENCLITIC DEFINITE ARTICLE AS CASE ASSIGNER

We now turn to the element -*L*, and begin our discussion with constructions in which it is hosted by an N. We will show that this element functions as definite article both in non-possessor and in possessor constructions, and we will demonstrate its GEN Case assigning role in the latter type of situation.

Consider the italicized non-possessor constructions in the following data, where -*L* attaches to the nouns *băiat/băieți* 'boy/boys' and *fată/fete*

159

'girl/girls'; the underlined expressions in the (a) subcases bear NOM Case, those in the (b) subcases bear GEN Case.

(2.16) a. *Băiatu-l înalt* a plecat.
boy -L tall has left
'The tall boy has left.'
b. Prietena *băiatu-lui* înalt a plecat.
friend(F)-L boy -L(GEN) tall has left
'The tall boy's girlfriend has left.'

(2.17) a. *Fat(*ă)-a înaltă* a plecat.
girl -L tall has left
b. Prietena *fet(*e)-ei* înalte a plecat.
friend(F)-L girl -L(GEN) tall has left
'The tall girl's girlfriend has left.'

(2.18) a. *Băieți-(*l)i înalți* au plecat.
boys -L tall have left
'The tall boys have left.'
b. Prietena *băieți-lor* înalți a plecat.
friend(F)-L boys -L(GEN) tall has left
'The tall boys' girlfriend has left.'

(2.19) a. *Fete -le înalte* au plecat.
girls-L tall have left
'The tall girls have left.'
b. Prietena *fete -l(*e)or* înalte a plecat.
friend(F)-L girls-L(GEN) tall has left
'The tall girls' girlfriend has left.'

In (2.16)–(2.19), *-L* has the same semantic value as English *the* and comparable elements in other languages. Syntactically, it exhibits the behaviour which characterizes determiners in Romanian, that is, it serves as (sole) locus for affixal Case realization. The latter point emerges from a comparison of the (b) subcases of (2.16)–(2.19) with the primed subcases of (2.13); note that, in the former set of examples, GEN Case affixes attach only to *-L*, which points to the functional Head status of this enclitic (the attachment of affixes to *-L* is not always fully transparent on the surface, but this is due to independently motivated phonological processes[5]).

We shall now demonstrate the role played by N-borne *-L* in licensing GEN Case on a possessor constituent. The data in (2.20) show that GEN possessors are not possible without a token of *-L*, and that the latter must moreover govern and occur adjacent to a possessor to be able to license GEN Case on it.

(2.20) a. Portretu-l rege-l-ui
portrait-L king-L-GEN
'the portrait of the king'

b. *Portretu-l acesta rege-l-ui
    portrait-L this   king-L-GEN
    'this portrait of the king'
c. *Portretu-l frumos   rege-l-ui
    portrait-L beautiful king-L-GEN
    'the beautiful portrait of the king'
d. *Ștefan Moldov -ei
    Stephen Moldavia-GEN
    'Stephen of Moldavia'
e. *Acest portret   rege-l-ui
    this portrait   king-L-GEN
    'this portrait of the king'
f. *(Nici) un portret   rege-l-ui
    no   a portrait king -L-GEN
    'no/a portrait of the king('s)'
g. *Rege-l-ui   portret
    king -L-GEN   portrait
    'the king's portrait'
h. *Rege-l-ui   a   sosit.
    king-L-GEN has arrived
    'the king's has arrived.'
i. *Rege-le [$_{CP}$[$_{NP/DP}$ cărui portret] atîrnă pe perete]
    king-L   whose portrait hangs on wall
    'the king whose portrait is hanging on the wall'
j. Întîlnire-a Mari -ei   cu   comandantu-l
    meeting   -L Maria-L(GEN) with commander -L
    'Maria's meeting with the commander'
k. Întîlnire-a cu   comandantu-l Mari -ei
    meeting   -L with commander -L Maria-L(GEN)
    'the meeting with Maria's commander/
    *Maria's meeting with the commander'

Observe that (2.20a, j, k), where the Head N *portret* 'portrait' hosts an instance of *-L*, which is adjacent to and governs the genitive phrase *regelui* 'of the king', is fine. In contrast, all the other data in (2.20) are ungrammatical because at least one of these three conditions is not satisfied. Thus, in (2.20d)–(2.20h) there is no instance of *-L* on the Head N (in (2.20h), there is in fact no overt Head N at all). In (2.21b) and (2.21c), there is an instance of *-L* on the Head N which governs the genitive, but the adjacency requirement is not satisfied. Finally, in (2.20i), there is an instance of *-L* which is adjacent to the genitive phrase, but the government requirement is not satisfied, because the genitive phrase is contained within another maximal projection which does not include *-L* (the bracketed NP or DP). The reality of the adjacency and government requirements is also demonstrated by the fact that (2.20k) cannot be construed as synonymous with (2.20j). That is to say, the genitive phrase *Mariei* can be understood as a complement of the Head N *întîlnirea* in (2.20j), but not in (2.20k). The reason is that, on such a construal of (2.20k), the token of *-L* on the Head N governs, but does not immediately precede the genitive phrase, while the token of *-L* on *comandantul* immediately precedes, but does not govern it.

Within the theory of Government and Binding, a natural interpretation of the state of affairs illustrated by the data in (2.20) is that *-L* functions as GEN Case assigner under government and adjacency, and that the ungrammatical subcases of (2.20) are out because an appropriate assigner of the Case is lacking.

I wish to note that, while the cooccurrence restriction between *-L* and genitive phrases has in general been recognized in the descriptive literature on Romanian (see, for example, Mallinson (1986)), the Case-assignment properties of *-L* have not always been recognized in earlier generative literature. For example, Dobrovie-Sorin (1987, Annexe), treats the cooccurrence facts at issue as purely accidental. In a personal communication, she has suggested to me that the cooccurence of *-L* with genitives may simply be due to the fact that nominal phrases with possessors are sometimes necessarily definite, as was argued, for example, in Woisetschlägger (1983) with respect to English constructions like *an old man's book*; on this view, GEN Case would be assigned not to governed elements (by their governor), but simply to items occupying certain configurationally-definable positions (echoing Chomsky (1981), who proposed that, in English, 'NP is genitive in [$_{NP}$ —— X']'). There are, however, good grounds for *not* espousing such a view.

First, the ungrammaticality of (2.20b)–(2.20e) shows clearly that semantic definiteness in the containing nominal phrase does not in and of itself license genitive phrases. Second, (2.20b)–(2.20i), and in particular the full version of (2.20f), which can by no stretch of imagination be viewed as a definite expression, do, after all, have minimally distinct grammatical realizations which preserve the (in)definiteness of the entire nominal phrase *and* the genitive phrases in corresponding positions; this latter point will be illustrated in the next section. These two facts clearly indicate that semantic definiteness in the containing nominal phrase is neither a sufficient nor a necessary condition for the occurrence of genitive phrases.

The data in (2.20) have demonstrated the need for the functional Head *-L* in a variety of possessor constructions. In the next three sections, we shall consider facts which, in conjunction with (2.20), will lead us to the conclusion that GEN Case can be assigned (under government and adjacency) only by *-L* and only when the latter is a functional category. In contrast to, for example, German, where GEN Case can be assigned by N, V and A without benefit of a determiner (as illustrated in (2.21a)–(2.21c) respectively), Romanian allows nothing of the sort.

(2.21) a. Das Bild   Napoleons
       the picture Napoleon(GEN)
      'Napoleon's picture'

b. Er bedarf deiner Hilfe.
   he needed your   help(GEN)
c. Sie ist des Englischen mächtig.
   she is the English(GEN) commanding
   'She has a good command of English.'

Note, in this connection, that the Head N in (2.20d)–(2.20f), which governs and is adjacent to a genitive phrase, is unable to assign Case to the latter. The only constructions other than the one illustrated by the grammatical subcases of (2.20) where genitive phrases are possible in Romanian exhibit prepositions or adjectives which immediately precede and govern the genitive phrase *and* which, as will be argued in the ensuing two sections, host a token of *-L* with the status of functional Head.

6.3 GENITIVE PHRASES AS OBJECTS OF COMPLEX PREPOSITIONS

Romanian GEN-assigning prepositions are, as hinted at in the conclusion to the preceding section, morphologically complex and analysable into a stem and a form of *-L*. We can distinguish two subclasses. In the first subclass, the stem is to varying degrees syntactically and semantically recognizable as a historical relic of an earlier noun (sometimes preceded by a preposition); in these cases, *-L* agrees with this nominal stem. In the second class, which has a single member, the stem is the preposition *a* (see example (2.15b)) and *-L* agrees with the 'possessed' N (that is, the N with respect to which the PP headed by *a+L* functions as complement or specifier). We shall discuss the two subclasses separately, as some of the problems they raise are distinct.

6.3.1. Prepositions with nominal stems

A number of illustrations exhibiting prepositions with nominal stems and their genitive complements are provided below.

(2.22) a. În spate-le   copacu-l-ui
        in back -*L*.M.SG. tree -*L*-GEN
        'behind the tree'
      b. Înainte-a   copacu-l-ui
        before -*L*.F.SG.   tree -*L*-GEN
        'before the tree'
      c. Dedesubtu-l   copacu-l-ui
        ?   -*L*.M.SG. tree -*L*-GEN
        'under the tree'
      d. Deasupr-a   copacu-l-ui
        ?   -*L*.F.SG. tree -*L*-GEN
        'over the tree'

```
       e. Contr-a           rege-l-ui
          ?    -L.F.SG.     king-L-GEN
          'against the king'
```

The fact that the above prepositions have been analysed as including tokens of *-L* can be justified on at least two grounds. First, the proposed enclitics have exactly the realizations that they would have if they were attached to nouns providing morphophonological contexts parallel to those provided by the proposed stems in (2.22). For example, the proposed enclitics in *spate-le, înainte-a, dedesuptu-l,* and *deasupr(*ă)-a/ contr(*ă)-a* in (2.22a)–(2.22d) are entirely parallel in form to, respectively, *rege-le* 'the king', *lume-a* 'the world', *băiatu-l* 'the boy' and *mostr(*ă)-a* 'the sample'. Second, when the various complex prepositions in (2.22) take pronominal complements, these agree in number/gender with the proposed instances of *-L* within the various prepositions just as they agree with instances of *-L* that are hosted by Ns. The parallel patterns of agreement can easily be detected by comparing (2.24) with (2.23).

```
(2.23) a. Prietenu        -l           tău
          friend.M.SG.-L.M.SG.  your.M.SG.
          'your (male) friend'
       b. Prieten         -a           ta
          friend.F.SG.-L.F.SG   your.F.SG.
          'your (female) friend'
       c. Prieteni        -i           tăi
          friend.M.PL.-L.M.PL.  your.M.PL.
          'your (male) friends'
       d. Prietene        -le          tale
          friend.F.PL.-L.F.PL.  your.F.PL.
          'your (female) friends'

(2.24) a. In spate-le tău/ *ta/ *tăi/ *tale
                      M.SG. F.SG. M.PL. F.PL.
       b. Inainte-a *tău/ta/*tăi/*tale
       c. Dedesubtu-l tău/*ta/*tăi/*tale
       d. Deasupr-a *tău/ta/*tăi/*tale
       e. Contr-a *tău/ta/*tăi/*tale
```

As far as I am aware, *all* Romanian prepositions which assign GEN Case to their objects can be shown, by utilizing the two tests just noted, to include an instance of *-L*. It thus seems natural to view *-L* as the Case assigner in such prepositional constructions.

To be sure, there are certain clear differences between the constructions in (2.22) and those addressed in section 6.2. both in respect to *-L*'s host and in respect to *-L* itself. Thus, in contrast to the constructions of section 6.2, the hosts of *-L* do not function as independent syntacto-semantic units elsewhere in the language. This can be seen even for the most 'transparent' combinations, for example, *în spatele* in (2.22a)); thus, although *în* and *spate* occur as independent formatives elsewhere in the language, they are not construed in exactly the same way; in particular, the noun *spate* 'back' is not otherwise applicable to plants, but only to animals and people (one cannot, for example, say **spatele copacului e lat* 'the back of the tree is broad'). In the remaining subcases of (2.22), it is even harder to detect a nominal stem that would justify the presence of a definite article. As for *-L* itself, it does not seem to have definite content; for example, it is far from clear in which sense, say, *contr-a* 'against' is more definite than *pentru* 'for'.

How can one reconcile the observations of the preceding paragraph with the fact that *-L* functions as a syntactic unit with Case-assigning properties in both the constructions of section 6.2 and those introduced in this section? The answer I wish to propose takes advantage of two refinements in the theory of Extended Projection which are motivated on numerous independent grounds. First, as Grimshaw (1991) notes, there exist *prima facie* counterexamples to her proposal that the lexical and functional components of an Extended Projection share categorial features; in particular, there are instances where some functional category seems to categorially select more than one type of complement. Grimshaw proposes to handle such situations through neutralization of some of the categorial features of the selecting Head. And second, as observed in Grosu (1992), Grimshaw's theory needs to permit neutralization of the functional/categorial distinction for at least certain types of categories in order to account for certain types of data which were not directly addressed in Grimshaw (1991). The need for this second type of neutralization stems from the fact that Grimshaw views the various maximal 'perfect' projections of an Extended Projection as ranked with respect to each other in terms of a 'functional rank'; the content of this claim is that certain types of categories must always occur 'higher' than certain other types of categories. In general, the lexical perfect projection is always 'lowest', and thus has rank F^o, but functional categories are also (potentially) ranked with respect to each other. In the specific case of *nominal* Extended Projections, Grimshaw explicitly proposes that prepositions have *higher* functional rank than determiners, in fact, *maximal* functional rank. None the less, as pointed out in a number of recent studies (van Riemsdijk 1990; Rouveret 1991), PPs sometimes arguably occur as complements of certain functional categories which appear elsewhere with *non-maximal* functional rank. In other words, Ps sometimes simultaneously behave as F^{max} *and* as F^o elements, a conflict which seems to require a neutralization of their lexical/functional status. Assuming these two neutralization options, I propose that the host of *-L* in constructions like those in (2.22) is a P neutralized as to lexical/functional status, and that *-L* is a functional Head obtained from the definite article by neutralizing the feature [N], so that this neutralized *-L* is to P what its non-neutralized counterpart is to N; the proposed neutralization entails, one may assume, de-semanticization, specifically, the loss of the definiteness specification, which would in any event not make much sense in relation to a P.

Given the difficulty of assigning distinct semantic content to -*L* and its host in the constructions illustrated in (2.22) and the non-word status of the host in many instances, it seems reasonable to assume that such complex prepositions are created in the lexicon. I return to this issue in section 7.

6.3.2 The preposition *a+L*

The complex preposition *a+L* stands apart from the prepositions discussed in section 6.3.1 in a number of ways.

First, -*L*'s host exhibits no detectable synchronic or diachronic nominal properties. The clearest indication of this is that its gender/number properties are not determined by the (morphology or earlier semantics of the) stem, but by the gender/number specifications of the 'possessed' noun, that is, the noun with respect to which the *a+L*-initiated phrase functions as complement or specifier. This agreement pattern is brought out by the following data.

```
(2.25) a. Un portret        a-l/        *a-i        băieti -lor
          a portrait(M.SG) a-L(M.SG)/ a-L(M.PL) boy(M.PL)  -L(GEN)
          'a portrait of the boys'
       b. Nişte fotografii    a-le/       *a-l        rege        -lui.
          some picture(F.PL) a-L(F.PL)/a-L(M.SG) king(M.SG)-L(GEN)
          'some pictures of the king'
```

The host of -*L* is the element *a-*, which, I suggest, may be identified with the prepositional marker *a* that occurs 'bare' in (2.15d).

A second difference between *a+L* and the prepositions discussed in section 6.3.1 is that not only -*L*, but its host as well, appears to make no contribution to meaning. Rather, *a+L* seems to fulfil a strictly syntactic function, namely that of assigning GEN Case to, and thus of 'salvaging' adnominal arguments that cannot, for some reason, receive GEN Case in the way indicated in section 6.2. This latter point emerges from the following considerations: first, observe that all the ungrammatical subcases of (2.20) become grammatical if an appropriate form of *a+L* is inserted, as illustrated in (2.26).

```
(2.26)   a. *Portretul al regelui
         b. Portretul acesta al regelui
         c. Portretul frumos al regelui
         d. Ştefan al Moldovei
         e. Acest portret al regelui
         f. (Nici) un portret al regelui
         g. Al regelui portret[6]
         h. Al regelui a sosit.
         i. Regele al cărui portret atîrnă pe perete
```

In fact, *a+L* can be used more than once per construction, if necessary, as illustrated below.

(2.27) A   cui   descriere a României   e cea mai
        a-L⁷ whose description a Romania(GEN) is the most
        convingătoare?
        convincing
        'Whose description of Romania is the most convincing?'

Second, *a+L* may not be used (in the kind of constructions under consideration) if it is not needed for overt GEN Case assignment. Thus, its use is disallowed when a *bona fide* definite article fulfils the conditions for GEN Case assignment (cf. (2.20a) with (2.26a)), or when the phrase in need of Case may not bear (overt) GEN Case (cf. (2.15b) with (2.28)).

(2.28) Ion este tată -l a/*a-l trei copii.
        Ion is   father-L a/ a-L three children
        'Ion is the father of three children.'

Despite the differences just noted, I see no reason for analysing *a+L* in a radically different way from the prepositions addressed in section 6.3.1. Thus, I propose to analyse *a+L* as a complex preposition which takes a 'possessor' nominal phrase as complement, and which consists of a prepositional base (*a-*), and a categorially (partly) neutralized and de-semanticized functional Head (*-L*), much like the other GEN Case assigning prepositions; for a more detailed consideration of the internal syntax of *a+L* (and of other genitive Case assigning Ps), as well as of the exact position of the complement, see section 7. The de-semanticization of *-L*, that is, the fact that it is voided of definiteness content, is reflected in the fact that the noun with which it agrees need not head a definite phrase, as illustrated by (2.26f)[8].

As for the differences noted above, they are traceable to two facts. First, *a*, whether 'bare' or not, seems to be empty of semantic content and to have no other function than that of *alternative* Case assigner; thus it occurs 'bare' when the Case recipient does not tolerate affixal Case (see (2.15)), and it carries the functional enclitic *-L* when affixal Case can and needs to be assigned, its role being largely analogous to that of the Spanish, Romanian and Hebrew 'accusative' prepositional markers *a*, *pe* and *et* respectively. Concerning the distinct patterns of agreement exhibited by *-L* when hosted by *a-* and by other prepositional stems, I suggest that the former pattern is attributable to the fact that *a+L*, but not the other Ps, initiate '*possessors*'. Note that it is a general feature of Romance that 'possessors' agree with their 'possessed' nouns. This generalization is often obscured in constructions with non-pronominal 'possessors', because only pronominal 'possessors' are standardly inflected for number/gender. However, in non-pronominal 'possessor' constructions with *-L*, the inflectional options available to this element enable the agreement pattern to find concrete realization. In contrast, the prepositions considered in section 6.3.1 do not introduce 'possessors', so that there is no basis for a comparable agreement pattern; rather, -*L* reflects the gender/number features associated with the morphology and/or the historical semantics of the stem.

Before concluding this section, I should like to take a closer look at constructions with *prænominal* genitives, such as (2.26g), in which the 'possessed' N may not carry a token of -*L*. This state of affairs has prompted certain workers (for example, Dobrovie-Sorin (1987, Annexe)) to propose that *a*+*L* is here a non-clitic variant of -*L* generated as Head of the entire construction, rather than a P which takes the 'possessor' as complement, as I have proposed. Specifically, Dobrovie-Sorin proposed that the D-Structure representation of a construction like (2.26g) is something essentially like (2.29a)[9], rather than, say, something like (2.29b) (if one assumes that semantically-empty Case-assigners are inserted into derivations at S-Structure, as has sometimes been maintained).

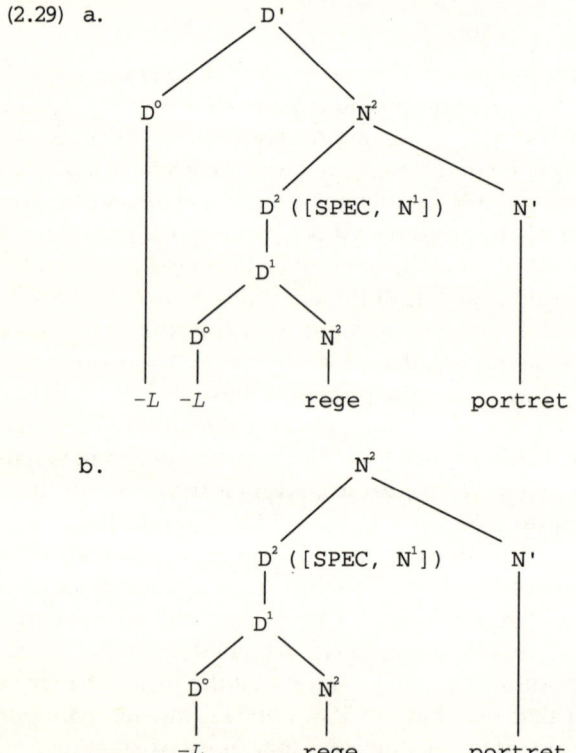

She also assumed that the rightmost token of -*L* in (2.29a) subsequently receives GEN Case and cliticizes on the ensuing noun, while the leftmost token of -*L* is realized in its presumed 'strong' form *a*+*L*, on the grounds that it is unable to cliticize on the D^2 in [SPEC, N'], which has its own token of -*L*. In arguing for her proposal, Dobrovie-Sorin further maintains that it can account for the deviance of (2.26a) on the reasonable assumption that the D° position may not host *two* instances of -*L* at D-Structure. Note also that *a+L* is in a position to function as Case-assigner for the DP in [SPEC, N']. (Dobrovie-Sorin did not, however, envisage such a role for it.)

There are a number of considerations which argue against the analysis just outlined.

First, there are cases where *a+L does* cooccur with an N-borne enclitic token of -*L*, for example, in (2.26b, c); clearly, -*L* cannot be held to originate in D°-position in such cases. Comparable remarks apply to constructions with two phrases introduced by *a+L* (for example, (2.27)), where at least one of the two *a*-borne instances of -*L* cannot have originated in D°-position. But if another source for *a+L* is in any event necessary, the case for viewing it as a 'strong' form of the definite article is weakened.

Second, even in cases like (2.26g), *a*-borne -*L* does not exhibit the syntactic behaviour which characterizes the determiners of nominal phrases in Romanian; that is to say, it cannot serve as locus of attachment for affixal Case, as illustrated by the contrast between (2.30a) and (2.30b).

```
(2.30) a.  M -am      adresat    fete -l-or  Mariei.
           me-have-I addressed  girls-L-DAT Maria(GEN)
       b. *M-am adresat a-l-or Mariei fete.
                        a-L-DAT
          'I addressed Maria's daughters.'
```

Observe that an N-borne instance of -*L* may host Case-endings (as shown in (2.30a)), while an *a*-borne instance of -*L* does not have this privilege (as shown in (2.30b)). This distinction is somewhat mysterious under Dobrovie-Sorin's analysis, but follows straightforwardly from mine. Thus, affixal oblique Case is realized, as pointed out in section 6.1, only on functional Heads that are construed as heading the nominal Extended Projection to which Case is assigned. Since *a*-borne -*L* in (2.30b) heads the 'possessor' phrase, rather than the larger nominal construction which is assigned Case, the deviance of (2.30b) is predicted.[10]

I thus conclude that *a+L* in constructions like (2.26g) and (2.26h) is the same *a+L* as elsewhere.

There is in fact another domain where *a+L* may seem to be an alternative realization of the definite article and where it turns out to have the basic properties it has elsewhere, that is, lack of definite content and partial categorial neutralization. The domain in question consists of the counterparts to all ordinal numerals other than *first* and *last*. While *prim* 'first' and *ultim* 'last' may bear an enclitic -*L*, all other ordinals must be preceded by *a+L*, as illustrated in (2.31).

```
(2.31) a. Ultimu-l băiat/ultim-a fată
          last   -L boy  /last -L girl
          'the last boy/the last girl'
```

b. A-l doilea băiat/a   doua   fată
   a-L second boy   /a-L second girl
   'the second boy/the second girl'

The fact that -*L* agrees in number and gender with the 'modified' N in both (2.31a) and (2.31b) and the fact that the expressions in both subcases of (2.31) are construed as definite make it look plausible that -*L* and *a*+*L* are mere positional variants here. Closer examination, however, refutes this first impression. Thus, while genuine instances of the definite article are incompatible with the indefinite article, as well as with pre-nominal demonstratives, as illustrated by (2.32a) and (2.32c), *a*+*L* shows no such incompatibility, as illustrated by (2.32b) and (2.32d). This clearly indicates that *a*+*L* is neutralized in respect to definiteness, and that it cannot occupy (or have originated in) the D° position of a nominal Extended Projection. This leads to the prediction that *a*+*L*, in contrast to -*L*, is not a possible bearer of affixal Case; as shown in (2.33), this prediction is fulfilled.

(2.32) a. Un ultim(*u-l) băiat îşi făcu apariţia.
          a last   -L boy REFL made the appearance
          'A last (*the) boy appeared.'
       b. Un *(a-l) doilea băiat îşi făcu apariţia.
          a   a-L second boy
          'A second boy appeared.'

(2.33) a. M -am   adresat ultimu-l-ui băiat.
          me-have-I addressed last   -L-DAT boy
          'I addressed the last boy.'
       b. *M-am adresat a-l-ui doilea băiat.
                        a-L-DAT
          'I addressed the second boy.'

I conclude from the above that -*L* in constructions like (2.31a) is a genuine nominal A-borne D (for discussion of A-borne -*L*, see sections 6.4 and 7), and that *a*+*L* in constructions like (2.31b) are functional Heads of an *adjectival* Extended Projection, neutralized for the feature [V] and for semantic content. The fact that *a*+*L* heads an adjectival projection is responsible for its inability to bear affixal Case (see section 6.4 for more discussion of this point). Its functional Head status is, I suggest, responsible for the fact that ordinals like those in (2.31b) may not also bear an encliticized token of the 'genuine' definite article, in addition to *a*+*L*. For discussion of a set of data which appear to contradict the latter prediction, but which upon closer examination turn out to support it, see the conclusion to section 6.4.

6.4 GENITIVES AFTER ADJECTIVES

In addition to Ns and Ps, As can serve as hosts of -*L*. These instances of -*L* need to be viewed as *bona fide* definite articles heading the DP whose noun nucleus is modified by A(P), because (i) these elements may bear affixal Case and (ii) have definite content (a property reflected in their incompatibility with indefinite determiners). These two points are demonstrated in (2.34) and (2.35) respectively.

```
(2.34) M -am       adresat   viteazu-l -ui  soldat.
       me-have.1 addressed  brave    -L -DAT soldier
       'I addressed the brave soldier.'

(2.35) Un viteaz(*u-l)  soldat se      cățără  pe zid.
       a  brave    -L   soldier REFL   climbed on wall
       'A brave soldier climbed on the wall.'
```

Just like N-borne and P-borne instances of -L, A-borne instances of -L can license genitive phrases, with one difference: the genitive phrases must be pronominal. This point is illustrated by the following contrast.

```
(2.36) a. Viteji -i tăi      fii
          brave  -L your(SG) sons
          'your brave sons'
       b. *Viteji -i țării           soldați
           brave  -L country-L(GEN) soldiers
           'the country's brave soldiers'
```

That the underscored pronoun in (2.36a) is licensed by -L is not in doubt, since pronominal, just like non-pronominal genitive phrases need to be immediately preceded by a governing token of -L. Thus, a noun may be immediately followed by a pronominal genitive only if it hosts -L, otherwise, recourse to *a+L* is necessary, as shown in (2.37). Similarly an adjective needs to bear -L to allow an immediately-following pronominal genitive, as shown in (2.38) (note that -L occurs only on the leftmost adjective).

```
(2.37) a. Caietu  -l tău
          copybook-L your(SG)
          'your copybook'
       b. Un caiet   *(a-l) tău
          a  copybook a-L   your(SG)
          'a copybook of yours'

(2.38) a. Ultim-a ta       senzațională idee
          last -L your(SG) sensational  idea
          'your last sensational idea'
       b. Senzațional-a ta          ultimă idee
          sensational-L your(SG)   last    idea
          'your sensational last idea'
       c. *Ultim-a senzațională ta idee
       d. *Senzațional-a ultimă ta idee
```

Now, if A-borne -L is able to license pronominal genitives by Case assignment under adjacency and government (on the latter point, see section 7.1.4. for more discussion), one may suspect that the ungrammaticality of data like (2.36b) is due not to inability on the part of *-L* to assign GEN Case, but to some independent cause. This suspicion is confirmed by the observation that (2.36b) cannot be salvaged by resorting to *a+L*, not even when the determiner is indefinite, as shown in (2.39).

(2.39) a. *Viteji -i a-i țării   soldați
          brave -L a-L country-L(GEN) soldiers
          'the country's brave soldiers'
       b. *O nouă a   Mariei   idee.
           a new a-L Maria(GEN) idea
          'a new idea of Maria's'

It is unlikely that the deviance of (2.39a, b) is due to some semantic incongruity, since they both become grammatical if the genitive phrases occur pre-adjectivally or postnominally, as illustrated in (2.40).

(2.40) a. A-i țării viteji soldați (cf. (2.39a))
       b. Viteji-i soldați a-i țării (cf. (2.39a))
       c. O nouă idee a Mariei (cf. (2.39b))

Nor can the deviance of (2.36b) be attributed to considerations of relative 'heaviness' of the various phrases, as appears to be the case with genitives sandwiched between a noun and a *post*nominal adjective. Thus, unlike (2.41a), (2.36b) is not improved when the element which follows the genitive (and/or the one which precedes it) increases in heaviness, as shown in (2.42).

(2.41) a. *Soldații   țării   curajoși
           soldiers-L country-L(GEN) brave
          'the country's brave soldiers'
       b. ?Soldații   țării   curajoși și neînfricați
           soldiers-L country-L(GEN) brave   and fearless
          'the country's brave and fearless soldiers'

(2.42) a. *Viteazul și neînfricatul Mariei   fiu
           brave-L and fearless-L   Maria(GEN) son
          'Maria's brave and fearless son'
       b. *Vitejii (și neînfricații) țării
           brave-L and fearless-L   country-L(GEN)
           soldați și ofițeri
           soldiers and officers
          'the country's brave and fearless soldiers
           and officers'

In short, the contrast between (2.36a) and (2.36b) does not seem to be attributable to failure of Case-marking, or to semantic or stylistic factors. I believe, however, that it can be attributed to the interaction of two independently-motivated mechanisms, specifically, certain adjacency effects involving Ns and modifying A(P)s, and the mechanism of (partial) neutralization of the categorial specification of D(P)s, something we have already appealed to in section 6.3 and which will be invoked again in section 6.5.

As pointed out in van Riemsdijk (1991), APs that occur within nominal phrases exhibit adjacency effects between A and N, especially when the AP is prenominal. This state of affairs is found, for example, in Dutch, as shown by the following data (adapted from van Riemsdijk).

(2.43) a. Een vader zo *TROTS*   zijn zoon dat...
           A   father so *PROUD* of his son that
       b. De *op zijn zoon TROTSE* vader.
           the *of his son PROUD* father
           'The father who is proud of his son.'
       c. *De *TROTSE op zijn zoon* vader

The complement of the adjective *trots* 'proud' can follow its Head when the AP is postnominal, as shown in (2.43a); when the AP is prenominal, however, the complement of this adjective must precede it, as shown by the contrast between (2.43b) and (2.43c). Note that the adjectival complement *op zijn zoon* intervenes between A and N in (2.43c), but not in (2.43b). Comparable adjacency effects are found in German and English, as illustrated in (2.44) and (2.45) respectively.

(2.44) a. Der Lehrer   is sehr *STOLZ auf unsere Errungenschaften*.
           the teacher is very *PROUD on our   achievements*
           'The teacher is very proud of our achievements.'
       b. Der *auf unsere Errungenschaften STOLZE* Lehrer
           the *of our   achievements   PROUD* teacher
           'the teacher who is proud of our achievements'
       c. *Der *STOLZE auf unsere Errungenschaften* Lehrer'

(2.45) a. John is *EASY to please*.
       b. John is an *EASY* man *to please*.
       c. *John is an *EASY to please* man.

Now, whatever the ultimate explanation of these adjacency effects may be (for a suggestion, see section 7.4.3), they are also found in Romanian; thus note the contrast between (2.46a) and (2.46c), which is parallel to the contrasts between the (a) and (c) subcases of (2.43)–(2.45) (for reasons which need not concern us here, Romanian permits neither the preposing of the adjectival complement, as in (2.43b) and (2.44b), nor its extraposition, as in (2.45b), so that (2.46c) does not have a grammatical alternative realization).

(2.46) a. Rege-le e *MÎNDRU de generali-i lui*.
           king-L is *PROUD of generals-L his*
           'The king is proud of his generals.'
       b. *MÎNDRU-L* rege.
           PROUD -L king
           'the proud king'

```
    c. MÎNDRU-L *de generali-i lui rege
       PROUD  -L  of generals-L his king
       'the king who is proud of his generals'
```

Given this adjacency requirement, the deviance of (2.36b) is predicted, since the 'possessor' nominal phrase intervenes between A and N. The proposal that the deviance of (2.36b) is due to a violation of the adjacency requirement is also supported by the observation that this example has a grammatical alternative realization, that is, (2.40a), in which A and N are adjacent.

It remains to provide an account of the well-formedness of (2.36a). Van Riemsdijk (1991) observes that the adjacency condition must be so formulated as to allow continuous sequences of prenominal adjectives, as in the following Dutch example:

```
(2.47) Een mooie     snelle auto
       a   beautiful fast   car
```

Such sequences are also permitted in Romanian, as illustrated by (2.48).

```
(2.48) Senzațional-a nouă idee a    Mariei
       sensational-L new  idea a-L Maria(GEN)
       'Maria's sensational new idea'
```

Therefore if it can be argued that pronominal 'possessors', in contrast to nonpronominal ones, can (also) function as adjectives, the acceptability of (2.36a), (2.38a) and (2.38b) will be explained.

The required argument is easy to construct. In Study 1, section 3.4 and n. 30 (p. 238), it was observed that overt definite pronouns may also function adjectivally in various languages, and it was proposed that the element *pro* may exhibit such double function as well (see discussion of example (1.123)). This state of affairs can be accounted for straightforwardly by assuming that definite pronouns and *pro* may in principle undergo neutralization, by losing the specification for the feature [V] and remaining specified as [+N] alone. It is this neutralization option, I submit, which enables the definite possessive pronouns[11] in (2.36a), (2.38a) and (2.38b) to occur in *adjectival position*, while permitting a *nominal interpretation* (since categorial neutralization does not automatically entail de-semanticization). Furthermore, under the assumption – made on independent grounds in Study 1, section 3.4 that Case is a property of [+N] categories, the fact that the possessive pronouns in the data under consideration receive (GEN) Case can also be accounted for. It is important to point out, however, that a [+N] functional Head is not automatically entitled to bear just any Case; rather, Case must be appropriate to the interpretation that (the projection headed by) the functional ultimately needs to receive. Thus, as pointed out in relation to (2.33b), pre-ordinal *a+L* may not bear GEN Case, since it heads an adjectival Extended Projection, which is moreover 'adjectively construed'; *a+L*-headed ordinal adjectival projections can, however, bear whatever Case predicative APs bear, since they are allowed in predicative position (demonstration omitted). In contrast, the possessive pronouns in (2.36) and (2.38) *may* bear GEN Case, because they are 'nominally construed'. Note also that the well-formedness of (2.33a) does not conflict with what has just been said because *-L*, while morphologically A-borne, is construed as heading the entire nominal Extended Projection *ultimului băiat*, in contrast to *a+L* in (2.33a), which is construed as heading just the adjectival projection **alui doilea*.

In support of the proposal made in the preceding paragraph, I wish to note that the neutralization of D in respect to its [V] specification is not an idiosyncratic property of the grammar of Romanian. Comparable phenomena are found, for example, in English and German.

Thus, consider the English data in (2.49).

```
(2.49) a.  This my sword
       b. *This the colonel's sword
```

While (2.49a) has a literary and archaic flavour to it, many informants still recognize it as a possible, if obsolescent type of construction; in contrast, everybody finds (2.49b) completely impossible (the same kind of contrast is found in literary German and, according to an anonymous referee, in literary Italian). Note that, given the analysis of English genitive constructions outlined in section 6.0.1, there is no coherent analysis for (2.49b), since *'s* must occur under D° (and *the colonel* in [SPEC, D']), but the D° position is filled by *this*. In contrast, an analysis *is* possible for (2.49a) if we assume that *my* has been neutralized for the feature [V], for this would enable it to occur in 'adjectival position', that is, adjoined to N^2 or N', and thus *after this*.[12]

Consider now the following data from German.

```
(2.50) a. Die Seele jedes(S)      guten(W)     Menschen
          the soul  every.GEN.    good.GEN.    person.GEN.
          'every good person's soul'
       b. Die Seele eines(S)  jeden(W)    guten(W)   Menschen
          the soul  a.GEN.    every.GEN.  good.GEN.  person.GEN.
          'every good person's soul'
       c. Die Seelen dieser(S)    guten(W)    alten(W)   Freunde
          the souls  these.GEN.   good.GEN.   old.GEN.   friends
          'the souls of these good old friends'
       d. Die Seelen guter(S)    alter(S)   Freunde
          the souls  good.GEN.   old.GEN.   friends
          'the souls of good old friends'
       e. Die Seelen aller(S)    dieser(S)    Menschen
          the souls  all.GEN.    these.GEN.   people
          'the souls of all these people'
```

Certain components of nominal phrases can be inflected according to either a 'strong' or a 'weak' pattern (which I have indicated above with (S) and (W) respectively). In general, when a nominal phrase includes both one or more functional Heads and one or more adjectives, the former are strong and the latter are weak, as illustrated in (2.50c); it is only when no overt functional Heads are present that the adjectives bear strong inflectional markers, as illustrated in (2.50d). Observe now the behaviour of the element *jeder* 'each'. In (2.50a), where it is strong *and followed by a weak A*, it behaves like a nominal functional Head, for if it were an A, the ensuing A *guten* would have been strong, just like *alter* in (2.50d). But in (2.50b), where *jeder* immediately follows a strong D *and is itself weak*, its behaviour is that of an A (just like that of the ensuing *guten*), for if it were a nominal functional Head, it would need to be strong, just like *dieser* in (2.50e). In addition, as indicated by the translations of (2.50a) and (2.50b), *jeder* seems to receive the same interpretation in both cases (according to my German informants, the only difference between these two examples seems to be one of register, (2.50b) being assignable to a more elevated one). This 'schizophrenic' morphological behaviour of *jeder* with retention of semantic interpretation suggests that this element, much like the 'possessor' pronouns of Romanian and English, can undergo neutralization of the categorial specification [-V].[13]

To sum up, as has just been shown, the contrast in (2.36) can be accounted for in terms of independently-needed mechanisms.

Before concluding this section, we shall take a look at another type of contrast found in an adjectival construction. Consider (2.51), where the translations of the (b)–(d) subcases indicate purported readings.

```
(2.51) a.  A doua        ta           carte
           second.F.SG.  your.F.SG.   book(F.SG.)
           'your second book'
       b.  *A doua       Mariei       carte
           second.F.SG.  Maria(GEN)   book
           'Mary's second book'
       c.  *Al doilea    tău          roman
           second.M.SG.  your.M.SG.   novel(F.SG.)
           'your second novel'
       d.  *Al doilea    Mariei       roman
           second.M.SG.  Maria(GEN)   novel(M.SG.)
           'Mary's second novel'
```

Here, the genitive 'possessors' are placed after an ordinal numeral (for which, see section 6.3.2). The contrast between (2.51a) and (2.51b), which is parallel to the one between (2.36a) and (2.36b), suggests that ordinals are adjectival categories. The contrast between (2.51a) and (2.51c) does not follow from anything that has been said so far. Before proposing a solution for this new contrast, it will be instructive to look at certain facts involving 'possessors' after N.

Thus observe the following facts.

(2.52) a. Ecaterina *(a)   Rusiei
         Ecaterina   a+L Russia(GEN)
         'Catherine of Russia'
      b. Construiți   Românânia (*a)   viitoru-l-ui!
         build.IMP.PL. Romania   a+L future -L-GEN
         'Build the Romania of the future!'

The fact that the F.SG. realization of *a+L* is required in (2.52a) and excluded in (2.52b) suggests that the personal proper name in the former bears no -L, while the place proper name in the latter does; note that the presence/absence of -L is not expected to be superficially 'visible' on feminine nouns whose stem ends in *a*, given the fact that the F.SG. realization of -L is also *a* and the existence of the vowel-deletion rule hinted at in n. 5. The correctness of this conclusion is reinforced by the observation that *masculine* names of individuals and countries show an overt contrast in the predicted direction, as shown in (2.53).

(2.53) a. Ștefan(*-ul) *(al) Moldovei
         'Stephan of Moldavia'
      b. Clădiți Sudan*(-ul) (*al) viitorului!
         'Build the Sudan of the future!'

That feminine proper names ending in *a* are potentially ambiguous as to the presence/absence of -L is also shown by the following data.

(2.54) a. Egipt*(-ul) e lîngă Sudan(*-ul).
         'Egypt is near Sudan.'
      b. Franța e lîngă Elveția.
         'France is near Switzerland.'

Owing to a curious restriction of Romanian which precludes -L on (definitely construed) single-word nominal phrases after certain prepositions, names of countries must occur 'bare' after such prepositions, as shown in (2.54a). This forces us to assume that in (2.54b), *Elveția* is 'bare' and *Franța* bears a token of -L.

Let us now return to the facts in (2.51). The deviance of (2.51c) is straightforwardly attributable to the fact that *al doilea* does not bear a M.SG. realization of -L. But what about (2.51a)? Given what has been said in the preceding paragraph, *a doua* could in principle bear a F.SG. realization of -L. To be sure, this could not be an instance of -L with *definite semantic content*, and this, for two reasons. First, as shown in (2.55a), constructions like (2.51a) are compatible with the *indefinite* article; second, *doua* cannot bear morphological Case, as shown in (2.55b) (recall the point made earlier in this section that de-semanticized instances of -L are not possible loci for morphological Case realization).

(2.55) a. O a doua ta   carte   ar   fi   de prisos.
          a second your book would be   of surplus
          'A second book of yours/by you would be superfluous.'
      b. Apariția   primei/   *a douei   ediții
          appearance-the first-L-GEN second-L-GEN edition
          'the appearance of the first/second edition'

None the less, as was abundantly shown in section 6.3, de-semanticized variants of -*L* with Case-assigning ability certainly exist. I suggest that the acceptability of (2.51a) and (2.55a) is due to the reanalysis of *a doua* as having the more abstract structure *a doua+L*, and this, due to the 'phonological plausibility' of such an analysis.

6.5 -*L*-BEARING COMPLEX DETERMINERS

6.5.1 -*L* as a non-Case assigner

In the preceding three sections, we have examined a variety of construction-types characterized by the presence of Case-assigning -*L*; de-semanticization, specifically lack of definiteness specifications, was seen not to prejudice -*L*'s Case-assigning properties (although it did prejudice its Case-hosting properties). In this section, we will address constructions which exhibit unquestionable instances of the morpheme -*L*, but in which this element does *not* have Case-assigning properties.

Indefinite and demonstrative determiners with an overtly headed N^2 complement have counterparts whose N^2 complement lacks an overt N-Head, as can be seen by comparing (2.56a, b) and (2.56c, d).

(2.56) a. *Un* băiat deștept
          a   boy   clever
          'a clever boy'
      b. *Acel* băiat deștept
          that boy   clever
          'that clever boy'
      c. *Unul* deștept
          one   clever
          'a clever one'
      d. *Cel* deștept
          that clever
          'the clever one'

A comparison of the various realizations of -*L* in the NOM Case (reproduced in (2.57a)) with the corresponding realizations of the italicized elements in (2.56c) and (2.56d) (which are provided in (2.57b) and (2.57c) respectively) shows that the latter two forms are analysable into an initial morpheme (*un*) or stem (*ce-*) and the morpheme -*L*.

(2.57) a. -(u)l, -a, -i, -(e)le
 b. unul, una, unii, unele
 c. cel, cea, cei, cele

Now the forms in (2.57b) and (2.57c) may be followed by 'possessors', as shown in (2.58). But, in contrast to constructions where it is hosted by N, P or A, -L is unable to assign Case in these contexts, as the obligatory presence of *a+L* reveals.

(2.58) a. Unul *(al) rege-l-ui
  one   a-L king-L-GEN
  'one of the king'
 b. Cel *(al) rege-l-ui
  that a-L king-L-GEN
  'that of the king'

Since -*L* is obviously the same *morpheme* (in the sense of Aronoff (1976: § 2.1.3.3) in the constructions discussed in sections 6.2–6.4. and in (2.58), why should it exhibit (GEN) Case-assigning abilities in the former only? The proposal I wish to defend here is that GEN Case assignment is not a property of the mere morpheme -*L* (as I earlier maintained in Grosu (1988a)), but of -*L qua* D, and – more generally – *qua* syntactic category.

Let us look at -*L* in (2.57b) more closely. This is clearly not an instance of the *definite* article, since the total forms are construed as indefinite. However, as we have seen in relation to GEN Case-assigning prepositions and to the construction in (2.55a), de-semanticization does not in and of itself detract from -*L*'s Case-assigning capabilities. At the same time, there are additional facts which suggest that -*L* is here not just a de-semanticized D, but rather no D at all. The facts in question concern the DAT/GEN forms of *unul*, which are listed in (2.59a).

(2.59) a. un-ui-a (M.SG.), un-ei-a (F.SG.), un-or-a (PL.)
 b. cel-ui (M.SG.), cel-ei (F.SG.), cel-or (PL.)

Observe that, under a D analysis of -*L*, this element would head a nominal Extended Projection, and should thus be able to serve as host to affixal Case-endings. That D-borne -*L* can in principle serve as locus for affixal Case realization is shown by the DAT/GEN forms of *cel* (listed in (2.59b)). But, curiously, -*L* is completely absent in the forms in (2.59a), affixal Case attaching directly to *un-*. This state of affairs suggests (to me) that -*L* in (2.57b) serves no more than a 'strengthening' *euphonic* role, with no *syntactic* import, much like the final *s* in *yours*,[14] and unlike the one in *girls*, *eats*, or *John's*. Now, in (2.59a), the 'strengthening' role seems to be taken over by the invariant morpheme -*a* (which is possible – and necessary – only when no N follows); that is to say, -*L* is disallowed is such forms, forms like **unului(-a)* or **unilor(-a)* being ungrammatical (presumably, some Economy Principle excludes the full versions, much like the one which disallows a redundant use of *a+L*; see (2.26a)). The fact that -*L* is retained in the oblique forms of *cel* (see (2.59b)) is attributable to the fact that its omission would yield vowel sequences of a kind that the language disallows (see n. 5 p. 243).

In short, I submit that a reasonable interpretation of the facts in (2.58) is that GEN Case in Romanian is assigned not by the morpheme -*L per se*, but by this morpheme with D status.

6.5.2 On neutralized CEL

The element CEL, whose realizations were listed in (2.57c) and which was shown in the preceding section to be unable to assign Case in spite of the fact that it includes the morpheme -*L*, raises further issues of interest for the theory of functional categories. Specifically, it illustrates the need to appeal to neutralization of categorial specifications and/or of the functional/categorial distinction, a state of affairs that has already been illustrated in section 6.3.

Thus in addition to contexts where it initiates an *argument* (see (2.57b) and (2.59b)), CEL may also initiate a *predicate*, much like *the* in the following construction.

```
(2.60) Peter [the Great]
```

One may think that the bracketed constituent, which functions as predicate with respect to the proper noun, is a nominal phrase with a null N-Head modified by an adjectival phrase. Such an analysis is not initially implausible, since nominal phrases with overt Heads can also function as predicates in comparable contexts, for example, *Jack the Ripper*. Furthermore, nominal phrases with a modified null Head arguably occur as arguments in other languages, for example, in French, as illustrated in (2.61a); note that the bracketed phrases in (2.61a) also have predicative uses comparable to that of *the Great* in (2.60), as shown in (2.61b).

```
(2.61) a. J'ai    vu    [le grand], mais pas [le petit].
          I have seen the big       but  NEG the  small
        'I saw the big *(one), but not the small *(one).'
       b. Pierre [le Grand]
```

None the less, there are reasons for not analysing the bracketed constituent in (2.60) as exhibiting a null nominal nucleus. Thus note that in English, phrases like the bracketed one in (2.60) cannot in general be used argumentally, as shown by the deviance of the reduced version of the English translation of (2.61a). But an overt nominal Head, in particular the element *one*, is not needed in (2.60) (it is in fact inappropriate in this context). To express this distinction, I propose to analyse the predicate in (2.60) as exhibiting an instance of *the* neutralized with respect to the feature

[V] and whose complement is *adjectival*, rather than *nominal*. A comparable conclusion is suggested by certain properties of CEL in predicative constructions, to which we now turn.

Predicative CEL-constructions can be productively formed in Romanian, and occur in a much larger set of contexts than their English counterparts. Thus, in contrast to English, the 'subject of predication' need not be a proper name, and the predicated phrase may be not only adjectival, but also prepositional, as illustrated in (2.62); these options do not exist in English, as shown in (2.63).

```
(2.62) a. Clădirea    [cea mare]  s'   a   prăbuşit.
          building-L  CEL  big    REFL has collapsed
          'The big building has collapsed.'
       b. Clădirea    [cea de peste drum] s'   a   prăbuşit.
          building-L  CEL of over  road   REFL has collapsed
          'The building across the road has collapsed.'

(2.63) a. *The building the big has collapsed.
       b. *The building the across the road has collapsed.
```

That the CEL-constructions in (2.62) do not exhibit a null nominal nucleus is suggested by two types of facts. First, the distribution of predicative CEL-constructions is more restricted than that of their argumental counterparts. Thus both construction types may include, in addition to CEL, an adjectival or prepositional phrase, as can be seen by comparing (2.62) with (2.64); however, only argumental CEL-constructions may include, in addition to CEL, an argument (of an 'understood' N) or a relative clause, as can be seen by comparing (2.65) and (2.66).

```
(2.64) a. [Cea mare]   s'   a   prăbuşit.
          CEL big      REFL has collapsed
          'The big (one.F.) has collapsed.'
       b. [Cea de peste drum]  s'   a   prăbuşit.
          CEL of over  road    REFL has collapsed
          'The (one.F.) across the road has collapsed.'

(2.65) a. Cei          ai  regelui     au   fugit.
          CEL.M.PL.    a-L king-L-GEN  have run
          'Those of the king have run away.'
       b. Cei          care luptă încă  sînt  epuizaţi.
          CEL.M.PL.    who  fight still are   exhausted
          'Those who are still fighting are exhausted.'

(2.66) a. *Soldaţi -i  cei         ai  regelui     au   fugit.
          soldiers-L CEL.M.PL.    a-L king-L-GEN  have run
          'The soldiers CEL of the king have run away.'
       b. *Soldaţ  -i  cei         care luptă încă  sînt  epuizaţi.
          soldiers-L CEL.M.PL.    who  fight still are   exhausted
          'The soldiers CEL who are still fighting are exhausted.'
```

Second, in predicative, but not in argumental constructions, CEL is typically unstressed, and in fact appears to cliticize on its immediate right context. Thus, as shown below, 'predicative CEL' contrasts with 'argumental CEL' in being unable to occur in conjunct-final position or followed by a parenthetical, that is, in (relatively) stressed positions.

(2.67) a. Am   vorbit [cu   cei]   şi   [cu   cele]
           have.1. spoken with CEL.M.PL. and   with those.F.PL.
           din   satul   învecinat.
           from village-L neighbouring
           'I spoke with those (men) and those (women) from the
           neighbouring village.'
       b. Cei,   aş   spune, incapabili să   se
          CEL.M.PL. would.1.SG. say   incapable   SUBJ REFL
          controleze, trebuie respinşi.
          control   must   rejected
          'Those, I might say, incapable of controlling,
          control must be rejected.'

(2.68) a. *Am   vorbit [cu   ţărani   -i cei]
           have.1. spoken with peasants.M.-L CEL.M.PL.
           şi [cu ţărănci   -le cele]   din   satul
           and with peasants.F.-L CEL.F.PL. from village-L
           învecinat.
           neighbouring
           'I spoke with those (men) peasants and those (women)
           peasants from the neighbouring village.'
       b. *Ţărani -i cei,   aş   spune, incapabili
           peasants.M. -L CEL.M.PL. would.1.SG. say   incapable
           să   se   controleze, trebuie respinşi.
           SUBJ REFL control   must   rejected
           'The peasants, I might say, incapable of
           controlling themselves, must be rejected.'

To see why these various facts argue against a nominal nucleus in predicative CEL-constructions, consider first the contrast between (2.65a) and (2.66a). If one assumes a (null) nominal nucleus in (2.66a), it is puzzling why *ai regelui* should not be interpretable as a 'possessor' argument of that nucleus. But if no such nucleus is assumed and *ai regelui* is viewed as a complement of CEL, the situation appears less mysterious. Thus, note that the purported complement is, as argued in section 6.3.2, headed by a (partly neutralized) D°, that is, -*L*, which selects a PP complement. If so, the deviance of (2.66a) is attributable to the fact that DP does not in general iterate; thus nominal phrases in general exhibit one determiner, and prepositional phrases may be assumed to be subject to a comparable constraint. Note that the proposal just made does not rule out (2.62b), where the complement of CEL is a PP, not a DP.[15]

Second, consider the contrast between (2.65b) and (2.66b). I suggest that the deviance of (2.66b) is derivable from the following considerations. On the one hand, restrictive relative clauses necessarily have a predicative operator in their [SPEC, C']; on the other hand, predicative CEL-constructions may be assumed also to necessarily exhibit a (null) predicative operator in their own Specifier. Now, under the assumption that no null nominal nucleus exists in (2.66b), we would seem to have two predicative operators that vie for the privilege of binding the same variable, a state of affairs that is in principle excluded within the theory of Government and Binding. But if a nominal nucleus is assumed, it is in principle possible for such a nucleus to serve as a variable bound by the 'higher' operator, while also serving as 'antecedent' with respect to the 'lower' operator. We thus have an additional argument for assuming that there is no nominal nucleus in (2.66b).

Third, consider the contrast between (2.67) and (2.68). There exist independent contexts in which the presence of an immediately-ensuing null element triggers an increase in stress level. For example, certain English auxiliaries cannot lose stress sufficiently to undergo contraction with a preceding subject when they are followed by the trace of a NO, as shown by the contrast in (2.69).

```
(2.69) a. John's willing to go.
       b. Mary's as intent on staying as John is/?*John's
          willing to go.
```

It is thus in principle possible to attribute the contrast between (2.67) and (2.68) to a comparable factor.

In short, there are a number of factors which point to the conclusion that the CEL in predicative constructions takes non-nominal complements and is thus appropriately neutralized in its categorial specifications.

Before concluding, I should like to briefly address the issue of the semantic content of CEL in predicative constructions. Given the absence of a nominal nucleus *and* the categorial neutralization of CEL, predicative CEL constructions do not designate some kind of entity, as (argumental or predicative) nominal phrases typically do, but rather properties, locations, etc. Should one then conclude that predicative CEL is also desemanticized? The answer to this question appears to be negative. That is to say predicative CEL appears to exhibit, just like argumental CEL, the kind of definiteness content which is found in (uncontroversial) demonstratives. Thus a CEL-predicate is incompatible with an indefinite D°, as shown in (2.70a), although it is compatible with a definite one, as shown in (2.70c). Furthermore, nominal phrases seem to allow a single demonstrative element, as suggested by (2.70b)-(2.70d) (demonstratives may occur either before or after the noun, but not in both positions). Now, a predicative CEL construction is incompatible with a demonstrative, an argumental CEL or another predicative CEL (see (2.70e), (2.70g) and

(2.70f, h) respectively), which strongly suggests that it has retained demonstrative content.

(2.70) a. Un băiat (*cel) deștept.
    a boy   CEL clever
    'a clever (*CEL) boy'
  b. Acel băiat
     that boy
  c. Băiatu-l acela
     boy -L that
     'that boy'
  d. Acel băiat (*acela)
     that boy   that
  e. Acel băiat (*cel) deștept
     that boy   CEL clever
     'that clever boy'
  f. Băiatu-l cel din vale (*cel) atît de deștept
     boy -L CEL from valley CEL so of clever
     'the boy from the valley (who is) so clever'
  g. Cel din vale (*cel) atît de deștept
     CEL from valley CEL so of clever
     'the (one) from the valley (who is) so clever'
  h. Băiatu-l (*cel) din vale cel atît de deștept
     (same meaning as (2.70f))

7

On the encliticization process

In the preceding four sections, we have examined in some detail the distributional links (or lack of them) between genitive phrases on the one hand and Ns, Ps, As and Ds that bear an *-L* enclitic on the other. In this section and the following two, I propose to explore the kinds of theoretical treatments that the theory of Government and Binding and the minimalistic programme make available with respect to generalizations uncovered in earlier sections.

In this section, we take up the question of how *-L* and comparable morphemes in other languages combine with their hosts.

7.1 ENCLITICIZATION WITHIN THE GOVERNMENT AND BINDING FRAMEWORK

7.1.1 General Considerations

A widely accepted view within the theory of Government and Binding is that complex morphological items arise through the operation of either syntactic or lexical processes. Borer (1984, 1988) took the interesting view that the rules which operate in the syntactic and in the lexical components are the *same* rules, and differ only in their modes of operation: regular and semantically transparent in the syntax, idiosyncratic and/or semantically opaque in the lexicon.

According to this logic, complex lexical items analysable as *P+L* and *D+L* (see sections 6.3 and 6.5 respectively) must be assumed to have arisen in the lexicon. In contrast, those constructions in which *-L* is N-borne or A-borne need to be viewed as having arisen in the syntax. Correspondingly, the English element *'s* and the Hebrew null Case-assigning D were assumed, in the studies reviewed in sections 6.3 and 6.5, to combine with their hosts post-lexically; as for the null GEN-assigning D which I proposed to assume for German (see section 6.0.2), I know of no compelling evidence that it needs to combine with anything (in overt representation).

I find the view that *P+L* and *D+L* formations arise in the lexicon unproblematic. I thus propose to accept it, and will have nothing more to say about it in what follows. We will thus direct our attention to *N+L* and *A+L* constructions; before this, however, I wish to note some facts which strengthen the assumption that the D° position is projected in such constructions, just as it is in constructions where it is superficially filled by some non-clitic D of some other sort.

7.1.2 Non-enclitic counterparts to definite -*L*

Most Romanian Ds are not clitics, and occur in pre-nominal position in superficial representation. Since definite -*L* behaves like other Ds in serving as locus for affixal Case realization, it is natural to assume that it originates in (pre-nominal) D° position at D-Structure and subsequently achieves enclitic status. This assumption is strengthened by the observation that there are at least two non-enclitic variants of -*L*, which occur pre-nominally, as expected.

One non-enclitic variant consists of 'bare' third person definite pronouns, which, as noted earlier, are viewed, within the DP Hypothesis, as simply elements of category D (which differ from 'definite articles' in having a null NP complement). That such pronouns are arguably special instances of -*L* is most transparent in the DAT/GEN Case; to see this, compare the corresponding underlined forms in (2.71) and (2.72).

```
(2.71) a. I       -am     scris  lui      /ei.
          him/her-have.1. written him(DAT) her(DAT)
          'I wrote to him/her.'
       b. Le -am     scris  lor.
          them-have.1. written them(DAT)
          'I wrote to them.'

(2.72) a. I       -am     scris  rege-lui  /regin-ei
          him/her-have.1. written king-L-DAT/queen-L-DAT
          'I wrote to the king/queen.'
       b. Le -am     scris  regi-lor  /regine-lor
          them-have.1. written kings-L-DAT/queens-L-DAT
          'I wrote to the kings/queens.'
```

The point just made can, however, also be appreciated in relation to the NOM/ACC Case, where pronouns are typically distinguishable from articles in exhibiting an initial *e* vowel, whose function is presumably to make pronominal forms pronounceable as separate words (cf. the corresponding underlined forms in (2.73) and (2.74)).

```
(2.73) a. El/ea   a    plecat.
          he/she has left
       b. Ei   /ele    au    plecat.
          they(M)/they(F) have left
```

(2.74) a. Băiatu-*l*/fata -*a* a   plecat.
       boy   -L/girl -L has left
       'The boy/girl has left.'
   b. Băieţi-*i*/fete -*le* au   plecat.
      boys -L/girls-L have left
      'The boys/girls have left.'

Another situation in which there is arguably an instance of (non-clitic) -*L* that occupies the D° position at both D- and S-Structure is found with DAT/GEN personal proper names, which, except for feminine names ending in -*a*, do not act as hosts for -*L*. In fact, the fact that feminine names in -*a* bear -*L* is probably the result of a reanalysis process, which is made possible by the fact that such names are ambiguously interpretable as bearing and as not bearing -*L* (for reasons noted in section 6.4). Such proper names are preceded by an invariant (M.SG.) form of -*L*+Case, as illustrated in (2.75).

(2.75) a. Frate -le *lui*   Ion.
          brother-L L-GEN   Ion.
          'Ion's brother'
   b. Frate -le *lui*   Jenny (cf. frate-le Mari -ei[16])
      brother-L L-GEN Jenny   Maria-GEN
      'Jenny's brother'
   c. Frate -le *lui*   Ion şi Gheorghe
      brother-L L-GEN Ion and Gheorghe
      'Ion's and George's brother'
   d. Frate -le *lui*   Jenny şi Lily
      brother-L L-GEN Jenny and Lily
      'Jenny's and Lily's brother'

The underlined elements in (2.75) in fact seem to occur in D° position not only at D- and S-Structure, but also at PF, because they do not procliticize on proper names. Note that, in the event of a coordination of definite nominals in the DAT/GEN, -*L*+Case must be realized on each conjunct (that is, it cannot attach to the coordination as a whole), as illustrated in (2.76).

(2.76) a. *Frate -le Maria   şi Zamfir-ei
          brother-L Maria(NOM) and Zamfira-GEN
   b. *Fratele Mari-ei   şi Zamfira
               Maria-GEN and Zamfira(NOM)
   c. Fratele Mari -ei   şi Zamfir-ei
              Maria-GEN and Zamfira-GEN
      'Maria's and Zamfira's brother'

In contrast, *lui* need not be realized on each conjunct of an ensuing coordination, as illustrated by (2.75c, d). There are thus no grounds for viewing it as a proclitic.

I wish to stress that, its invariant status notwithstanding, *lui* in cases like

(2.75) needs to be viewed as a D, because it includes the GEN/DAT Case-ending *-ui*. That the latter is indeed a Case-ending is brought out by the fact that, when interpretable as a GEN, it is subject to exactly the same licensing conditions as common or garden-variety GEN forms. To illustrate this briefly, note that the *lui*-initiated phrases in (2.75) need to be viewed as licensed by the immediately preceding token of enclitic *-L*, because if some other phrase intervenes between the latter and the former (as is the case, for example, in the reduced version of (2.77)), the use of *a+L* is necessary, as indicated.

```
(2.77) Frate  -le cel mare *(a-l) lui   Jenny și Lily
       brother-L the big      a-L   L-GEN Jenny and Lily
       'Jenny's and Lily's big brother'
```

This concludes our discussion of the two constructions in which some variant of *-L* superficially occurs in its D-Structure position.

7.1.3 N-borne *-L*

Recent work within has envisaged at least two ways in which an affix/clitic can be joined to an X°-host: by raising the host, or by lowering the affix/clitic (see Pollock (1989) and Chomsky (1991), on illustrations of these options in French and English). Ritter (1988, 1991) appealed to the former mechanism in proposing an analysis of the CS construction in Hebrew, and especially in attempting to account for the construction-initial position of the Head N (see section 6.0.3). In respect to Romanian, since both *-L*-bearing Ns and non-clitic Ds are DP-initial, a raising analysis appears entirely appropriate.

There is in fact some independent evidence in favour of a raising analysis for the Romanian constructions under consideration. Thus, *-L* may cooccur with a (strong form of a) demonstrative element, as illustrated in (2.78), in which case the latter must immediately follow *-L*, as illustrated in (2.79).

```
(2.78) Caietu  -l acesta/acela
       copybook-L this  /that
       'this/that copybook'
(2.79) a.  Bățu -l acesta mic
           stick-L this    small
           'this small stick'
       b.  *Bățu-l mic acesta
       c.  Bățu -l acesta de lemn
           stick-L this    of wood
           'this wooden stick'
       d.  *Bățu-l de lemn acesta
```

The adjacency facts in (2.79) can be accounted for by assuming that the demonstrative is generated under D° as a right-sister to *-L*. Given such an assumption, a raising analysis is more plausible, since Head-to-Head movement operations are usually viewed (within pre-minimalistic frameworks) as justified by the need to provide affixes/clitics with a host; under a lowering analysis, it is unclear why the entire *-L+DEM* complex should have to lower, that is, why lowering cannot apply to *-L* alone.

To sum up, an analysis in terms of raising of N appears to be optimal for *N+L* constructions.

7.1.4 A-borne *-L*

In contrast to the constructions addressed in the preceding subsection, constructions where *-L* is a definite article and is hosted by A are not amenable to an analysis such that the lexical host raises to D°.

First, a *nominal* Extended Projection whose determiner combines with an adjective would probably be uninterpretable, since the combined items conflict in their specifications for the feature [V].

Second, if A could raise to *-L*, we would expect (2.80) to be grammatical, just like (2.78); however, it is not.

```
(2.80)  *Viteazu-l  acesta  soldat
         brave  -L  this    soldier
        'this brave soldier'
```

Third, and most important, *-L*-bearing As may head higher adjectival projections, as shown in (2.81b) and (2.81c). Observe that raising AP to D° would violate widely-accepted principles of structure preservation.

```
(2.81)  a. Frumoas -a prinţesă
           beautiful-L princess
           'the beautiful princess'
        b. Prea frumoas-a prinţesă
           too
           'the exceedingly beautiful princess'
        c. Atît de frumoas-a prinţesă
           so   of
           'the so beautiful princess'
```

Two analytical possibilities remain: either AP raises out of NP and left-adjoins to DP, after which *-L* moves out of D° and encliticizes to it, or *-L* lowers to A. Neither analysis is unproblematic. Under the former analysis, it is unclear why other APs cannot also adjoin to DP, yielding patterns like (2.82a') (as an alternative realization of (2.82a)) and why N cannot raise to D°, yielding patterns like (2.82b) (as an alternative realization of (2.81c)).

```
(2.82)  a. Ultim-a interesantă idee a    Mariei
           last -L interesting idea a+L Maria.GEN
           'Maria's last interesting idea'
```

```
a'.*Ultimă  interesant -a idee a   Mariei
    last    interesting-L idea a+L Maria.GEN
   'Maria's last interesting idea'
b. *Atît de frumoasă  prinţes -a
    so  of beautiful princess-L
   'the so beautiful princess'
```

Under the latter analysis, it is somewhat unexpected that -*L* lowers to the Head of an adjunct, rather than to a Head of its Extended Projection (as in the cases considered by Pollock (1989)). Furthermore, it is unclear why it can only lower to the leftmost A. Note that if one assumes it encliticizes to the closest *AP*, rather than to its *Head*, one makes the strange assumption that -*L*, which is a lexical affix in every other construction where it appears, is a phrasal affix just in this construction.

To sum up, both raising and lowering analyses seem to be unable to yield a satisfactory account of -*L*'s encliticization to adjectives.

7.2 ENCLITICIZATION WITHIN THE MINIMALISTIC FRAMEWORK

The minimalistic framework, as outlined in Chomsky (1992), does not envisage the joining of functional affixes/clitics to lexical stems through syntactic raising or lowering operations. Rather, inflected words are created in the lexicon, and their inflectional properties are checked against the featural content of functional Heads, the latter being removed if the two sets of features match. Unremoved features on functional Heads cause a derivation to 'crash'. 'Weak' features may be removed after 'spell out', since they are invisible at PF, and they must in fact be removed late on the grounds that late movement is more economical; 'strong' features must be removed prior to 'spell out', forcing overt movement.

The view that inflected items are created in the lexicon makes it very easy to account for the encliticization of -*L* to various stems. All that is needed is to define -*L* as a lexical enclitic and to specify the Heads to which it can encliticize. The assumption that constituents never raise overtly except when strong features on some functional Head would otherwise cause a derivational 'crash' permits a straightforward explanation of the leftmost position of Ns or As that bear an -*L* enclitic. On the assumption that only such items need to be checked against definiteness features on (an abstract) D, they alone will raise into DP, thereby reaching a leftmost position within DP.

To sum up, the minimalistic framework seems much better equipped than the earlier theory of Government and Binding to deal with the *A+L* constructions of Romanian.

7.3 THE LINEAR ORDER OF GENITIVE PHRASES AND THEIR LICENSERS

The four languages that were discussed in preceding sections fall into two groups according as genitive phrases precede or follow their D licensers in overt representation; English and German belong to the former category, Hebrew and Romanian to the latter. I illustrate in (2.83) the relative positions of genitive phrases (in square brackets) and of their presumed licensers (in curly brackets) according to the analyses of sections 6.0 and 6.2.

(2.83) a. [Mary] {'s} picture
     b. [Marias] {D} Bild
     c. Tmuna {-t} [Miriam]
     d. Fotografi {-a} [Mariei]

The linear order illustrated in (2.83d) is also found in Romanian in constructions like (2.84), where -L is A-borne.

(2.84) Foarte interesant {-a} [ta] carte
     very interesting -L your book
     'your very interesting book'

7.3.1 An analysis within the Government and Binding Framework

One possibility offered by this framework is to parametrize the direction of Case-assignment on a language-specific and category-specific basis. Specifically, it may be proposed that English and German Ds assign Case to the left, while Hebrew and Romanian Ds assign Case to the right. Proposals in this sense were made in Ritter (1988) and Grosu (1988a). In the constructions in (2.83a)–(2.83b), D assigns Case into its Specifier; in the constructions of (2.83c)–(2.83d), D assigns Case into the Specifier of its complement. In the construction in (2.84), where D is borne by the Head of an AP that has left-adjoined to DP, its Case-assignee has presumably also raised and adjoined to DP (possibly after a 'stopover' in [SPEC, D']) in order to receive Case from a D in the Head position of a co-adjunct (on the grounds for assuming that genitive *pronouns* may occur in adjunct position, see section 6.4). Observe that this configuration for Case-assignment is unusual in that the assigner does not govern the assignee. I return to this issue at the end of section 7.4.

7.3.2 Analytical Options within the Minimalistic Framework

The approach outlined in the preceding subsection is not available within the minimalistic framework, where Case-licensing (that is, -checking) always involves the Spec-Head configuration, which, we may assume, is constant in the four languages, at least in so far as DP is concerned. The differences in linear order between the first two and the last two subcases of (2.83) can, however, be attributed to differential strength in those features on D that check the Case of the genitive phrase. To get the pattern in (2.83a)–(2.83b), we need to assume that the features at issue are strong (and thus require *overt* raising of the genitive to [SPEC, D']); to get the pattern in (2.83c)–(2.83d), we need to assume that the features in question are weak (and thus require, in conjunction with 'procrastinate', that the genitive raise only *covertly*). Concerning the construction in (2.84), the fact that the -*L*-bearing AP precedes the possessive pronoun is attributable to the fact that the AP is necessarily DP-initial, for reasons that were detailed in section 7.2.

7.4 ADJACENCY EFFECTS

In earlier sections, adjacency effects were detected in a number of constructions. In particular, it was pointed out (i) that English *'s* must be adjacent to the pre-nominal 'possessor'; (ii) that Hebrew and Romanian genitive DPs must be adjacent to a word that bears a specific encliticized determiner; (iii) that APs which precede the N they modify must form a sequence adjacent to N (with certain exceptions to be noted below); (iv) that prenominal genitive DPs in German must be N-final; and (v) that in Romanian (as well as in other languages), post-nominal APs must in general be adjacent to the N they modify, but may be shifted rightwards if sufficiently 'heavy'.

As far as I can tell, there is nothing in the syntactic Case- and agreement-licensing mechanisms assumed by the two frameworks we are considering here that can straightforwardly account for the effects in (iii)–(v). Concerning (i)–(ii), certain solutions have been proposed, or are easy enough to imagine. I shall concentrate primarily on (i)–(ii) in what follows, and will confine myself to a few conjectural remarks in respect to (iii)–(v).

7.4.1 Analytical Options within the Government and Binding Framework

The phenomena in (i) and (ii) can be handled by assuming that structural Case assignment is subject to an adjacency condition. This assumption was made in Chomsky (1981) and Stowell (1981) in respect to objective Case assignment by V in English, and in Ritter (1988) and Grosu (1988a) with respect to the phenomena under consideration here. To the extent that the adjacency effects in (i) and (ii) are of the same kind as those found in other contexts of structural Case assignment, they are straightforwardly accounted for. However, the effects in (i)–(ii) are stricter than those found elsewhere. Thus, while objective Case constructions need not satisfy adjacency when the object is sufficiently 'heavy', as illustrated in (2.85), and while VSO languages typically allow the right-shifting of 'heavy' subjects (demonstration omitted), *'s* can never license a non-adjacent possessor, as illustrated in (2.3a)–(2.3b) (reproduced below as 2.86), and the post-nominal 'possessors' of Hebrew and Romanian can never occur in a non-adjacent position, no matter how 'heavy' they might be, as illustrated in (2.87).

(2.85) a. John met Mary last night.
b. *John met last night Mary.
c. John met last night the girl he had
always dreamed of.

(2.86) a. John's initiative
b. *John initiative's

(2.87) a. Tmunat   gever yafa
picture(F) man   beautiful(F)
'a man's beautiful picture'
b. *Tmunat   yafa   gever xazak u -meod gavoha
picture(F) beautiful(F) man   strong and very tall
'the beautiful picture of a strong and very tall man'
c. Portretu-l   regin-ei cel nou
portrait-L(M) queen-GEN   DEM new(M)
'the queen's new portrait'
d. *Portretu-l   nou   regin-ei
portrait-L(M) new(M) queen-GEN
celei mai frumoase din lume
DEM   more beautiful from world
'the new portrait of the most beautiful
queen in the world'

It thus seems that additional factors are at work in the phenomena in (i) and (ii).

It may also be noted here that, given an internal structure for DPs essentially as in (2.12) and given the assumption that modifiers (in this case, APs) are adjoined to the *lexical* maximal projection (in this case, NP), it is not even clear how structures like (2.87a) and (2.87c) can arise, since APs ought to be hierarchically higher than, and thus left of [SPEC, N'], where 'possessors' are taken to occur. This *prima facie* difficulty can, however, be circumvented if one can argue for a functional category which is hierarchically intermediate between D and N. As alluded to in section 6.0.3, Ritter (1991) argued on independent grounds for exactly such a category, which she proposed to call NUM(ber). Under Ritter's assumptions, the possessor may raise to [SPEC, NUM'] in order to receive Case from D (under government and adjacency); under the further assumption that APs do not move from the position of adjunction to NP, which Ritter explicitly makes, only the (a) and (c) subcases of (2.87), but not the (b) or (d) subcases, can be generated.

7.4.2 Analytical Options within the Minimalistic Framework

In contrast to the framework of assumptions just examined, the minimalistic framework – more exactly, the assumption that inflected lexical items are built in the lexicon, rather than by syntactic operations – makes available a straightforward solution to the phenomenon in (i). If the logic applied to inflected lexical items is extended to phrases bearing phrasal clitics, we may assume that *'s* is (i) directly encliticized to a DP by structure-building generalized transformations (on this mechanism, see Chomsky (1992)), (ii) is a sort of Case, rather than a D, and (iii) that the D° position being filled by a null D which checks the presence of *'s* on the phrase in [SPEC, D']. Under this view, the adjacency of *'s* to a 'possessor' becomes a matter of necessity, as desired.

Concerning the facts in (ii), however, the minimalistic framework seems to encounter more descriptive problems than the framework of Government and Binding, and this, because it allows Case-licensing in configurations other than those which surface in overt representation. Since the Case of 'possessors' is checked at LF in Hebrew and Romanian (see section 7.3.2), and since [SPEC, D'] is assumed to lie left of D°, the necessary adjacency of a 'possessor' to a preceding determiner enclitic cannot be 'blamed' on an adjacency condition on Case-checking. Can one find alternative grounds for forcing the 'possessor' to raise to the Spec of D's complement? The answer is 'yes', but this result is not in and of itself sufficient.

One way to force the raising of 'possessors' is to reinterpret the category NUM (whose basic rationale in Ritter's analysis was to license number inflection on N) as a form of AGR and to assume that 'possessors' covertly agree with N, and thus need to be checked for number specifications in [SPEC, AGR']. Such an analysis is made quite plausible by the facts of Romanian, where pronominal and prepositional 'possessors' overtly agree with the 'possessed' N (in number and gender). One catch in this approach is that Ritter's assumption that APs never move out of NP has no place in the minimalistic framework, which assumes that constituents move if they have to (for checking purposes). Since not only 'possessors', but also APs agree with the 'possessed' N, it would seem natural to assume their agreement properties need to be checked in the Minimal Domain of AGR. If so, it is incorrectly predicted that patterns like (2.87b) and (2.87d), rather than like (2.87a) and (2.87c), ought to arise. There is, of course, a way to avoid this result, namely, by assuming that AGR's features which check APs are weak (so that APs raise *after* 'spell out') and that those which check 'possessors' are strong (so that 'possessors' raise *before* 'spell out').[17]

In addition to what has just been said, it needs to be pointed out that the *absolute* character of the adjacency effects in Hebrew and Romanian 'possessor' constructions, in particular their insensitivity to 'heaviness', is as much a problem for the framework under consideration here as it is for the alternative one.

7.4.3 Conjectures and Problems for Subsequent Research

The upshot of the two preceding sections is that the two frameworks we have considered make available no particularly interesting explanation for the strictness of the adjacency requirements in (ii). Furthermore, as noted already, the phenomena (iii)–(v), which were described and illustrated in some detail in van Riemsdijk (1991) do not seem to follow in any obvious way from the Case- and agreement-licensing mechanisms assumed by the two frameworks. These various phenomena call for an in-depth study which goes way beyond the scope of this chapter. None the less, I would like to offer a conjecture concerning a possible way to approach them.

Van Riemsdijk (1991) observed that some of the adjacency effects he noted are sensitive to the (c)overtness of inflectional morphology; for example, the constraint in (iii), which is supported by data like (2.43)–(2.46), is suspended when the AP ends in an adjunct (rather than in a complement), but only if A bears no overt agreement markers (the overt/covert contrast and the complement/adjunct contrast are illustrated, respectively, by the Dutch data in (2.88) and the English data in (2.89)).

```
(2.88) a.  Een [snel   (genoeg)]  vliegtuig    [NEUTER]
           a    fast    enough    airplane
       b.  Een [snell-e (*genoeg)] auto        [NON-NEUTER]
           a    fast    enough    car

(2.89) a.  *a [hard to crack] nut (cf. a hard nut to crack)
       b.  a [hard enough] problem
```

Furthermore, as pointed out in section 2, -*L*'s ability to license Case on a 'possessor' depends on the ability of the latter to host overt Case-markers. These facts suggest (to me) that there may be PF processes which license Case and agreement and which operate independently of the Case- and agreement-licensing mechanisms that operate in the syntax, sometimes providing redundant (or perhaps 'reinforcing') licensing; the envisaged picture is analogous in certain respects to that found in respect to the Kase properties of *pro* in realis FRCs, which – as prominently noted in Study 1 – may be redundantly licensed by percolation from the FRC-node and by 'matching' with a phrase in the FR's Specifier.

One mechanism which may perhaps be fruitfully 'revived' in this connection is that of 'local rule' in the sense of Emonds (1976), the most salient feature of which is that it operates on just two constituents, one of which is non-phrasal. If suitable local rules can be formulated and if it can be ensured that, in the desired instances, failure of such rules to apply to constituents involved in agreement and Case relations results in ungrammaticality, there are grounds to hope that many of the effects we have noted will be accounted for in motivated ways. At the very least, we may expect the existence of adjacency effects to follow from the fact that the rules alluded to are constrained to operate on adjacent constituents by definition.

In a slightly more specific vein, suppose that the local rules at issue can somehow recognize elements that can be involved in agreement or Case relations, and suppose furthermore that, in languages which exhibit effects like those in (ii)–(v), the rules are so stated that they only operate on ordered pairs of elements such that the non-phrasal one is leftmost. Under such circumstances, we may expect that the effects in (iii) (illustrated by the contrasts between the (b) and (c) subcases of (2.43)–(2.46)) will follow from the fact that the A-Head of an AP can agree with an ensuing N, while a complement of A cannot. Furthermore, the contrast between the (c) subcases of (2.43)–(2.46) and (2.89a) on the one hand and (2.88a) and (2.89b) on the other could in principle be accounted for by assuming that adjuncts, but not complements of A may in principle agree with A in phi-features; a local agreement rule may then operate iteratively from left to right, first on A and its adjunct, and then on the latter and N. The contrast between (2.88a) and (2.88b) suggests that the rule in question can iterate either in an overt or in a covert mode, but without switching modes midway. As for the contrast between the full and reduced version of (2.8) (see p. 154), it will hopefully fall out of the fact that the Head N of a 'possessor', but not N's complement, can bear the Case assigned by D.

Van Riemsdijk (1991) observed that unbroken sequences of pre-nominal adjectives are possible, even though only one adjective can be adjacent to N (as illustrated in (2.47)–(2.48)). In fact, unbroken sequences of APs are allowed, so long as they terminate in an element that can agree with N, in particular, the head A; this possibility is illustrated in (2.90).

```
(2.90) a. O [extrem  de interesantă   (*de citit)]
          a extreme of interesting     to read
          [complet   nouă] propunere
          completely new   proposal
       'a completely new proposal that is extremely
        interesting (to read)'
```

This phenomenon can also in principle be accounted for by assuming that the agreement-licensing mechanisms can operate not just on an A and a following N, but also on an A and an ensuing AP, provided that the two APs modify the same N (and thus agree with each other by transitivity). Finally, if the ability to operate in the way just indicated can be extended to Case-licensing operations, we can account for the properties of constructions like (2.84) (where, as pointed out in section 7.3, -L fails to govern the possessive pronoun it licenses).

In short, if a theory of local PF rules in the above sense can be devised, most of the adjacency effects we have considered will not need to be stipulated.[18]

7.5 SUMMARY OF RESULTS

This study has pursued a number of issues that concern the internal syntax of DP in general and of DP in Romanian in particular.

A result which strengthens the 'DP Hypothesis', that is, the claim that determiners are functional Heads (of a nominal Extended Projection), is that GEN Case in Romanian is licensed by the single morpheme *-L*, but only when the latter has D status. This does not mean that that *-L* needs to be *syntactically active* as a D in order to be able to license GEN Case; thus, when hosted by a P, *-L* is a derivational enclitic, in contrast to constructions where it is hosted by an N or an A, where it is an inflectional enclitic; none the less, *-L* can assign GEN Case in all three types of situation, in contrast to constructions where it is hosted by a D (-stem), where it plays a merely euphonic role and has no categorial status.

The relation of genitive phrases to *-L*'s host varies with the latter's category. When the host is an N, the genitive is related to it as argument or 'possessor'; when it is an A, it is related to it as co-adjunct to an N; and when it is a P, it is related to it as object. The hosting of *-L* by N and A, as well as the relative linear order of *N+L/A+L* and the genitive phrase were analysed from the perspective of the theory of Government and Binding and of the minimalistic programme outlined in Chomsky (1992). It was found that the latter framework yields a more straightforward account of the facts at issue than the alternative one.

-L and the genitive licensed by it must also be strictly adjacent in overt representation. No solution was proposed for this effect; none the less, it was suggested that it, as well as other adjacency effects that are found within DP in a variety of languages, are due to the operation of PF processes of a special sort.

Study III

On Null Operators in Romanian

INTRODUCTION

In Study 1, it was seen that the syntactic operators which occur in [SPEC, C'] at S-Structure may be either overt or null, without noticeable semantic contrast. Furthermore, specific languages may use, in specific constructions, either just overt operators, or just NOs, or both. As we shall see below, establishing whether a certain construction does or does not use NOs is not always a very simple matter. None the less, once a decision has been reached, it is reasonably clear how to *state* such states of affairs; for example, C°-s carrying specific combinations of values of the features [NAOP], [COIND] (and possibly others) may be marked on a language specific basis, as [+wh], [-wh], or be left unmarked (and thus allow both types of specification). Whether such markings can be derived in an interesting way from independent properties of language is, however, often unclear.

This study will examine the distribution of NOs in Romanian, making occasional comparisons with other languages. One reason for undertaking this endeavour is that the constructions in which NOs potentially occur are of interest in their own right. Another reason is that, due to morphological homonymy of various kinds, Romanian exhibits situations of the kind hinted at above, that is, where it is not immediately obvious whether NOs are employed or not. In fact, such homonymy is arguably responsible for the claim made by Dobrovie-Sorin (1987, 1990) to the effect that Romanian has no NOs.

The remainder of the study is organized as follows. In section 8.1, I briefly note a number of construction types in which NOs have been invoked in earlier literature. I then proceed to an examination of specific types of construction in sections 8.2 to 8.6, illustrating distributional patterns of null and overt operators in each of them with languages other than Romanian, and then undertaking a detailed investigation of the specific patterns found in Romanian. The results of this study are summarized in section 8.7, and are then compared with those achieved by Dobrovie-Sorin.

One last preliminary remark. In this study, I shall be concerned with operators that bind syntactic variables, that is, traces of extraction and RPs. Such 'NOs' as the 'unselective' ones proposed in Pesetzky (1987) (see section 3.2.3 of Study 1), which are assumed to bind *wh*-phrases, are thus left out of consideration.

8

pro-Operator Constructions

There a number of constructions in which *pro*-NOs have been argued for in past research. These include: cleft constructions, comparative constructions, relative constructions of all kinds, that is, restrictive, appositive and amount (both 'free' and 'headed'; see section 3.2.1. of Study 1), and a variety of constructions which, in English, exhibit infinitival subordinate clauses (*tough*-constructions, *ready*-constructions, irrealis relatives, purpose constructions and *too/enough* constructions). In addition, some languages also allow (predicative) NOs in main clauses, where the subject-of-predication is a null (*pro*) topic, which, as noted in section 3.3.2.1 of Study 1, is identified by reference to the earlier linguistic or non-linguistic context; such constructions are thus expected just in those languages which possess the type of *pro*-identifying mechanism in question.

8.1 CLEFT CONSTRUCTIONS

In English, cleft constructions may be formed both with [+wh] and with [-wh] operators (subject to a variety of constraints which need not concern us here), as illustrated below.

```
(3.1) a. It's John [who won the first prize].
      b. It's John [with whom Mary refused to work].
      c. It's John [NO (that) you met at the party].
```

In Italian, however, only NOs can be used, as pointed out by Grewendorf and Poletto (1990), and as illustrated by the following data, which they provide (cf. (3.1b)).

```
(3.2) a.  E  a Paolo que l'  ho          dato.
          is to Paolo that it have.1.SG. given
          'It's to Paolo that I gave it.'
      b. *E  Paolo  a cui   ho          parlato.
          is Paolo  to whom have.1.SG.  spoken
          'It's Paolo to whom I spoke.'
```

In German, on the other hand, only overt operators may be used (Grewendorf and Poletto 1990), as illustrated by the following examples. J. Horvath informs me that this generalization applies to Hungarian as well.

(3.3) a. Johann ist es, [*den* sie liebt].
         Johann is it   whom she loves
         'It's Johann that she loves.'
     b. *Johann ist es, [*NO* (dass) sie liebt].
         Johann is it   that she loves
         (same purported meaning as in (3.3a)).

Thus, all three logically-possible patterns of null and overt operators are attested.

Which of these three patterns is found in Romanian? The answer is 'none', and this because, for some unclear reason, Romanian has no cleft constructions at all (the semantic import of the construction can, of course, be expressed in alternative ways). I illustrate below the fact that clefts cannot be formed in any of the following ways: (i) with or without the complementizer *că*, which introduces indicative complement and adverbial clauses; (ii) with the complementizer *ca*, which introduces subjunctive complement and adverbial clauses; (iii) with the relative complementizer *ce* (justification for which is offered in section 8.4); and (iv) with relative pronouns (a possibility which exists in English and German). Accordingly, no conclusions concerning NOs in Romanian can be derived from cleft constructions.

(3.4) a. *E Maria [*NO* (că) vreau   să   întîlnesc].
         is Maria   that want.1.SG. SUBJ. meet.1.SG.
         'It's Maria (that) I want to meet.'
     b. *E Ion [*ce* a cîştigat premiul întîi].
         is Ion   has won   prize-L first
         'It is Ion that won the first prize.'
     c. *E Ion [*care* a cîştigat premiul întîi].
         is Ion who   has won   prize-L first
         'It is Ion who won the first prize.'
     d. *E Ion [*pe care* (l-) am   întîlnit ieri].
         is Ion ACC which him-have.1.   met   yesterday
         'It is Ion whom I met yesterday.'

8.2 COMPARATIVE CONSTRUCTIONS

English is a language which uses only NOs in comparative constructions. This can be seen both in *non-equative* and in *equative* comstructions, and both when *identical* and when *distinct* qualities, kinds of entities, etc. are compared; illustrations are provided in (3.5).

(3.5) a. We own more of the books than [NO they own].
 b. We own as many of the books as [NO they own].

(3.6) a. We own more of the books than [NO we own of the magazines].
 b. We own as many of the books as [NO we own of the magazines].

Any attempt to substitute some semantically appropriate *wh*-phrase for NOs, such as *how many*, results in ungrammaticality (demonstration omitted).

In contrast, Hungarian uses an overt *wh*-element under comparable circumstances, as illustrated by the following data (*amilyen* is also used with interrogative force to request information about a quality, roughly like *how* in *How is she? Nice*).[1]

(3.7) a. János magas-abb mint [amilyen magas Mari valaha is volt].
 János tall -er than how tall Mari ever also was
 'János is taller than Mari ever was.'
 b. János olyan magas mint [amilyen magas Mari lesz].
 János as tall as how tall Mari will-be
 'János is as tall as Mari will be.'

(3.8) a. János magas-abb mint [amilyen kövér Mari volt].
 János tall -er than how fat Mari was
 'János is taller than Mari is fat.'
 b. János olyan magas mint [amilyen kövér Mari].
 János as tall as how fat Mari
 'János is as tall as Mari is fat.'

The fact that *amilyen* is a *wh*-element is shown not only by its morphology, but, more importantly, by the fact that it has triggered the Pied-Piping of the AP which functions as its complement (I assume that *amilyen* is a functional Head). A noteworthy feature of (3.7), which distinguishes it from (3.5), is that, although identical adjectives form the basis of comparison, overt tokens MUST occur both in the matrix and in the subordinate clause. Furthermore, Pied-Piping is obligatory in these constructions.

Hungarian may, however, also use NOs in comparatives. Thus, the data in (3.7), but not those in (3.8), have counterparts with NOs; these are shown in (3.9).

(3.9) a. János magas-abb mint [NO Mari valaha is].
 b. János olyan magas mint [NO Mari lesz].

In this case, no token of the adjective *magas* may occur in the subordinate clause, either *in situ* or in Pied-Piped position.

The fact that, in Hungarian, Pied-Piping is obligatory with an overt operator and NOs may be used just in case they do not originate (in Head or Spec position) within a larger overt XP, and the fact that NOs may be used in English even when they do originate within such an XP, but without the option of 'dragging' the latter along, can be accounted for in terms of assumptions justified in a number of sections of Study 1. These are (i) the assumption that the 'residues' of overt XPs may be left *in situ* just in case the language independently allows their separation from NOs (for some discussion of this point see section 2.4); and (ii) the assumption that NOs cannot trigger Pied-Piping (except perhaps of null material), while overt operators may drag along overt material (sections 3.2.3 and 3.5). Thus, the fact that the *of*-complements of NOs can be left *in situ* in (3.6) is attributable to the fact that they can undergo prior separation from the NO, an assumption independently justified by data like (3.10b), where an overt *wh*-phrase has been reordered (Grimshaw 1987).

(3.10) a. *How many of these magazines* do you own?
       b. *How many* do you own *of these magazines*?

Given the null status of the operator, these complements *must* be left *in situ*, as shown in (3.11).

(3.11) a. *We own more of these books than
          [NO of these magazines we own].
       b. *We own as many of these books as
          [NO of these magazines we own].

The Hungarian data in (3.7) and (3.8) contrast in grammaticality with the English data in (3.11) because the reordered operator is here overt, and can therefore trigger the Pied-Piping of overt material. The fact that (3.7)–(3.8) have no counterparts with the adjectives *in situ* indicates that the language does not allow their separation from operators. Note that a comparable assumption is needed for English data like (3.12b) or (3.12d) (adapted from Grimshaw).

(3.12) a. *How many magazines* do we own?
       b. **How many* do we own *magazines*?
       c. *How beautiful* was she?
       d. **How* was she *beautiful*?

Finally, the grammaticality of (3.9) can be attributed to the fact that the (non-separable) AP residue is *null*, and may thus be Pied-Piped along with the latter.

We have thus illustrated the fact that there are (i) languages in which only NOs may be used in comparatives and (ii) languages in which both overt and null operators may be used in comparatives (there may conceivably be languages which utilize overt operators only, but I have no actual examples). Let us now turn to Romanian.

Romanian has constructions with identical compared properties like the following.

(3.13) a. Ion e și mai puternic decît a fost tatăl lui.
       Ion is and more strong than has been father-L his
       'Ion is even stronger than his father was.'
   b. Ion e tot atît de puternic pe cît
      Ion is all so-much of strong as how
      a fost tatăl lui.
      has been father-L his
      'Ion is just as strong as his father was.'

In both subcases of (3.13), there exist elements morphologically identical to an interrogative/exclamative degree word, that is, *cît* 'how much'. In interrogative/exclamative constructions, this element can be reordered either alone, as in (3.14a, b) or together with its complement, as in (3.14c, d) (cf. with (3.10)).

(3.14) a. *Cît de frumoasă* e Maria?
          how of beautiful is Maria
          'How beautiful is Maria?'
    b. *Cît de frumoasă* e Maria!
       how of beautiful is Maria
       'How beautiful Maria is!'
    c. *Cît* e Maria *de frumoasă*?
       how is Maria of beautiful
       'How beautiful is Maria?'
    b. *Cît* e Maria *de frumoasă*!
       how is Maria of beautiful
       'How beautiful Maria is!'

Morphological identity is, however, not sufficient. To check whether the tokens of *cît* in (3.13) are indeed *wh*-operators, we must check whether they can trigger the Pied-Piping of complements. This is done in (3.15).

(3.15) a. Maria e cu mult mai deșteaptă decît
          Maria is with much more clever than-how-much
          e Zamfira *de frumoasă*.
          is Zamfira of beautiful
          'Maria is far cleverer than Zamfira is beautiful.'
    b. *Maria e cu mult mai deșteaptă decît *de frumoasă* e Zamfira.
    c. Maria e tot atît de deșteaptă pe *cît*
       Maria is all so-much of clever on how-much
       e Zamfira *de frumoasă*.
       is Zamfira of beautiful
       'Maria is just as clever as Zamfira is beautiful.'
    d. Maria e tot atît de deșteaptă pe *cît de frumoasă*
       e Zamfira.

As shown by the contrast between the (b) and (d) subcases, Pied-Piping is possible *in the equative construction only.* We must conclude from this that, while *cît* is a *syntactically*-independent element in (3.15c, d), it does not have this status in (3.15a, b). Rather, it needs to be construed in the latter case as a *morphological* subelement of the (complex) preposition *decît* 'than', that is, as an element which combines with *de-* *in the lexicon*. This in turn leads to the conclusion that non-equative constructions like (3.13a) and (3.15a, b) utilize NOs only. On the other hand, equative constructions like (3.13b) and (3.15c, d) utilize overt *wh*-operators only.

The homonymy of *cît* in interrogative, exclamative, equative, and comparative non-equative constructions is one of those sources of potential confusion that I alluded to in the Introduction to this study. The confusion is moreover potentially compounded by the fact that both the element *de-* and the element *pe* which immediately precede *cît* in (3.13) and (3.15) function as prepositions in other contexts, so that it might be tempting to assume that they have the same status here. In fact, Dobrovie-Sorin (1987: § 1.3.6.8; 1990: n. 34) explicitly proposes that *decît* comparatives are formed with an overt operator. The evidence presented above, however, shows otherwise.

I note that the results we have arrived at converge with the fact that conventional orthography represents *decît* as one word and *pe cît* as two words, and also with the fact that *decît*, but not *pe cît*, can take nominal complements, as shown in (3.16).

(3.16) a. Ioana e mai inteligentă *ca* /*decît* Maria.
          Ioana is more intelligent than   Maria
       b. Ioana e la fel de inteligentă *ca*/**pe cît* Maria.
          Ioana is as   intelligent as   Maria.

Before concluding this section, I wish to note that the pattern of null and overt operators found in Romanian comparative constructions is strikingly similar to the one found in German (except that no potentially-confusing homonymy seems to exist). Thus, non-equative and equative comparative clauses are introduced by the elements *als* and *wie* respectively, only the latter of which functions as a *wh*-element elsewhere. As shown below, Pied-Piping is allowed in equatives only, so that non-equatives must be assumed to utilize NOs.[2]

(3.17) a. Sie ist dicker als [*NO* er *groß* ist].
          she is fatter than   he tall   is
          'She is fatter than he is tall.'
       b. *Sie ist dicker als [*NO groß* er ist].
       c. Es ist in Island eben so kalt [*wie* es in Israel *warm* ist].
          it is in Iceland just so cold as it in Israel warm is
          'It is just as cold in Iceland as it is warm in Israel.'
       d. Es ist in Island eben so kalt [*wie warm* es in Israel ist].

8.3 RELATIVE CLAUSES

Just as we saw in respect to cleft constructions, languages may construct relative clauses of various types with overt operators only, with NOs only and with a mixture of overt and null operators; furthermore, NOs may be placed in [SPEC, C'] by reordering, or by direct base-generation in that position (the latter type of situation is typically found when the bound variable is an RP; see sections 2.2. and 2.3. of Study 1).

A language in which restrictive, appositive and free relatives are formed with reordered NOs only seems to be Turkish, illustrations from which are provided in (3.18).

(3.18) a. [Geçen yaz   ada -da gör-düg -üm *NO*] kişiler...
           last summer island-LOC see-PARTIC-AGR   people
           'The people that I saw on the island last summer...'
       b. [Geçen yaz   ada -da gör-düg -üm *NO*] Christina...
           last summer island-LOC see-PARTIC-AGR   Christina...
           'Christina, whom I saw on the island last summer...'
       c. [Geçen yaz   ada -da gör-dük -ler-üm *NO*] pro...
           last summer island-LOC see-PARTIC-PL -AGR
           '(Those) whom I saw on the island last summer...'

A language in which all types of relative clauses are formed with overt operators only is standard contemporary German (J. Horvath informs me that Hungarian has comparable properties); this is illustrated below in respect to restrictive, appositive and free (amount) relatives.[3]

(3.19) a. Der Mann, [*den* sie liebt]...
           the man   whom she loves
       a'. *Der Mann, [*NO* (dass) sie liebt]...
           the man   that   she loves
       b. Johann, [*den* sie liebt]...
           Johann whom she loves
       b'. *Johann, [*NO* (dass) sie liebt]...
           Johann   that   she loves
       c. *pro* [*was* sie tut]
                  what she does
       c'. **pro* [*NO* (dass) sie tut]
                        that   she does

A language which exhibits a partly 'pure' and a partly 'mixed' distributional pattern of reordered overt and null operators is English, in which patterns vary from subtype to subtype. Thus restrictive relatives employ both overt and null operators, appositive and free relatives employ overt operators only, and headed amount relatives employ NOs only, as illustrated in (3.20).

(3.20) a. the people [*whom* you saw]
       a'. the people [*NO* (that) you saw]
       b. Mary, [*whom* you know]
       b'. *Mary, [*NO* (that) you know]
       c. *pro* [*what* you say] pleases me.
       c'. **pro* [*NO* (that) you say] pleases me.

d. *All [what/which there is to be said] scares me.
d'. All [NO (that) that there is to be said] scares me.

Another language with a complex distributional pattern of overt and null operators which is rather different from that found in English is Hebrew, where restrictive and appositive relatives are formed with NOs alone, while amount relatives are formed with both overt and null operators; furthermore, NOs may be either reordered to [SPEC, C'] or base-generated in it. I confine illustration here to restrictive and appositive relatives (for illustrations of amount relatives, see n. 9 of Study 1 (p. 228) and sections 2.1–2.3 of Chapter 2).

(3.21) a. Ha -iš [NO še   rayta   (oto)]...
           the man   that saw.2.SG. him
           'The man that you saw...'
       b. Ilana, [NO še   Dan ohev *(ota)]...
          Ilana   that Dan loves her
          'Ilana, whom Dan loves...'

With this background in mind, let us turn to Romanian.

Romanian disallows 'bare' relative clauses, such as the reduced versions of (3.20a') and (3.20d'). All three major (semantic) subtypes, that is, restrictive, appositive and amount, may utilize overt operators, as illustrated in (3.22).

(3.22) a. Fata   [pe care mi-ai   prezentat   -o
          girl-the ACC who me-have.2.SG. introduced   her
          ieri]   nu   mi-a   plăcut.
          yesterday not me-has pleased
          'The girl you introduced to me yesterday was not to my liking.'
       b. Maria, [pe care mi-ai   prezentat   -o
          Maria   ACC who me-have.2.SG. introduced   her
          ieri],   nu   mi-a   plăcut.
          yesterday not me-has pleased
          'Maria, whom you introduced to me yesterday, was not to my liking.'
       c. pro [pe cine nu   laşi   să   moară]
                 ACC who not let.2.SG. SUBJ die
          nu te lasă   să   trăieşti.
          not you let   SUBJ live
          '(He) whom you won't allow to die won't let you live.'

That the italicized phrases are reordered operators is shown by the fact that they carry the ACC P-marker *pe*.

Does Romanian also use complementizer-introduced relative clauses, that is, relative clauses with NOs? I propose to argue that NOs are used in two types of relative constructions. These constructions, which belong to specific 'stylistic registers', are (i) *colloquial* restrictive and appositive relatives with RPs, and (ii) literary and slightly archaic restrictive relatives introduced by *ce*.

Prior to presenting this argument, let us consider the kinds of complementizers that occur outside of relative constructions. In both complement and adverbial clauses, the complementizers *că* and *ca* cooccur with indicative and subjunctive mood respectively; I confine illustration to adverbial constructions (see (3.23)).

(3.23) a. Pentru că   {e   /*să   fie}   mulţumit...
           for   that is(INDIC)/ SUBJ be.3. satisfied
           'Because he is satisfied...'
       b. Pentru ca   {*e   /să   fie}   mulţumit...
           for   that is(INDIC)/SUBJ be.3.   satisfied
           'In order that he be satisfied...'

Furthermore, in certain adverbial clauses (but not in V-complement clauses) the complementizer *ce* is utilized, as illustrated in (3.24).

(3.24) a. A   băut pînă ce   a   crăpat.
           has drunk until what has croaked
           'He drank until he croaked.'
       b. De vreme ce   a   murit, îi   putem   împărţi averea.
           of time what has died   him can.1.PL. divide fortune-the
           'Since/as he has died, we can divide his fortune up.'
       c. El e harnic,   în timp ce   ea e leneşă.
           he is industrious in time what she is lazy
           'He is hard-working, while she is lazy.'
       d. Nu îl mai scoate   nimeni din casă, o dată ce
           not him yet take-out nobody from house a time what
           a   apucat să se   instaleze.
           has managed SP REFL install
           'No one can throw him out of the house, once he has
           moved in.'

Now, this *ce* is homophonous with the *wh*-pronoun *ce* 'what', which occurs in interrogative, free relative and 'headed' quantifying relative constructions (see (3.25)).

(3.25) a. Ce   vrei?
           what want.2.SG.
           'What do you want?'
       b. Ce   te   supără   pe tine mă supără şi pe mine.
           what you bothers ACC you   me bothers and ACC me
           'What bothers you bothers me as well.'
       c. Tot ce   te   supără   pe tine mă supără şi pe mine.
           all what you bothers ACC you   me bothers and ACC me
           'All that bothers you bothers me as well.'

None the less, *ce* may not be analysed as a *wh*-operator in (3.24), because there is no variable for it to bind.

Having established that Romanian has uncontrovertible complementizers homophonous with *wh*-pronouns, let us turn to relative clauses.

In contrast to English and Hebrew, there are no NO-relatives, either with or without RPs, that are introduced by those complementizers which introduce V-complement clauses, as shown in (3.26)–(3.27) (the italicized pronouns in (3.26) purport to be either RPs or 'doubling' clitics of the kind found in (3.22a, b); the italicized pronoun in (3.27) purports to be an RP, because it is internal to an extraction island, and is furthermore not a clitic).

```
(3.26) a. *Fata       că    mi-ai           prezentat (-o) e
          girl-the    that  me-have.2.SG.   introduced her
          ieri        nu    mi-a    plăcut.
          yesterday   not   me-has  pleased
          'The girl you introduced to me yesterday was not
          to my liking.'
       b. *Caut         un roman ca    Ion să    (-l) poată   citi e
          seek.1.SG.    a  novel  that Ion SUBJ  him  can.3.  read
          într -o după -amiază.
          within a after-noon
          'I am looking for a novel that Ion could read
          in an afternoon.'
(3.27)    *Băiatul  că   ți -am        spus că    am        lucrat
          boy-L    that  you-have.1    said that  have.1    worked
          cu    el...
          with  him
          'The boy who I told you that I worked with him...'
```

None the less, NO-relatives do exist, and they invariably exhibit complementizers that are homophonous with *wh*-elements. The *colloquial* RP-relatives are introduced by *care*, a complementizer homophonous with a relative *wh*-pronoun that is found in (register-unrestricted) restrictive and appositive relatives (see (3.22a, b)). Illustrations are provided in (3.28).

```
(3.28) a. Băiatul  [care ți -am        spus că    am        lucrat
          boy-L    who  you-have.1    said that  have.1    worked
          cu    el]...
          with  him
          'The boy such that I told you that I worked with him...'
       b. Băiatul  [care ți -am        arătat o fată care
          boy-L    who  you-have.1    shown  a girl  who
          îl simpatizează]...
          him has-sympathy-for
          'The boy such that I showed you a girl that likes him...'
```

In contrast to (3.22a, b), the *care* forms in (3.28) may not be construed as relative pronouns, and this, for the following reasons. In (3.28b), *care* lacks the ACC marker *pe* which characterizes definite human direct objects; furthermore, the putative extraction site (that is, the direct object position of *simpatizează*), is internal to a 'strong' island (in the sense of Cinque (1990)). Importantly, adding *pe* to *care* in this example results in ungrammaticality. It thus seems necessary to conclude that the italicized clitic pronoun *îl* (more exactly, the chain formed by this clitic and the empty category it binds) is an RP. Accordingly, a base-generated NO must be assumed. As for (3.28a), the same conclusion follows from the observation that the italicized pronoun *el* occurs in an A-position, and can thus only be an RP.

Let us now turn to the second type of NO-relatives, which, as noted above, have a literary and slightly archaic flavour. These are introduced by *ce*, which – as already seen in relation to the data in (3.24) – may be a complementizer. Some illustrations from nineteenth-century poetry are provided in (3.29); in (3.30), I provide some constructed data, whose acceptability ratings refer to the contemporary non-literary language.

(3.29) a. căci   moşneagul *ce* priveşti   [e] nu e   om de rînd...
          because old-man-L *ce* look-at.2.SG not is man of file
          'because the old man you are looking at is no ordinary
          person...'
       b. Capul   *ce* [e] se   pleacă sabia   nu- l   taie...
          head-L *ce*   REFL bends   sword-L not him cut
          'The sword does not cut the head that bends...'

(3.30) a. ?Persoanele *ce* [e] s-   au   adresat preşedintelui...
          persons-L   *ce*   REFL have   addressed president-L(DAT)
          'The persons who approached the president...'
       b. ?Munţii   *ce* [e] se   înalţă la orizont...
          mountains-L *ce*   REFL loom   at horizon
          'The mountains which loom at the horizon...'
       c. ?*Cartea *ce* sperai   să   poţi termina de citit [e]
          book-L *ce* hoped.2.SG SUBJ can finish of read
          la timp...
          at time
          'The book you were hoping to be able to finish
          reading in time...'
       d. ?Nişte cărţi *ce* am   înţeles   dela d-l profesor că
          some books *ce* have.1 understood from Mr teacher that
          doriţi   să   *(le)   cititi...
          wish.2.PL   SUBJ   them   read.2.PL
          'Some books which I understood from the teacher
          that you wish to read (them)...'
       e. ?Moşneagul *ce* priveşti   fără
          old-man-L *ce* look-at.2.SG without
          a   *(-l) recunoaşte...
          INF. him recognize
          'The old man you are looking at without
          recognizing him...'

Examples (3.30a)–(3.30c) show that such constructions are still basically acceptable in current Romanian so long as the extraction gaps are in relatively 'accessible' positions; when the gaps are in less 'accessible' positions, for example, in an indicative complement clause, or when they are 'parasitic', acceptability is further reduced, and RPs must in general be used, as shown in (3.30d)–(3.30e).[4]

Given that the morpheme *ce* occurs elsewhere both as complementizer and as *wh*-pronoun (see (3.24) and (3.25) respectively), either analysis is in principle conceivable in respect to the data in (3.29)–(3.30). I now proceed to argue that only the complementizer analysis is tenable for these constructions.

A first test for distinguishing between complementizers and relative pronouns, which was noted at the beginning of this section, is the inability/ability to occur in Pied-Piping contexts. As shown by the contrast between (3.31) and (3.32), Pied-Piping of a preposition is possible in interrogatives, non-matching nominal FRCs, missing-P FRCs and amount relatives with an external functional Head, but completely impossible in *ce*-initiated restrictive relatives. The deviance of the data in (3.32) is fully expected under a complementizer analysis for *ce*, but mysterious under a *wh*-pronoun analysis.

(3.31) a. *Cu ce* te speli?
with what yourself wash.2.SG
'What do you wash with?'

b. *La ce* se uită Maria costă deobicei o avere.
at what REFL looks Maria costs usually a fortune
'What Maria looks at usually costs a fortune.'

c. Mă gîndesc *la ce* te gîndeşti şi tu.
me think at what you think and you
'I am thinking (of that) of which you are also thinking.'

d. Tot *la ce* te referi îmi trezeşte
all at what yourself refer.2.SG me(DAT) wakens
curiozitatea.
curiosity-L
'Everything you refer to excites my curiosity.'

(3.32) a. *Moşneagul *la ce* te uiţi e tare bătrîn.
old-man-L at *ce* you look is very old
'The old man you are looking at is very old.'

b. *Săpunul *cu ce* se spală Maria e parfumat.
soap-L with *ce* REFL washes Maria is perfumed
'The soap that Maria is washing with exhales perfume.'

Note the minimal contrast between (3.31d) and (3.32), both of which exhibit superficially quite similar OHRCs, except that the relative clause is of the amount type in the former and of the restrictive type in the two subcases of the latter. This semantic distinction between the two construction types correlates not only with a different status for *ce* (*wh*-pronoun versus complementizer), but also with different stylistic values. Thus, unlike *ce*-restrictive relatives, *ce*-amount relatives are fully acceptable in all registers, a state of affairs reflected in the lack of restrictions on 'relatively inaccessible' positions of the kind that were noted in relation to (3.30d)–(3.30e); to see this, contrast the reduced versions of these data with (3.33a)–(3.33b).

(3.33) a. Tot ce   mi-ai   povestit că   ai   făcut e
          all what me-have.2.SG. told   that have.2.SG. done
          mă nemulțumește.
          me not-satisfies
          'Everything you told me that you did causes
          me dissatisfaction.'
      b. Tot ce   repeți   e fără   a înțelege   e
          all what repeat.2.SG. without IP understand
          te pune într-o lumină proastă.
          you puts in   a light bad
          'Everything you repeat without comprehending makes
          you look bad.'

A second argument for viewing *ce* as a complementizer in restrictive relatives is provided by the fact that *ce* fails to exhibit agreement with the Head of the OHRC, something which is atypical for uncontroversial *wh*-pronouns, but typical for complementizers. Thus observe that the oblique forms of the relative pronoun *care* 'which' display strict agreement with the Head in respect to all the features for which they are inflected, in particular number and gender, as illustrated in (3.34).

(3.34) Fata   *căruia   /căreia   /*cărora
       girl-L who.DAT.M.SG who.DAT.F.SG   who.DAT.PL
       i   -am   scris...
       him/her(DAT)-have.1 written
       'The girl to whom I write...'

Now, the *wh*-pronoun *ce* 'what' has a [+HUMAN] counterpart, *cine* 'who', which MUST be used when a specifically human referent is intended; this state of affairs is demonstrable in respect to both interrogatives and FRs (see (3.35)).

(3.35) a. Cine/*ce   vorbește   acuma?
          who/ *what is-speaking now
      b. Cine/*ce   vorbește   prea mult va   fi pedepsit.
          who *what talks   too much will be punished

Observe that amount OHRCs like the one in (3.31d) are consistent with this generalization, since the clause external 'bare' quantifiers (such as *tot* 'all', *nimic* 'nothing') are not marked for the feature [HUMAN], and *ce* may thus be viewed as agreeing with them. In contrast, restrictive OHRCs like those in (3.29)–(3.30) are inconsistent with the generalization at issue if *ce* is analysed as a *wh*-pronoun, because *ce* is invariably used regardless of [+HUMAN] specifications on the Head. For example, if *cine* is substituted for *ce* in (3.29a), the result is completely impossible, rather than merely register-restricted. In conclusion, we have a second argument for the complementizer status of *ce* in restrictive relatives.

A third and particularly compelling argument for the complementizer status of *ce* in restrictive relatives emerges from a consideration of data like the full version of (3.30e), reproduced below for convenience.

```
(3.30) e. Moşneagul ce priveşti      fără
         old-man-L ce look-at.2.SG without
         a    -l recunoaşte...
         INF. him recognize
         'The old man you are looking at without recognizing him . . . '
```

Under the view that *ce* is a pronoun, it serves as antecedent for the italicized clitic pronoun. But in cases where *ce* is uncontroversially a *wh*-pronoun, for example in interrogative constructions, it may NOT antecede such a pronoun, as shown in (3.36).

```
(3.36) Ce   priveşti      fără     a   (*-l) recunoaşte?
       what look-at.2.SG without INF. him recognizing
       'What are you looking at without recognizing (it)?'
```

The deviance of (3.36) is due to a constraint which is found in other Romance languages as well (for example, French and Italian), and whose effect is to disqualify maximally unspecified 'bare' quantifiers from serving as antecedents for pronouns derived from the Latin form *ille*; that is to say, the constraint concerns bare quantifiers like *nimic* 'nothing', *ceva* 'something' and *ce* 'what' on the one hand and pronouns like *el* 'he' and the clitic -*l* 'him' on the other, but neither [+HUMAN] 'bare' quantifiers like *nimeni* 'nobody', *cineva* 'somebody' or *cine* 'who', nor pronouns that fail to be derived from *ille*, such as the reflexive clitics *se*(ACC)/*îşi*(DAT) or the null element *pro*. Illustration of these points is provided below.

```
(3.37) a. *Nimic_i nu trebuie repetat numai pentrucă publicul
          nothing not must     repeated only because audience-the
          nu  l_i- a     auzit.
          not him has heard
          'Nothing needs to be repeated just because the audience has
          not heard it.'
       b. Cine_i a    fost arestat din   cauză că    Maria
          who    has been arrested from cause that Maria
          nu  l_i -a   recunoscut?
          not him has recognized
          'Who was arrested because Maria did not recognize him?'
```

c. Ce$_i$ și$_i$ -a dovedit utilitatea?
    what REFL.DAT. has proven usefulness
    'What has proven its usefulness?'
d. Ce$_i$ a   trebuit repetat din cauză că   pro$_i$ nu
    what has must   repeated from cause that   not
    fusese înțeles?
    had-been understood
    'What needed to be repeated because it has not been understood?'

This constraint is, as far as I can tell, completely exceptionless. Accordingly, the acceptability of the full version of (3.30e) constitutes an argument of the strongest kind for *not* analysing the item *ce* in it as a *wh*-quantifier, and thus for assuming that the missing direct object of *privești* in the reduced version of (3.30e) is a trace bound by an NO.

The arguments presented above show, I submit, that despite the complicating and potentially confusing factor of homonymy with a genuine *wh*-element,[5] *ce* in restrictive relatives is a complementizer. Accordingly, an analysis of these constructions in terms of a reordered NO is clearly optimal.

To summarize, while the 'major' (in the sense of 'register-unrestricted') relative constructions of Romanian utilize overt operators, there are two register-restricted constructions which utilize NOs.

8.4 SUPINE CONSTRUCTIONS WITH NOs

In addition to the kinds of constructions examined in the two preceding sections, there exists a third class of Romanian constructions in which homonymy potentially 'masks' the need for an analysis in terms of NOs. This class includes (at least) the *tough*-construction and the nonfinite relative construction, which, in English and in Western Romance languages, exhibit an *infinitival* subordinate clause. In Romanian, however, these constructions are realized on the basis of the *supine* mood, a form homophonous with the passive participle, and apparently the only reflex of the Latin supine in a major modern Romance language.[6]

In English, infinitival relatives utilize overt operators only when PPs are reordered, and NOs otherwise, while *tough* constructions utilize NOs only, as illustrated below (for an alternative analysis of English *tough* constructions, see n.8 (p. 247)).

(3.38) a. *John is tough [*with whom* to work]
       b. John is tough [*NO* to work with]

(3.39) a. People [*with whom* to work closely]
       b. People [*NO* to work closely with]

In Romanian, on the other hand, no overt operators can be used. The following data show that *tough* and non-finite relatives may be formed with supines, but not with infinitives.

(3.40) a. *Cartea$_i$ e uşor de PRO$_k$ a   citi   e$_i$.
           book-L is easy of   INF. read
           'The book is easy to read.'
       b. *Caut   o carte$_i$ de PRO$_k$ a   citi e$_i$
           seek.1.SG a book   of   INF. read
           'I am looking for a book to read.'

(3.41) a. Cartea e   uşor de citit.
           book-L is easy of read(SUP)
           'The book is easy to read.'
       b. Caut   o carte de citit.
           seek.1.SG a book of read(SUP)
           'I am looking for a book to read.'

The homophony with passive participles is undoubtedly in part responsible for the view, put forward in a number of earlier studies, that constructions like those in (3.41) are based on passive configurations of some sort (for example, in Dobrovie-Sorin (1987: § 1.3.6.6, 1.3.6.7) where S-Structures essentially like those in (3.42) are proposed).[7]

(3.42) a. Cartea$_i$ e uşor de PRO$_i$ citit e$_i$
       b. Caut o carte$_i$ de PRO$_i$ citit e$_i$

The structures in (3.42) rest on the assumption that the Case which a transitive verb can in principle assign to its direct object is 'absorbed', owing to the passive character of the participle (n.7 (p. 247)). Under this assumption, the null category in object position is an anaphor, rather than a variable, and the supine clause can contain no NO. Conversely, if a passive-type analysis is untenable for the supine constructions at issue, the null object must be viewed as a syntactic variable bound by an NO, because it is unclear what factor other than the passive can deprive the direct object of a transitive verb of Case, and thus of variable status.[8] In the remainder of this section, I argue against a passive analysis for data like those in (3.41).

As alluded to in n.7 (p. 247), the supine is homophonous not only with passive, but also with active participles, which, as noted there, do not absorb Case (note that the supine in (ii) of n.6 (p. 247) has an overt direct object, which requires Case). It is thus necessary to provide positive support for a choice between the two a priori possible analyses. I now proceed to do just this, using passive participles without auxiliary verbs (like the capitalized one in (3.43)) for purposes of comparison with the supine, and this, in order to keep the contrast as 'minimal' as possible.

(3.43) CRITICAT   de către toţi, copilul   izbucni în plîns.
        criticized by   all   child-the burst   in crying
        'Criticized by everyone, the child burst into tears.'

A first point concerns the agreement properties of participles. While active (past) participles are invariant (see (3.44a)), passive participles obligatorily agree with their subjects (see (3.44b, c)); now the supines at issue are invariant, as shown in (3.44d, e), which is unexpected under the envisaged passive-like analysis.

```
(3.44) a. Profesoarele      au    CRITICAT(*E)       elevele.
          teachers(F)-the have criticized(F.PL) students(F)-the
          'The female teachers have criticized the female students.'
       b. Fetele     au    fost CRITICAT*(e)     de toată lumea.
          girls-the have been criticized(F.PL.) by all   world
          'The girls were criticized by everybody.'
       c. CRITICAT*(e)      de toată lumea, fetele     izbucniră
          criticized(F.PL.) by all    world girls-the burst
          în plîns.
          in crying
          'Criticized by everyone, the girls burst into tears.'
       d. Fetele    sînt imposibil de CRITICAT(*e).
          girls-the are  impossible    criticized(F.PL.)
          'The girls are hard to criticize.'
       e. Nişte probleme de REZOLVAT(*e)  pînă mîine...
          some  problems    solved(F.PL.) till tomorrow
          'A number of problems to solve by tomorrow...'
```

A second contrast concerns the (im)possibility of 'long movement'. Thus, while such movement is completely excluded in (both 'full' and 'bare') passives, as illustrated in (3.45), it is definitely possible in supines, as illustrated in (2.46).

```
(3.45) a. *Problemele    au    fost TERMINATE   DE REZOLVAT(E) e
          problems-the have been finished.F.PL. solved(F.PL.)
          la timp.
          at time
          'One finished solving the problems on time.'
          (purported meaning)
       b. *TERMINATE    DE   REZOLVAT(E)    e în scurt timp,
          finished.F.PL.  solved(F.PL.)    in short time
          problemele   au    încetat să mai  constituie un mister.
          problems-the have stopped SP more constitute a  mystery
          'Having finished solving (them), the problems ceased
          constituting a mystery.'
          (purported meaning)

(3.46) a. Cartea asta e   imposibil de terminat     de citit
          book-L this is impossible of finished(SUP) of read(SUP)
          înainte de sfîrşitul lunii.
          before of end-L    month-L(GEN)
          'This book is impossible to finish reading before
          the end of the month.'
```

b. Cartea asta e imposibil de continuat   de citit
                            of continued(SUP) of read(SUP)
   în condiţiile   existente.
   in conditions-L existing
   'This book is impossible to continue reading under
   existing conditions.
c. Cartea asta e imposibil de început   de citit
                            of begun(SUP) of read(SUP)
   înainte de întîi Ianuarie.
   before   of first January
   'This book is impossible to begin reading before
   the first of January.'

It is difficult to see how the contrast between (3.45) and (3.46) can be accounted for without assuming that an NO has undergone reordering to [SPEC, C'] in the derivation of the various subcases of (3.46). It thus seems that the supine constructions represent a third class of Romanian constructions for which the assumption of NOs is motivated.

The conclusion we have just reached is partly obscured by the fact that the supine constructions illustrated in (3.41) do not exhibit the full range of extraction dependencies that is found, for example, in interrogative and relative *wh*-type constructions. In particular, dependencies with a 'gap' that is internal to an indicative or subjunctive clause, or belongs to the 'parasitic' variety, are in general unacceptable, as illustrated by the data in (3.47) and (3.48) respectively.[9]

(3.47) a. ?*Asemenea formulare sînt greu de forţat
            such   forms   are hard of forced(SUP)
          pe elevi să   completeze.
          ACC pupils SUBJ complete.3
          '?Such forms are hard to force the pupils to fill out.'
      b. ?*Nişte formulare de cerut   tuturor elevilor
            some forms   of asked(SUP) all   pupils-L
          să   completeze mi-au   fost trimise ieri.
          SUBJ complete.3 me-have.3.PL been sent   yesterday
          '?Some forms to ask the pupils to fill out
          were sent to me yesterday.'

(3.48) a. Cartea e imposibil de analizat   fără
          book.L is impossible of analysed(SUP) without
          a   *(o) citi mai întîi cu atenţie.
          INF. her read more first with attention
          'This book is impossible to analyse without first
          reading ??(it) carefully.'
      b. O carte de citit   fără   a   *(o) analiza
          a book of read(SUP) without INF. her analyse
          în mod prea detaliat mi-a   fost trimisă ieri.
          in way too detailed me-has been sent   yesterday

'A book to read without analysing ??(it) in too much
detail was sent to me yesterday.'

Such facts need not, however, be unduly worrisome. It has been known for some time that 'tough' constructions, and more generally, constructions with nonfinite clauses that have an NO in [SPEC, C'] are restricted in ways analogous to those illustrated in (3.47) and (3.48) in languages where the nonfinite verb is an *infinitive* (for example, English and Western Romance languages), so that a passive-like analysis is not particularly plausible. For example, Ross (1967: § 6.1.3.3) observes in relation to the English 'tough' construction that 'this rule appears not to be able to delete elements of clauses containing finite verbs', and offers the following datum as illustration:

(3.49) ?*These flowers would be easy for you to say that you
       had found.

Chomsky (1977) and Stowell (1985) echo these remarks with respect to English nonfinite constructions with NOs in general, and numerous informants that I have personally consulted have expressed similar judgements (which are expressed in the two question marks awarded to the English translations of the data in (3.47)). For further discussion of these stricter constraints and of some cross-linguistic linguistic variation in their strictness, see Grosu (1988b). In respect to parasitic gaps, I note that French, for example, also requires pronouns in constructions like those in (3.50) (in the places indicated with brackets), although these constructions exhibit infinitives where the data in (3.48) exhibit supines; furthermore, as indicated by the question marks in the English translations of the data in (3.48), parasitic gaps have marginal status even in English (Chomsky and Lasnik 1977: Appendix I).

(3.50) a. Ce   livre est impossible à   discuter
          this book is impossible to discuss
          sans   *(l-) avoir lu au   préalable.
          without him have read at-the previous
          'This book is impossible to discuss without having first
          read ?(it) carefully.'
       b. Voici un livre à lire sans   devoir   *(le) discuter
          here-is a book to read without having-to him discuss
          plus tard.
          more late
          'Here is a book to read without needing to
          discuss ?(it) later.'

But if the constructions at issue are subject to special restrictions regardless of the particular nonfinite form they exhibit, then the data in (3.47)–(3.48) need not be viewed as weakening the conclusion that the constructions of (3.41) exhibit null operators.

In fact, such data improve in acceptability, at least for some informants,

THREE STUDIES IN LOCALITY AND CASE

(3.51) a. ?*Nimic*   nu e imposibil de convins   pe un copil
          nothing   not is impossible   persuade(SUP) ACC a child
          să   facă e.
          SUBJ do
          '?Nothing is impossible to persuade a child to do.'
      b. ?*Ceva*   important de cerut   tuturor copiilor   să
          something important of asked(SUP) all-DAT children-L-DAT SUBJ
          facă mi-a   fost explicat ieri.
          do.3 me-has been explained yesterday
          '?Something to ask all the children to do
          was explained to me yesterday.'

(3.52) a. ?*Aşa ceva*   e imposibil de reparat   e fără
          such something is impossible of repaired(SUP)   without
          a   atinge e mai întîi cu   mîinile.
          INF. touch more first with   hands-L
          '?Something like this is impossible to repair without
          first touching with one's hands.'
      b. ?*Ceva*   de reparat   e fără   a   atinge în vreun
          something of repaired(SUP) without INF. touch in any
          fel e cu   mîinile mi-a   fost trimis prin   poştă
          way   with hands-L me-has been sent through post
          ieri.
          yesterday
          '?Something to repair without touching in any way with
          one's hands was sent to me by post yesterday.'

Note that the variables in (3.51)–(3.52) cannot be operator-bound by the corresponding italicized elements, because these are not in appropriate positions (for example, the italicized elements in the (a) subcases are subjects, and thus occupy an A-position). Furthermore, if these elements could bind the corresponding variables, we might expect (3.47), where the main clause subjects also have quantifier content, to exhibit a comparable degree of acceptability, and this expectation is not fulfilled.

These facts show that – under certain circumstances – NOs are possible even in constructions like (3.47)–(3.48), and that the claim that certain Romanian supine constructions utilize NOs stands on firm ground.

8.5 *TOO/ENOUGH* CONSTRUCTIONS

One last context in which Romanian appears to allow NOs under special circumstances consists of the counterparts to the English *too/enough* constructions.

English constructions like the reduced version of (3.53) are usually analysed in terms of an NO in the infinitival clause (the full version probably does not require an NO, since an RP is not necessary, as shown in (3.54)).

```
(3.53) John is too dangerous for us to be willing to hire (him).
(3.54) John is too dangerous for us to simply adopt
       a wait-and-see attitude.
```

In general, Romanian exhibits only constructions like the full version of (3.53) and (3.54), which are formed with either an infinitive or a subjunctive subordinate clause, but not constructions like the reduced version of (3.53), as shown in (3.55).

```
(3.55) a. Ion e  prea periculos pentru a      *(-l) angaja.
          Ion is too  dangerous  for    INF.  him   hire
       b. Ion e  prea periculos pentru ca     să *(-l) angajăm.
                                       that SUBJ
       'Ion is too dangerous for us to hire(him).'
```

Data like the reduced version of (3.53) seem to be excluded in at least some Western Romance languages as well, as shown by the French data in (3.56).

```
(3.56) Jean est trop dangereux pour qu'  on *(l-) embauche.
       Jean is  too  dangerous for  that one him  hire
       'Jean is too dangerous for anyone to hire(him).'
```

None the less, data like the reduced versions of (3.55) can be somewhat improved by means of maximally nonspecific bare quantifier antecedents, as illustrated below (cf. (3.51))–(3.52)). This shows that, under special circumstances, NOs are marginally possible in these constructions, too.

```
(3.57) a. ??Nimic   nu e destul de important pentru a
           nothing not is enough of important for    INF.
           întreprinde e înainte de sosirea    şefului.
           undertake     before  of arrival-L boss-L-GEN
           'Nothing is important enough to undertake before
           the boss's arrival.'
       b. ??Nimic   nu e destul de urgent ca    să  discutăm
           nothing not is enough of urgent that SUBJ discuss.1.PL
           e la o oră  atît de tîrzie.
           at a hour so  of late
           'Nothing is pressing enough for us to start discussing
           at such a late hour.'
```

8.6 SUMMARY AND CONCLUSIONS

In the preceding four sections, I have argued that NOs must be assumed to occur in a number of Romanian constructions, in particular, in certain comparative and relative clauses, in supine clauses with an object 'gap' and – as a marked option – in *too/enough* constructions; in addition, they need, of course, to be assumed in RP constructions.

While Romanian makes a more restricted use of NOs compared to other languages (for example, English or Chinese), it is certainly not the only language that seems to 'prefer' overt operators to null ones. For example, German and Hungarian are at least as restricted in respect to NO options (as noted in earlier sections, they tolerate NOs in comparatives, but not in relatives or clefts), which points to the possibility of an areal phenomenon.

As alluded to in the Introduction to this study, Dobrovie-Sorin (1987, 1990) maintains that Romanian makes no use of NOs,[10] and proposes to derive this presumed state of affairs from independent properties of Romanian. I have presented evidence in this study which refutes her claim. In the remainder of this section, I will show that her argumentation for the conclusion that Romanian is an NO-free language is based on faulty reasoning. If my argument goes through, there are at the moment no grounds for even expecting that Romanian should have this property.

Dobrovie-Sorin's argument takes as its point of departure certain (unobjectionable, as far as I can see) results she achieves in relation to a distinction between Romanian and other languages (such as French, English, etc.). This distinction concerns S-Structure *wh*-dependencies which are *not* overt reflexes of the subsequent LF operator-variable configurations. As was pointed out in section 3.2.3 of the first study, S-Structure/LF discrepancies arise in (at least) two types of situation: (i) when the *wh*-phrase in [SPEC, C'] is of the D-linked type; and (ii) when the phrase in [SPEC, C'] properly includes a non-D-linked *wh*-phrase that belongs to a distinct Extended Projection. Under such circumstances, the empty category in an A-position bound by the phrase in [SPEC, C'] must be 'doubled' by a clitic (unless that phrase is itself non-D-linked, in which case it exhibits quantifying properties). In contrast, when the phrase in [SPEC, C'] is a possible LF operator with clausal scope (and in particular a *wh*-phrase of the non-D-linked type), no such clitic is allowed. The distribution of clitics in *wh*-dependencies is illustrated below.

(3.58) a. *Pe care băiat *(l-) ai văzut?*
       ACC which boy   him have.2.SG. seen
       'Which boy did you see?'
   b. *Pe al cui fiu *(l-) ai întîlnit?*
       ACC a+L whose son him have.2.SG. met
       'Whose son did you meet?'

(3.59)   *Pe cine (*l-) ai întîlnit?*
         ACC who him have.2.SG. met
         'Whom did you meet?'

Note that the contrast between (3.58) and (3.59) in respect to clitics is not found between the corresponding English translations. Looking at this in a slightly different way, data like (3.59) are clitic-less in both languages, while data like (3.58) exhibit clitics in Romanian, but not in English. On the whole, Western Romance languages pattern with English, rather than with Romanian.

Dobrovie-Sorin proposes to characterize this parametric distinction by assuming that, in languages like English, but not in languages like Romanian, the [SPEC, C'] position confers *syntactic quantifier* status upon any phrase that fills it at S-Structure, something which enables it to operator-bind a *syntactic variable*, that is, an extraction trace in an A-position. Under this assumption, the clitics in (3.58) are needed to license the empty categories in an A-position, since these cannot be interpreted as syntactic variables because there is no syntactic quantifier to bind them. In contrast, the absence of clitics in (3.59) is dictated by the need to construe the empty category in an A-position as a syntactic variable; this need follows from the fact that the phrase in [SPEC, C'] qualifies as a syntactic quantifier in virtue of its inherent properties, and a quantifier must bind a variable (vacuous quantification being excluded in natural languages (Chomsky 1982)).

Now, Dobrovie-Sorin (1990: § 1.4.2) maintains that a positive setting for the 'structural quantifier parameter' is necessary to license NOs on the grounds that 'Quite obviously, a "null" operator is not marked with intrinsic *qu*-features; its quantifier status is due exclusively to its position in [Spec, C']. It is then natural to assume that the existence of null operators depends on the positive value of the structural quantifier parameter'. In section 3.3.2.3 of the first study, I also proposed that NOs must move to [SPEC, C'], but for an entirely different reason; specifically, I proposed that an NO must occur in [SPEC, C'] in order to have its specifications in respect to (at least) the features [NAOP] and [COIND] identified by C^o. Note that this account is inherently non-parametric, because it relies on (presumably universal) mechanisms, namely (i) the licensing of appropriate specifications on CP by its context; (ii) the percolation from CP to C^o; and (iii) Spec-Head agreement. But if so, there is no need for a positive setting of the Syntactic Quantifier Parameter to assign operator status to NOs. In fact, note that such a setting finds its justification, in Dobrovie-Sorin's account, in those instances where the phrase in [SPEC, C'] cannot, due to its inherent specifications, function as *semantic* operator. But this state of affairs is not applicable to NOs. Furthermore, observe that the licensing mechanism I have proposed is needed even in languages which are positively specified for the Syntactic Quantifier Parameter, because – as pointed out in section 3.2.2 of the first study – NOs must be differentiated in terms of various feature specifications, and a mere positive setting of the Syntactic Quantifier Parameter cannot accomplish this purpose. In short, Spec-Head agreement, which is needed over and above the Syntactic Quantifier Parameter, renders the latter superfluous with respect to NOs. Accordingly, a negative setting of the parameter implies nothing with respect to the distribution of NOs, a conclusion reinforced by the observation that Hungarian and German, which are *positively* specified for the parameter (because they exhibit no clitics in *wh*-dependencies), exhibit NO-distribution patterns highly reminiscent of the one found in Romanian.

In conclusion, the assumption of null operators does not conflict with any known principles of Romanian grammar, and empirical evidence shows that such an assumption is well motivated with respect to a number of Romanian constructions.

NOTES

STUDY I THE SYNTAX OF FREE RELATIVE CONSTRUCTIONS

1 This distinction between restrictive and amount relatives also has consequences for the interpretation of coordinate clauses. Thus, the coordinate restrictive relatives in (i) may be construed as purporting to identify a single set of boys all of whom both sang and danced. The coordinate clauses in (ii), on the other hand, do not purport to identify the same set of people, and (iii) does not carry the implication that John bought and Mary sold the same thing(s).

(i)   The boys who sang and who danced...

(ii) The people that there were at Bill's party and that there had been at Mary's party...

(iii) What(ever) John bought and what(ever) Mary sold...

2 Groos and van Riemsdijk do not directly address the issue of how their account of matching effects applies to extraposed FRs (as in (1.23e)).

If Extraposition-from-NP can be viewed as a 'stylistic' rule in the sense of Chomsky and Lasnik (1977), that is, a rule which applies in PF, structures like (1.23e) pose no special problem. Such a position is, however, difficult to espouse in view of the convincing arguments given in Guéron (1980) and Guéron and May (1984) that Extraposition-from-NP is a rule of the core grammar, that is, one that applies before S-Structure.

If so, there are two alternatives to consider, depending on whether one assumes that the extraposition process leaves a trace or not. If one assumes the former, then the by-pass option must permit application to [SPEC, C'] via the FR's trace; if one assumes the latter (which is argued for, for example, in Baltin (1987)), it is unclear what the natural extension of Groos and van Riemsdijk's account might be.

As will be seen below, the analysis of FRCs and matching effects that is proposed in Chapters 3 and 4 encounters no special difficulties in relation to extraposed structures. For some evidence which favours an analysis with a trace, see n. 24 (p. 236).

3 The fact that the bracketed constituents in (1.33), but not left-dislocated constituents, undergo reconstruction can be inferred from facts like the following:

NOTES

(i) *That you *ever* stole anything, I will never believe it.

(ii) I will never believe it, that you *ever* stole *anything*.

(iii) I will never believe this sort of rumour:
that you *ever* stole *anything*.

4 Observe that if the Head by-pass hypothesis is formulated in terms of Kase, rather than of Case/subcategorization, it is the facts of fully-matching languages, such as French and English, that are straightforwardly predicted when the by-pass option is taken, and it is restricted-matching languages of the kind illustrated by Spanish and Catalan that emerge as requiring some additional treatment. Under a formulation in terms of Case/subcategorization, the situation is reversed (see discussion of Hirschbühler and Rivero's work in section 1.2.2).

5 As Suñer notes, non-finite FRCs are not necessarily possible in all languages which allow finite FRCs. I address the reason for their highly restricted distribution in section 3.2 and in Chapter 5.

6 Suñer does not, of course, use the term 'Kase', but 'Case'. The former term, however, correctly reflects her intentions in this case.

7 While the basic objections to Suñer raised in Grosu (1989) are maintained here, the positive proposals made in that earlier article have been significantly changed, as will become clear in what follows.

8 Further complexities are possible, since Ps may take PP complements, as in (i).

(i) He emerged [from [under the table]].

Furthermore, Ps may, in some languages, be neutralized as to functional/lexical status and exhibit their own functional projections (see section 6.3 in the second study for elucidation and illustration of this point).

I also wish to note that Kase needs to be viewed as a property of [+N] categories, rather than just of *nominal*, that is, [+N, −V] categories, as stated above in the text. This further refinement is of no importance at this stage; its justification is thus postponed until later (see section 3.4).

9 The glossing of the italicized sequence in (1.52a) points to the possibility of analysing the bracketed structure as an OHRC with *mi* as Head and *še* as complementizer introducing the relative clause. If this were the structure of constructions like those in (1.52), the deviance of (1.52b) would have no bearing on the hypothesis we are investigating. But while such an analysis seems to be a reasonable one for *mi še* constructions that exhibit a R(esumptive) P(ronoun), such as (ia) (note the contrast between (ia) and the full version of (ib) on the one hand and the reduced version of (ib) on the other, where, respectively, an RP and a 'gap' are contained in an extraction island),

(i) a. Carix la'azor gam le mi še   eynenu ohavim
       must to-help also to who that not-we like
       et [ha -anašim še   tomxim b -o].
       ACC the-people that support in-him
       'One must also help (him) who we don't like the people that
       support him.'
    b. Carix la'azor gam le 'ele še   eynenu ohavim
       must to-help also to those that not-we like
       et [ha -anašim še   meodedim *(otam)].
       ACC the-people that encourage them
       'One must also help those that we do not like the
       people who encourage *(them)'

228

it does not seem to be the optimal analysis for corresponding constructions with a 'gap' instead of an RP, and this, for two reasons.

First, (iib) is distinctly worse than (iia), which is surprising if the gap is due to the movement of an NO, since NO gaps in direct object position are certainly possible in incontrovertible OHRCs (see (iii)).

(ii) a. mi še e sirev   le-hazmin oti le-beyt -o...
        who that refused to-invite me to-house-his
        '(He) who refused to invite me to his house...'
    b. *mi še   siravta   le-hazmin e le-beyt -xa..
        who that refused-you to-invite to-house-your
        '(He) whom you refused to invite to your house...'

(iii) a. ha -anašim še siravta   le-hazmin e
         the-people that refused-you to-invite
         le-beyt -xa ...
         to-house-your
         'The people that you refused to invite to your house...'

However, the deviance of (iib) becomes understandable if *mi* or *mi še* has been moved to [SPEC, C'] from the direct object position, since the ACC marker *et* is missing, and this marker is obligatory with direct object *mi* elsewhere (cf. the interrogative construction in (iv), where removal of *et* results in ungrammaticality).

(iv) [*(et) mi   raita]?
      ACC who saw-you
      'Who did you see?'

Note that constructions comparable to (iia), that is, apparent OHRCs which, upon closer examination, turn out to be FRCs, have been signalled by Hirschbühler and Rivero (1981, 1983) in Catalan; a case in point is the non-matching FRC in (v).

(v) [Al   que li pique] que se   rasque.
      to+he that him itches that self scratch
      'He who itches, let him scratch himself.'

Note that, in the sequence *al que*, which is a contraction of *a+el que*, the element *el* is PRECEDED by the preposition *a*, which forces the conclusion that *el* is in [SPEC, C'], rather than in Head position.

A second argument for analysing *mi še* constructions with 'gaps' as FRCs, rather than as OHRCs, is furnished by constructions with 'missing' prepositions (analogous to those in (1.21)), which have the superficial properties of (vi) (*non-matching* constructions like (v) cannot be constructed, as already noted in relation to (1.52b)).

(vi) ani muxan le-hazmin [et mi še   ata hizmanta e].
      I   ready to-invite ACC who that you invited
      'I am prepared to invite (him) whom you invited.'

Note that *mi (še)* is taken to be in Head position so (vi) ought to be deviant, just like (iib), and this is not the case.

Further evidence for the point just made is provided by data with non-omissible prepositions (*et* is, under certain circumstances, omissible; see, for example, (iii)).

(vii) a. ani mityaxes *le ma   še*   gam ata hityahasta.
         I   refer   to what that too you referred.2.SG.
         'I am referring (to that) to which you also referred.'
     b. ani mityaxes *la   uvdot še* gam ata hityahasta
         I   refer   to-the facts that too you referred.2.SG.
         *(eleyhen).
         to-them
         'I am referring to the facts that you also referred to.'

(viii) a. ani oved *im   mi še* ata oved.
          I work with who that you work.2.SG.
          'I work with (the one/those) with whom you work.'
      b. ani oved *im   ha -anašim še* ata oved *(itam).
          I work with the-people that you work   with-them
          'I work with the people that you work with.'

Note that if the (a) subcases in (vii) and (viii) include an OHRC, the incontrovertible OHRCs in the reduced version of the corresponding (b) subcases should also be grammatical. However, (viib) and (viii) are ungrammatical because the non-omissible prepositions *le* and *im* (the former occurs in the corresponding full version in an allomorphic variant) are missing. I interpret the grammaticality of (viia) and (viiia) as resulting from the fact that the entire sequences *le ma še* and *im mi še* have undergone reordering; for justification of this claim and for further details concerning my proposed analysis of constructions with 'missing' prepositions (such as (1.21) and (1.22)), see section 3.4.

I conclude from the above that the bracketed strings in (1.52) are FRCs, not OHRCs, and that the deviance of (1.52b) indicates that non-matching subject FRCs are disallowed in Modern Hebrew.

10 For discussion and illustration of Case-Markedness hierarchies in relation to a variety of processes, see section 4.1.
11 In subsection 1.4.3.3, it will be seen that this generalization applies to at least some non-governed positions as well.
12 Comparable assumptions would need to be made with respect to a variety of other constructions, such as the Romanian data in (i) and the English data in (ii). In relation to the latter, Grimshaw (1987) argues for an analysis along these lines on independent grounds.

(i) *Cît   îţi   închipui   că   sînt de bogat?*
     How-much REFL fancy.2.SG that I-am of rich?
     'How rich do you think I am?'

(ii) John has drunk more of the wine than [*NO* it is suspected he has drunk of the beer].

13 Cole (1987a) proposed to account for the Subjacency effects in Quechua by assuming (i) that Subjacency holds in some languages (in particular, in Quechua) not only of the 'overt' syntactic component, but also *of LF*; and (ii) that Subjacency violations may occur in Head-Internal relatives due to the fact that the internal Head raises at LF *to the position occupied by pro.*

The assumption that Subjacency effects in Head-Internal relatives is due to LF movement was argued against at some length in Watanabe (1991) in relation to comparable facts of Japanese (see n. 21 (p. 234)).

As for the assumption of movement to the position of external Head, rather than to [SPEC, C'], Cole's sole motivation was that Quechua OHRCs and Head-Internal relative constructions can in this way exhibit the same configuration at

NOTES

LF, and thus undergo semantic interpretation by the same rules. It is not clear, however, that the two kinds of relative constructions *ought* to be interpreted in the same way. G. Hermon (p.c.) informed me that the Head-Internal relatives of Quechua do not stack, while those with external Heads do. This points to the conclusion that the latter are, unlike the former, restrictive constructions, which means that the process envisaged by Cole is unmotivated, and in fact undesirable.

14 Rizzi's remark concerning identification is echoed in Borer (1989), who considers – as already noted in section 1.4.3.1 – that the identifier of a null category must be a 'local antecedent'.

15 The exact position of *pro* within the various subjunctive clauses is not at issue here (Dobrovie-Sorin (1987, 1993) argues that it is post-verbal at S-Structure).

16 This assumption is minimal. Without it, Kase-matching effects would be hard to make sense of (as already noted in 3.1.2.1 in relation to Authier's proposals).

17 There is also another area where the discontinuous character of the relation between correlatives and their external nominals has empirical consequences. Thus, correlatives, unlike headed amount relatives, may exhibit multiple *wh*-phrases, each of them related (via CP) to a distinct external nominal within IP. An illustration of this state of affairs is provided in (i).

(i) [jis laRkiiNE$_i$ jis larkeKO$_j$ dekhaa]
    REL girl-ERG   REL boy-ACC   saw
    usNE$_i$ usKO$_j$ passandkiyaa.
    DEM-ERG DEM-ACC liked
    'Which girl saw which boy, she liked him.'

That correlatives with multiple *wh*-phrases are indeed possible just in cases of structural discontinuity is brought out by the fact that multiple *wh*-phrases are excluded when the correlative is adjoined to a DP (as in (1.98b')).

The kind of analysis envisaged in the text with respect to correlatives with single *wh*-phrases extends straightforwardly to correlatives with multiple *wh*-phrases. Each such *wh*-phrase is a weak DP with a corresponding weak DP in some A-position, each of the latter being (overtly or implicitly) bound by a strong non-partitive D. CP bears an ordered n-tuple of indices corresponding to the ordered n-tuple of indices that are borne by the various *wh*-phrases it contains. CP now designates a relation which is jointly defined by the n-tuple of *wh*-phrases and the remainder of CP. The weak DPs in A-positions define a corresponding relation with *resumptive* status, hence the strong non-partitive character of their overt or implicit binders.

The extension from simplex to multiple correlatives is thus basically unproblematic.

18 One such auxiliary hypothesis is that *wh*-phrases need not count as operators (at some level of representation) if they do not occupy a scope position, such as [SPEC, C']. Thanks to this assumption, English multiple questions like the following do not violate (1.103a) at S-Structure, since the *wh*-phrase *in situ* does not count as an operator at that level.

(i) I wonder [$_{CP}$ what [$_{C'}$ you gave to whom]].

Of course, Rizzi's (1.103a) requires that *whom* move at LF to be properly interpreted (other linguists, for example, Chomsky (1992), take the position that such *wh*-phrases *in situ* do not move at LF, but achieve operator status through 'long distance' absorption with the *wh*-phrase in [SPEC, C']).

An interesting point, which Rizzi does not discuss, is that his auxiliary assumption is not true of ALL *wh*-phrases. In particular, it is true neither of exclamatory *wh*-phrases, nor of interrogative *wh*-phrases of the *what the hell* type (which, as J. Horvath pointed out to me, are arguably exclamatory, too, in the sense that one exclaims at the fact that something is *not* known, rather than at that which *is* known). To see this, observe that the data in (ii) are not well-formed.

(ii) a. *Who the hell spoke *with who the hell*?
    b. *What a nice girl went out *with what a stupid boy*!

That *what the hell*-type phrases are not well-formed *in situ* in languages with overt *wh*-Movement was noted in Pesetzky (1987: n. 20). Pesetzky, however, did not consider data like (ii), but rather contrasts like the one in (iii), and suggested on this basis that *what the hell*-type phrases must move to [SPEC, C'] before 'ordinary' interrogative phrases.

(iii) a. Who the hell caught what?
    b. *Who caught what the hell?

Pesetzky's suggestion is, I believe, on the right track, but it is insufficient with respect to data like (ii), where no 'ordinary' *wh*-phrases exist. A more accurate descriptive generalization is that in languages with overt *wh*-Movement, ALL exclamatory *wh*-phrases must move to [SPEC, C']. This proposal is not testable with respect to English, which does not tolerate multiple applications of *wh*-Movement to the same [SPEC, C']. It is however, testable with respect to Romanian, which allows such movement (see (iv)); as illustrated in (v) and (vi), the prediction is confirmed.

(iv) a. *Cine* a întîlnit *pe cine*?
       who has met   ACC who
      'Who met who(m)?'
    b. *Cine pe cine* a întîlnit?

(v) a. **Cine naiba* a întîlnit *pe cine naiba*?
      who devil has met   ACC who devil
     '*Who the hell met who the hell?'
    b. *Cine naiba pe cine naiba* a întîlnit?

(vi) a. **Ce băiat drăguț* s' a încurcat
      what boy nice REFL has entangled
      cu ce fată tîmpită!
      with what girl stupid
     '*What a nice boy got involved with what a stupid girl!'
    b. *Ce băiat drăguț cu ce fată tîmpită* s'a încurcat!

Why do exclamatory phrases behave in this way? The answer lies, I suggest, in the fact that data like (iva) and (ivb) are not completely synonymous, the rightmost *wh*-phrase in (iva) (and the corresponding English translation) being 'focus dependent' on the corresponding leftmost phrase, while the rightmost *wh*-phrase in (ivb) is not. Thus, (iva) can be construed as a family of questions like (viia), but not like (viib).

(vii) a. Well, what about BOB? Whom did HE meet?
     b. Well, what about MARY? Who met HER?

Example (ivb), on the other hand, seems to be a simultaneous question about the person(s) who met some other person(s) and the person(s) that some other person(s) met. It appears that that the independent/dependent status of interrogative foci is reflected in the following syntactic requirement: independently construed *wh*-phrases must have their scopal properties established at the earliest level permitted by the grammar, dependently construed ones need not. If so, the inability of *what the hell*-type phrases, and, more generally, of exclamatory phrases to occur *in situ* at S-Structure in English and Romanian is attributable to the fact that such phrases, in view of the complete novelty implied by their content, must receive a focus-independent interpretation, and therefore necessarily occur in [SPEC, C'] at S-Structure.

The proposal just made appears to be consistent with the fact that such phrases may occur *in situ* in languages like Turkish (see (viii)–(ix) below) and Japanese (see Pesetzky's article for illustrations), under the assumption that the *wh*-Criterion holds in these languages at LF only and that scopal properties cannot be established earlier.

(viii)   John *hangi cehenneme* kayboldu?
         John which hell-DAT   disappear.PAST
         'Where the hell did John disappear?'

(ix) Dün   partide   *ne güzel* eğlendik!
      yesterday party-LOC what pretty enjoy.PAST.1.PL
      'What a great time we had at the party yesterday!'

But if so, we may also expect the languages at issue to allow multiple exclamatory phrases *in situ*, and this, according to the informants I consulted, is not the case. This state of affairs is derivable, I would maintain, from the fact that, despite 'masking' appearances, scopal properties need to be established at S-Structure in these languages under certain circumstances, and in particular, for exclamatory *wh*-phrases. For elaboration and justification of these claims, see below in the text and n. 21.

19 Grimshaw's view is too restrictive in general, because [wh] appears to be sometimes transmissible from positions comparable to that of *whom* in (1.104), except that they are not within English embedded interrogatives. This effect is found, for example, in English appositive and restrictive relatives, as can be seen by contrasting (1.104d) with (i), and (iii) with (ii).

(i)   John, [$_{DP}$ several books about whom] have just been written,
       is a great guy.

(ii)   *I wonder [$_{DP}$ the height of the lettering on the covers of
       which reports] the government prescribes.

(iii) Reports [$_{DP}$ the height of the lettering on the covers of which]
       the government prescribes are invariably boring.

While constructions like (i) and (iii) may perhaps have a more 'marked' status than constructions like (104c) (as suggested by Emonds (1976: § V.7)), they are clearly acceptable, and their acceptability furthermore depends on the presence of a *wh*-pronoun within the Pied-Piped phrases (for example, replacement of *which* with *them* in (iii) results in ungrammaticality).

Some languages are arguably considerably laxer than English in respect to [*wh*] transmission. For a set of facts which implies this conclusion with respect to Japanese, see n. 21.

I will not attempt to identify the mechanisms which make possible [*wh*] spread beyond the limits envisaged by Grimshaw, and neither will I attempt to discover the factors responsible for the cross-constructional and cross-linguistic

NOTES

differences noted above. I will, however, argue below in the text that the extremely tight restrictions on Pied-Piping found in *wh*-FRCs result from requirements unrelated to [*wh*] spread *per se*.

20 According to Haegeman and Zanuttini (1991), all languages possess a Neg X°, which may or may not have a morphological realization in a given language. Thus, West Flemish possesses a Neg X° which may, but need not be morphologically realized; in contrast, the English counterpart of this element is never realized, as indicated by the contrast between, e.g., (1.106a) and (1.106c). Furthermore, English is – as Rizzi (1990, 1991) puts it – a 'residual' V2 language, in particular one in which V2 structures occur only when 'licensed' by 'criteria' like those in (1.103) and (1.105), while West Flemish is a 'full' V2 language, that is, one in which initial phrases of V2 structures need not bear particular features. This latter distinction accounts for the contrast in grammaticality between (1.106d) and the reduced version of (1.106b).

21 One of a number of reasons put forward by Watanabe for assuming NO movement prior to S-Structure is the existence of certain Subjacency effects in the distribution of interrogative phrases. Thus, when an interrogative *wh*-phrase occurs within a *wh*-island, as in (i), the result has the kind of marginality found in the corresponding English translation.

```
(i)  ?John-wa [Mary-ga nani-o    katta ka dooka]
      John-Top Mary-NOM what-ACC bought whether
      siritagatte iru no?
      want-to-know    Q
      'What does John want to know whether Mary bought?'
```

The Subjacency effects of Japanese exhibit a curious relaxation, with interesting implications. Thus, interrogative *wh*-phrases may occur within a complex NP, but not if they are of the exclamatory (*what the hell*) type, as illustrated below.

```
(ii)  Mary-wa [Tom-ni  (*ittai) nani-o    ageta
      Mary-TOP Tom-DAT the hell what-ACC gave
      hito-ni    atta no?
      person-DAT met   Q
      'What (the hell) is such that Mary met the person who gave it to John?'
```

To account for the well-formedness of the reduced version of (ii), Watanabe suggests that the moved NO originates in the specifier of the bracketed (complex) DP, rather than in the specifier of the *wh*-phrase. This view requires the assumption that the [*wh*] feature can somehow spread in Japanese out of a relative clause and into a superordinate DP, ultimately reaching the specifier of this DP, something which is disallowed in English (this greater laxity of Japanese was alluded to in n. 19). The NO is then in a position to satisfy the version of the *wh*-Criterion which applies at S-Structure in Japanese.

Concerning the fact that the mechanism of [*wh*] propagation is unable to salvage the full version of (ii), it is derivable from the proposal made in n. 18 to the effect that exclamatory phrases must have their scopal properties established at the earliest level permitted by the grammar. Note that this condition is stronger than the simple anticipatory version of the *wh*-Criterion, which, in languages like Japanese, requires only an S-Structure 'signal' to the effect that some phrase which lies arbitrarily deep within the DP that launched the NO will ultimately achieve CP-scope at LF. In particular, the scope of an exclamatory *wh*-phrase can only be marked by an NO coindexed with it; hence the inevitability of a Subjacency violation in the full version of (ii). I note in passing that the

NOTES

scopal requirement on exclamatory *wh*-phrases is also reflected in the fact that, in languages with overt *wh*-Movement, such phrases exhibit a sort of anti-Pied-Piping effect, as illustrated in (iii) (I am indebted for this observation to H. Obenauer, personal communication).

(iii) a. The boyfriend of which actress was invited to the party?
      b. *The boyfriend of who the hell was invited to the party?

One last remark. Under the assumption that Japanese (and Turkish) interrogatives require NO-Movement prior to S-Structure *and* that an exclamatory phrase must launch an NO, the observation made in n. 18 to the effect that these languages disallow multiple exclamatory phrases *in situ* can receive a reasonable explanation. All that needs to be assumed is that Japanese, just like English, disallows multiple displacements to [SPEC, C'] prior to S-Structure.

22 In section 2.4, I noted the existence of an analysis, put forward by certain writers (for example, Watanabe (1991)), according to which elements like the capitalized one in (i) are assigned to [SPEC, D'], much like the capitalized element in (ii).

(i) WHATEVER books
(ii) WHOSE books

Even under such an analysis, the account I outlined above in the text predicts that *wh*-FRs may exhibit phrases like (i), but not like (ii) in the specifier. The reason is that, in cases like (i), in contrast to cases like (ii), the *wh*-element contains no phi-specifications that conflict with those of the Head noun.

23 Jacobson (1988) cites marginally acceptable data like (i), which she attributes to John Richardson, and which appear to conflict with the claim just made.

(i) ?Whoever's book appears first will get drunk.

Jacobson/Richardson attribute the marginality of such data 'to some morphological problem with having a genitive form of *whoever*'. This proposed explanation is vitiated by the fact that (ii), where no obvious morphological problem exists, seems no better than (i).

(ii) ?Whatever man's book appears first will get drunk.

None the less, both (i) and (ii) seem somewhat better than (iii), and this fact does require an explanation.

(iii) *Whose book appears first will get drunk.

Safir (1986: § 5) observes that the raising of a *wh*-element within [SPEC, C'] out of a Pied-Piped phrase, which constitutes his own analysis of 'reconstruction' and typically applies at LF, is sometimes marginally possible in overt syntax. I suggest that the greater acceptability of (i)–(ii) is due to this kind of process, which is made easier by the semantically and intonationally added prominence of *-ever* forms. That this suggestion is on the right track is shown by the fact that (iv), where the embedded *wh*-phrase has clearly *not* been overtly reordered within [SPEC, C'], is completely out (on the intended reading), despite the presence of an *-ever* form.

(iv) *The book of whatever writer appears first will get drunk.

In a nutshell, the slightly improved status of (i)–(ii) with respect to (iii) is not due to the use of a form with *-ever per se*, but to the fact that such a form facilitates overt raising of a *wh*-phrase within [SPEC, C'], something which enables the raised phrase to transmit its features to CP at S-Structure, and to make possible in this way the identification of *pro* at that level.

24 Observe that the relation between a correlative and a *pro* argument must be different from the one that holds between an FR extraposed (to the right) and a (non-adjacent) *pro*-Head, as in (1.23e), reproduced (with modifications) in (i).

```
(i) Max hat pro empfangen, [wen Gretchen ihm geschickt hat].
```

The reason is that *pro* occurs in (i) in a position where it is not in general licensed (in German). To enable the FR to function as *local* antecedent of *pro*, it appears to be necessary to assume that *pro* is sister to a null category that functions as the trace of the FR.

25 In general, a governing functional X° assigns to its NP-complement (and thus, to *pro* in (1.109)) the Case it itself inherits from the extended maximal projection to which it belongs. It may, however, also act as a Case-assigner in its own right under certain circumstances (for an illustration, see Babby (1987)).

26 Some speakers of French find animate third person null P-objects more marginal than inanimate ones, but still distinctly better than their non-third person counterparts. For these speakers, the default specification must be [3PERSON, –ANIMATE].

27 In the literature, it is often assumed that *predicative* NOs are identified by their 'subject of predication' (see, for example, Browning (1987)). Under such a view, predicative NOs constitute a counterexample to Rizzi's linkage hypothesis, since the subject of predication is usually neither a governor of nor an assigner of Case to the NO. I do not believe, however, that the view in question is justified, and this, for the following reasons.

Predicative NOs, like NOs of other types, are identified *qua operators* by the governing C°. The fact that they may receive additional content, in particular, phi-features, from the subject of predication is a state of affairs which is independent of their *null* status; rather, it is a consequence of the *predicative* status of their CP, since predicates require a 'subject of predication'. This ability to pick up extra-content from a more distant element is no different from the fact that the relative pronoun *who* in OHRCs may pick up gender and/or number specifications from the OHRC's Head, or from the fact that *pro* in constructions of the kind illustrated in (1.111c) may pick up number specifications from a distant antecedent, as illustrated in (i).

```
(i)  Ce    collier /ces    colliers    m'  inspire(nt)    le  désir
     this necklace/these   necklaces   me-inspire.SG/PL   the desire
     de m' enfuir    avec pro.
     of me-run-away with
     'This/these necklace(s) make me feel like running
     away with (it/them).'
```

28 It is not in principle impossible for an FR with an NO to assign more than just [3PERSON] specifications to its *pro*-Head. This happens, for example, in Turkish FRs, which – presumably due to the nominal properties of the participial forms with which they are constructed – bear inherent number specifications, as illustrated by the following data (adapted from Kornfilt (1984: Ch. 5); plural specifications have been capitalized).

```
(i) a. [[Bu     hava-    da e deniz-e   gir-   en-      LER] pro]
        this weather-LOC   sea  -in enter-PARTIC-PL
```

```
            fazla    açıl-na-  sin(lar).
            too-much open-NEG- IMPER(PL)
```
'(Those) who go into the sea in such weather shouldn't swim too far.'

```
   b. [[Geçen yaz    ada-  da e gör-dük-   LER- in] pro]
         last   summer island-LOC  see-PARTIC-PL  -1.SG
         bu    yaz    gel- ne- di(LER).
         this summer come-NEG-PAST(3.PL)
```
'(Those) who(m) I saw on the island last summer didn't come this summer.'

That such specifications are inherent is shown by the fact that they interact with the external context of the FRC, while features inherited through Spec-Head agreement are 'deactivated' (see section 3.2.4). Thus, in (ib), the participle bears the plural suffix *-ler* and the [1PERSON, SG] suffix *-in*, which reflects agreement with an implied subject; as shown by the plural marking on the main verb, it is the plural marking on the participle that is syntactically active.

It is also of interest to note that the [3PERSON] default value of an FR does not apply if a different value can be explicitly provided. Literary German allows subject-resumptive pronouns of any person in free relative clauses introduced by pronouns from the *d*-set, as illustrated in (ii).

```
(ii)   [pro [die ihr      für ihre      Rechte kämpfet]]
             who you.PL. for your.PL. rights fight.2.PL.
           werdet      siegen.
           will.2.PL. prevail
```
'(You) who fight for your rights will prevail.'

In this class, *pro* must be assumed to receive [2PERSON, PL] specifications from the FR.

29 In view of the fact that the account in section 3.2 rules out configurations that violate the 'anti-Pied-Piping constraint', the following data from French (brought up in Hirschbühler (1976b: n. 3)), are *prima facie* problematic.

```
(i) a. Pierre a    joué   ce    concerto
       Pierre has played this concerto
       [sous la direction de qui tu voulais qu'  il le joue].
       under the direction of who you wanted that he him play
```
'Pierre has played this concerto under the baton of (the conductor) under whose baton you wanted him to play it.'

```
   b. Pierre s'    est assis [à   côté de qui
       Pierre REFL is  seated at side of who
       tu voulais qu' il s'    assoie].
       you wanted that he REFL seats
```
'Pierre sat down near (the person) near whom you wanted him to sit down.'

```
   c. Pierre a réussi [avec l'aide de qui
       tu espérais qu'il réussirait].
```

As Hirschbühler points out, the italicized sequences in the above data cannot simply be viewed as (lexically generated) complex Ps, because they are not frozen (they allow, for example, such variants as *sous ta direction* 'under your direction', *à tes côtés* 'at your side' and *avec ton aide* 'with your help', in contrast to sequences like *par rapport à* 'in relation to', which allow no comparable manipulation).

NOTES

However, the problem created by such data is more apparent than real. To see why, observe that such data cannot be freely constructed; for example, (ii) is not acceptable.

(ii) *Jean est sorti   avec la soeur de qui tu voulais
     Jean is gone-out with the sister of who you wanted
     qu' il sorte.
     that he go-out

I suggest that an important distinction between the italicized sequences in (i) and (ii) is that the former are semantically equivalent to uncontroversial Ps, in particular, to *sous* 'under', *près de* 'near', and *grâce à* 'thanks to' respectively, while the latter sequence has no such obvious prepositional counterpart. It thus seems likely that the sequences in (i), but not the one in (ii), have undergone reanalysis into complex Ps (cf. the widely assumed reanalysis of *make the claim* into [$_V$ make the claim] in constructions like *what did he make the claim that she saw?*).

In short, data like (i) are not really problematic for the theory of *pro* developed in preceding sections.

30 The assumption that *pro* may be adjectival, as well as nominal, derives some plausibility from the observation that, in certain languages, the *same* overt elements can serve as either nominal or adjectival pro-forms. Illustrations from French and German are provided below.

(i) a.   Ich mag *dieses Mädchen*, aber Peter mag *es* nicht.
         I   like this   girl   but Peter likes it not
         'I like this girl, but Peter does not like her.'
    b.   Die Männer sind *stark*, aber die Frauen sind *es* nicht.
         the men   are strong but the women are   it not
         'Men are strong, but women are not.'
    c.   Je connais *Jean*, mais Marie ne *le* connait pas.
         I know   Jean but Marie not him know   not
         'I know Jean, but Marie does not know him.'
    d.   Les hommes sont *forts*, mais les femmes ne *le* sont pas.
         the men   are strong but the women not him are not
         'Men are strong, but women are not.'

Interestingly, overt pro-PPs (for example, the *en* and *y* forms of French) are usually different from those that serve as pro-NPs/APs, which reinforces the objection to a PP-*pro* raised earlier in the text (see discussion of (1.112d) in section 3.4.4).

31 In the Introduction, it was stated that restrictive relative constructions are invariably nominal. If this generalization is correct, the reduced version of (1.124a) ought to be an amount construction. This prediction is confirmed by the fact that the construction at issue disallows stacking, as shown by the contrast between the full version of (ia) and (ib).

(i) a.   By 1999, I will have lived in every city that John has
         lived in (that Mary has lived in).
    b.   By 1999, I will have lived in every city that John has
         lived (*that Mary has lived).

32 For illustration of Hierarchy-controlled Kase-interaction effects of other sorts, see, for example, Harbert (1983) and Babby (1987).

33 This example uses the sequence *lo que* (literally: 'that which'), rather than the form *qué* found in interrogative constructions like (i), because the latter may not introduce FRCs, as shown in (ii).

NOTES

(i) ¿Qué haces?
     what do-you
     'What are you doing?'

(ii) a. *Que haces me sorprende.
         what do-you me surprises
     b. Lo que haces me sorprende.
         it that
        'What you are doing surprises me.'

One might object that the relative constructions in (iib) and (1.133b) are OHRCs, but this is not necessarily so, because the sequence *lo que* is (also) analysable as a complex relative pronoun (for justification, see (1.135) and n. 34), much like comparable sequences in Catalan (see Hirschbühler and Rivero (1981, 1983)). I note in passing that Romanian also has a complex relative pronoun, *ceeace* 'that which', which contrasts with true *Head+Relative Pronoun* sequences like *cei care* 'those who', as shown below:

(iii) a. Maria se ocupă [de ceeace te ocupi și tu].
         Maria REFL occupies of that-which REFL occupy and you
         'Maria takes (of that) of which you, too, take care.'
      b. Maria se ocupă [de cei *(de) care te ocupi și tu]
                           of those of whom
         'Maria takes care of those of whom you, too,
         take care.'

Example (iiia) is interpretable as a missing-P FRC, which indicates that *ceeace* is a relative pronoun; in (iiib), no preposition may be missing, because the bracketed string is an OHRC.

34 These data provide support for the view that that the sequence *lo que* is analysable as a complex relative pronoun (see n. 33), because the preposition *con* 'with' precedes, rather than follows, the subelement *lo*.

35 (1.132d) seems worse than (1.131d). Apparently, the juxtaposition of two prepositions such that the 'higher' fails to select the 'lower' (as, for example, in *he emerged from [under the table]*) is an additional acceptability-reducing factor. To the best of my knowledge, attested instances of constructions like (1.132d) or (1.29d) are exceedingly hard to find even in languages which allow counter-hierarchical non-matching.

36 A somewhat surprising result was that some informants more readily accepted non-matching *object* FRCs, such as (1.144)–(1.145), than non-matching *subject* FRCs, such as (1.143); no such tendency was detectable in respect to the Spanish data in (1.135) or the Romanian data in (1.136)–(1.137). I suspect this is due to the fact that non-matching subject FRCs are 'at a disadvantage' in German in that a 'better alternative' is available. Thus, while non-matching FRCs (which conform to the German-specific Kase-Hierarchy) tend to be somewhat marginal, as noted in the text, constructions like the full version of (i), which appear to exhibit a non-matching FRC in Left-Dislocation position, are judged impeccable by native informants.

(i) a. Wem   du   auch schreiben wirst,
        whom (DAT) you ever write   want
        (der)   wird dir nie   antworten.
        that-one will you never reply
        'Whoever you may want to write to, that one
        will never reply to you.'

NOTES

This is entirely expected if, as suggested in section 3.2.6, constructions of this type exhibit no FR at all, but rather some sort of correlative, where *pro* occurs as a complement to the demonstrative in the main clause, rather than as sister to the relative (so that the former, rather than the latter, is responsible for identifying *pro*). Now, what I am suggesting is that the reduced version of (i) (= (1.143a)) is less acceptable than might be expected because the minimally different full version is fully acceptable. No such effect arises in connection with data like those in (1.144)–(1.145), because no comparable 'repair' strategy is available.

37 Note that this type of situation does not arise in OHRCs, where the output of attraction processes is in no way 'preferable' to the corresponding input, as nothing needs to be 'identified'. As one may expect, attraction is accordingly typically optional in such cases.

38 Schwyzer provides no instances of possible but unrealized attraction, but Auberger (personal communication) informs me that constructions like (i) were possible, if infrequent.

(i) Kratō [*pro*(GEN) hon(ACC) phileis
     command-I   who   love-you
     'I command (those) whom you love.'

39 An issue which is addressed in section 4.4 is whether the tripartite characterization of language variation which follows immediately in the text needs to be viewed as *parametric* or can be *derived* from independent language-specific properties.

40 In these forms, [ANIMATE] is not entirely independent from [GENDER], as its '+' value coincides with the union of M and F, and its '−' value, with N.

41 These data are from Harms (1964). The lists are unfortunately incomplete, as Harms refrains from listing a number of Case forms, in particular, the translative, allative, ablative and abessive. His use of 'etc.' does, however, imply that such Case forms also exist.

42 Harbert (1983) writes that Russian is an unrestricted non-matching language, and marshalls this 'fact' in support of his proposal that FRC-external rich Case can effect Head-*pro* identification (Russian is reasonably rich in Case distinctions). He appears to be in error, however. The only example with which he supports his claim is one in which the FR is NON-FINITE (reproduced in (i)), and such FRCs are typically non-matching (see Chapter 5).

(i) On iščit [s   kem   poexat']
     'He seeks with whom to go.'

Finite FRCs must match in Russian everywhere, as Pesetzky (1982: § 4.4.1) notes; informant work of mine confirms this claim. I illustrate the point in (ii).

(ii) Ja vstretil *(tovo) [o   kom ty mne govoril]
     I met   that-one about whom you me spoke
     'I met *(the one) *about whom* you spoke to me.'

43 The only contemporary reflex of the earlier demonstrative-based relative pronouns is the relative *complementizer that*.

44 It may be of interest to compare the approach to irrealis FRCs developed in this section, which rests on the assumption that that they are 'bare' CPs, with the one put forward in Suñer (1984), which assumed that CP has a *pro*-sister (and thus, that they have the same gross structure as realis FRCs). To note just one consequence of this assumption, recall that Suñer proposed to account for the lack of matching effects in irrealis FRCs in terms of a particular feature of the

NOTES

filter in (1.39), namely, the stipulative limitation of its applicability to tensed (that is, realis) relatives. Now, the import of this stipulation, in conjunction with the fact that the only identifier Suñer proposes for Head-*pro* is the CP-internal *wh*-phrase, is that, in non-matching irrealis FRCs, *pro* remains unidentified. I do not find this an acceptable result, and therefore cannot countenance Suñer's analysis as a viable alternative to mine.

There is an additional assumption in Suñer's article which strikes me as worth refuting. It is clear from her discussion and choice of examples that she views Spanish *subjunctive* FRCs as falling together with *indicative*, rather than with *infinitival* FRCs. Since the subjunctive FRCs of Romanian were shown to fall together with infinitival, rather than with indicative FRCs, one may wonder whether these two rather closely related languages differ so radically in respect to their subjunctive FRCs. I believe that Suñer's position turns out to be wrong on closer examination.

The basis for Suñer's assumption was that certain non-matching subjunctive constructions, such as (i), have low acceptability.

```
(i) *Briana no  encuentra [con  quien tu       puedas      salir].
     Briana not finds      with who   you.SG   can(SUBJ)   go-out
    'Briana doesn't find (anyone) with whom you can go out.'
```

There are, however, a number of considerations which argue against interpreting this contrast in the way Suñer did. First, as noted above in the text, Spanish subjunctive FRCs pattern with infinitive, rather than with indicative constructions in respect to the (in)ability to bear the marker *a*. Second, a contrast comparable to the one invoked by Suñer exists in Romanian as well, as can be seen by comparing the reduced version of (1.167b) and (ii) of this note.

```
(ii) *Maria nu  are [cu  cine să poți       tu       pleca].
      Maria not has  with who  SP can.2.SG  you.SG   leave
     'Maria doesn't have (anyone) with whom you can leave.'
```

But as was seen in relation to (1.162), Romanian subjunctive FRCs systematically allow non-matching in constructions parallel to Suñer's (1.37), that is, where the FR's subject is controlled by the matrix subject, which indicates that the deviance of (ii) – and by implication, of (i) – cannot simply be blamed on the subjunctive mood of the verb.

I suggest that the key to the contrast between (1.37), (1.161) and (1.162) on the one hand and (i) and (ii) on the other can be partly traced to the fact that the former three, unlike the latter two, are control constructions. Control ensures an automatic 'relevance' of the content of the subordinate clause to the content of the matrix, which is apparently required in these constructions. But in (i) and (ii), the relevance of the content of the FR to the content of the matrix is far from obvious. That this must be the the reason for the low acceptability of (i) and (ii) is shown by the fact that the acceptability of non-control constructions can be substantially improved through a more judicious choice of words, as, for example, in (iii) and (iv), which are distinctly better than (i) and (ii), if perhaps somewhat more awkward than (v) and (vi).

```
(iii) (?)María no  tiene [con  quien su  hija
         Maria not has    with whom her daughter
         se    pueda    casar].
         REFL  can.SUBJ get-married
        'Maria does not have (someone) with whom her daughter
         could get married.'
```

NOTES

(iv) (?)Maria nu are [cu   cine să   se   mărite fiica   ei]
     Maria not have with whom SUBJ REFL marry   daughter her
     (same meaning as (iii))

(v) María no tiene [con quien casar(SUBJ) a   su   hija].
                                marry   ACC her daughter
     'Maria does not have (someone) to whom to marry her daughter.'

(vi) Maria$_i$ nu are [cu cine să   -și$_i$ mărite fiica].
                                SUBJ REFL marry daughter
     (same meaning as (v))

I thus do not see that data like (i) and (ii) seriously threaten the generalization that subjunctive FRCs fall together with infinitival, rather than with indicative FRCs.

STUDY II ROMANIAN DETERMINERS AS FUNCTIONAL CATEGORIES

1 Haider offers the following data in support of this point:

(i) a. Die Erfindung Edisons
        the invention Edison's
        'Edison's invention'
    b. Die Erfindung der Glühlampe
        the invention the lightbulb(GEN)
        'The invention of the lightbulb'
    c. *Die Erfindung Edisons   der Glühlampe
        the invention Edison's the lightbulb(GEN)
    d. Edisons Erfindung der Glühlampe
        Edison's invention the lightbulb(GEN)
        'Edison's invention of the lightbulb'

Note, however, that the ungrammaticality of (ic) is ambiguously attributable to the fact the rightmost genitive phrase fails to be adjacent to the Head N *and* to the fact that the Head N is called upon to assign GEN Case twice. It is for this reason that I have used the data in (2.6), where such ambivalence does not arise.

2 The Head N in CSs sometimes exhibits a phonological realization different from the one it has elsewhere (in (2.10b), it has an additional final *t*). These phonological effects may be viewed as triggered by an encliticized abstract D (see below in the text).

3 In general, the (in)definiteness of a CS construction is a function of the (in)definiteness of its (abstract) genitive constituent.

In Ritter (1988), this state of affairs is given a rather inelegant and not fully coherent account along the following lines: the D° of the CS construction may be filled in D-Structure with either the null GEN assigner, or *-ha*, or both, or none. When this node is doubly filled, *-ha* moves downwards and cliticizes on the genitive constituent. This account not only tacitly presupposes an *ad hoc* deletion rule of one token of *-ha* when the genitive constituent is already endowed with one, it also fails to explain why CS constructions with a surface token of *-ha* on the genitive constituent do not also exhibit an indefinite reading, which is expected under a D-Structure without *-ha* under the highest D° and with *-ha* on the genitive constituent; furthermore, it fails to explain why the genitive constituent cannot be construed as indefinite when it bears a surface

NOTES

token of -*ha*, which, according to the proposed account, may have been transferred by downwards movement.

A considerably improved account was put forward in Ritter (1991), where the D° of the CS construction is unspecified for definiteness and acquires (in)definiteness specifications from the genitive constituent. The mechanism for (in)definiteness transmission is Spec-Head agreement between the genitive phrase, which occurs in [SPEC, N'] at D-Structure, and N°; subsequent movement of N to D makes it possible for N to convey its acquired (in)definiteness specifications to DP. This account is consistent with the proposal made in section 3.2.4 to the effect that specifications inherent in an Extended Projection have primacy over 'immigrant' features (see discussion of (1.107)); since the D of the CS construction is taken to be unspecified for (in)definiteness at D-Structure, 'immigrant' features face no competition, and can thus be conveyed to the host Extended Projection.

4   It may be noted that this state of affairs is not universal. For example, Hungarian 'possessor' constructions exhibit a POSS morpheme and overt agreement with the 'possessor' on the 'possessed' N, as well as NOM (rather than GEN) Case on the 'possessor' (as illustrated in (i)). This situation is strikingly reminiscent of clausal contexts, where V bears Tense and Agreement morphology and the subject exhibits NOM Case. Presumably, Case is here assigned by POSS which has raised to AGR, much as clausal subjects receive Case from Tense that has raised to AGR.

```
(i)  a      te(NOM)   vendég-e  -d
     the    thou      guest     -POSS-2.SG.
     'thy guest'
```

5   A very general process which deletes the first of a sequence of two vowels under circumstances which need not concern us here accounts for the ungrammaticality of the full versions of (2.17a), (2.17b) and (2.19b). The vowel which precedes the realization of -*L* in (2.16a, b) belongs to the stem, and drops when -*L* is not present. Finally, a process which drops word-final *l* before the masculine plural marker is responsible for the ungrammaticality of the full version of (2.18a)

6   Prenominal genitives of the kind illustrated in this example are uncommon in current standard colloquial usage, and have a literary flavour. An exception to this generalization is formed by interrogative and relative pronouns, which are perfectly natural in all styles. For example, (2.26i) is at least as colloquially acceptable as (i), where the genitive relative pronoun appears postnominally.

```
(i)   Regele portretu-l căruia atîrnă pe perete.
                    -L whose
      'The king whose portrait is hanging on the wall'.
```

7   The element glossed in this way, which is derived from the sequence *a-a*, is reduced to a single *a* by a process of vowel deletion that has already been alluded to (see n. 5).

8   To eliminate any suspicion of a definite specification on *a+L*, observe that *a+L* is possible when neither the 'possessed' nor the 'possessor' nouns head definite phrases, as illustrated in (i).

```
(i)   Un portret al unui rege.
      'A portrait of a    king.'
```

9   Example (2.29a) constitutes an adaptation to the framework assumed here of

NOTES

Dobrovie-Sorin's representation in her (6.54), in ways which do not affect the thrust of her proposals.

10 There is one construction where *a+L* may receive affixal Case. The construction is of the general type illustrated in (2.26g), but the 'possessor' must be a plural masculine definite pronoun and the implied 'possessed' element must be construed roughly as 'folks', in the sense of relatives (the M.PL. markings on the 'possessor' are due to agreement with the implied 'possessed' entity). As shown below, any deviation from the restrictions just listed results in ungrammaticality.

(i) Trimite salutări *al-or tăi*   (*părinți).
    Send   greetings al-DAT your.M.PL. parents
    'Send greetings to your folks/parents.'

(ii) a. *Trimite salutări *al-ui tău/ al-ei tale/ al-or tale.*
                          your.M.SG/ your.F.SG./ your.F.PL.
     b. Asta aparține *al-or tăi*
        this belongs al-DAT your.M.PL.
        'This belongs to your folks/*shoes, etc.'

I suggest that *ai tăi* 'your folks' is a set expression with idiosyncratic syntax.

11 I wish to note that my neutralization proposal is unrelated to the fact that the possessive pronouns which are not historically derived from Latin *ille* agree with their 'possessed' Ns in Romance languages and are usually called 'adjectives' in traditional grammar books. My proposal applies to the pronouns derived from *ille* as well, which do not agree with possessed Ns (for example, *ei* 'her' may be substituted for *tăi* in (2.36a) with preservation of grammaticality), and it does not apply to *a+L*-introduced nominals, even though *a+L* does agree with a possessed N; in connection with the latter point, note the ill-formedness of (ii), which purports to convey the meaning of (i).

(i) Trei viteji ostași   *ai regelui.*
    three brave soldiers a+L king-the.GEN
    'the brave soldiers of the king'

(ii) *Trei *ai regelui* viteji ostași.

12 That (at least restrictive) modifiers of a lexical Head are normally adjoined to some perfect (in Grimshaw's sense, that is, 'non-extended') projection of that lexical Head seems to have been assumed in every pertinent study known to me (see, for example, Pollock (1989) and Haider (1987)).
13 Note that neutralized *jeder*, in contrast to neutralized 'possessor' pronouns, does not head an Extended Projection distinct from that of N. This indicates that weak inflection is not, strictly speaking, a property of non-initial *lexical* adjectives, but rather a property of non-initial Heads that fail to be marked [−V].
14 Another comparable case is that of the inserted *-t-* in certain auxiliary inversion contexts in French, for the purpose of avoiding two consecutive vowels (an illustration is provided below).

(i) Il a   mangé.
    He has eaten.

(ii) A *(-t-) il mangé?
     Has   he eaten?

15 The assumption that CEL can take PP complements implies that the PP is neutralized for functional/lexical status, for reasons made clear in section 1.4.1.

244

NOTES

16 In colloquial speech, the use of *lui* is sometimes extended to feminine forms in -*a*, yielding expressions like (i).

(i) Frate -le lui   Maria.
    brother-L L-GEN Maria
    'Maria's brother'

This phenomenon is probably the reflection of a tendency to regularize personal proper names, in the sense that names in -*a* are analysed as *not* bearing -*L*, just like all other personal names. Observe that names of countries, which *must* bear -*L* (see section 2.0), never give rise to forms like (i); for example, (ii) has no counterpart like (iii) in any register.

(ii) Victori-a Franţ   -ei.
     victory-L France(-L)-GEN
     'France's victory'

(iii) *Victoria lui Franţa.

17 One initial problem raised by adnominal APs is that there can be an arbitrarily large number of them, and it is unclear how to ensure that an exactly equal number of checking features are generated on AGR. A possible way out of this difficulty might be to allow stacked APs to be treated like coordinations, so that a single checking feature on AGR can check them all across the board.

18 I do not, at the moment, see an interesting way of accounting for the fact that the adjacency restrictions on Hebrew and Romanian 'possessors', as well as on German GEN phrases licensed by N (see (2.6)), have a strict character, while the restrictions on post-nominal APs and English verbal objects are lifted for 'heavy' constituents.

STUDY III ON NULL OPERATORS IN ROMANIAN

1 The Hungarian data were kindly provided to me by J. Horvath.
2 While *wie* is clearly a *wh*-element in (3.17d), in view of Pied-Piping, it is not obvious that it has this status in (3.17c), since interrogative *wie* may not be separated from its complement, as shown in (i).

(i) a. Wie groß ist er?
        how tall is he
    b. *Wie ist er groß?

Observe that *wie* also occurs in reduced comparatives, as shown in (ii); presumably, *wie* is a preposition here.

(ii) Er ist so groß wie du.
     He is as tall as you.

Furthermore, the comparative clause in (3.17d) is not introduced by any overt preposition (that is, 'subordinating conjunction'). It is thus possible that equative comparative clauses are generated with the introductory *preposition wie*, which is presumably deleted when immediately followed by the *wh*-operator *wie*, to avoid haplology (presumably, this happens in (3.17d)). As for (3.17c), one may assume, in view of (ib), that it utilizes an NO, *wie* being a preposition. If so, the distributional pattern of overt/null operators in German comparatives is slightly more complex than envisaged in the text, namely, NOs only in non-equatives, and either NOs or overt operators in equatives.

NOTES

3 It is possible that German also has headed (realis) amount relative constructions of the kind studied by Carlson (1977) in respect to English. A possible illustration is provided by constructions like (i), which, according to Engel (1988, p. 662), contrast with constructions like (ii) in the following way:

(i) Das Spannendste, [was ich je   erlebt   habe].
     the most-exciting what I   ever experienced have
     'The most exciting thing (that) I have ever experienced.'

(ii) Das Spannendste, [das ich je   erlebt   habe].
     the most-exciting which I   ever experienced have
     'The most exciting thing which I have ever experienced.'

Voraussetzung für die relative Verwendung von was *ist, daß an eine unbestimmte Größe bzw. Menge gedacht wird. Sind Größe bzw. Menge und deren Elemente hingegen bekannt und klar umrissen, so kann stets . . . auch das reguläre Relativpronomen verwendet werden* ('a precondition for using *was* as a relative pronoun is that one have in mind indefinite amounts or sets. If amounts or sets and their members are known and clearly defined . . . the regular relative pronoun can also be used'). It seems to me that the first type of interpretation is more naturally rendered into English by using an NO, rather than a *wh* relative pronoun, and I have indicated this in the English translations of the above examples. In view of the fact that English amount OHRCs require the use of NOs (see the Introduction to the first Study), one may suspect that (i) is an amount construction and (ii), a restrictive one.

If this conjecture is correct, the constructions in (i) and (ii) ought to, respectively, disallow and allow stacking. Unfortunately, the informants to whom I had access did not seem to accept stacked relatives in general. Be this as it may, (i) and (ii) have no counterparts with NOs. In the event that (i) is an amount construction and amount OHRCs require the use of *was*, then we have an additional instance of a German relative clause which must be formed with an overt operator.

4 There exist contexts in which an RP may not be used, in particular, when the 'relativized' element is the direct object of a verb in the supine mood, and this because supines (and past participles in general), may not host clitic pronouns in Romanian. In such cases, the acceptability of relativization without RPs 'into' contexts like those of (3.30d)–(3.30e) appears to be enhanced, as can be seen by contrasting the reduced versions of (i) and (ii) with those of (i') and (ii') respectively (the vowel between square brackets in the primed examples is suppressed in the full versions, due to the vowel reduction rule mentioned in n. 5 of the second study.

(i)   Cartea ce pretinzi   că   ai   terminat
      book-L ce claim.2.SG that   have.2.SG finished
      de citit ??(*-o) acum o jumătate de oră ...
         read(SUP) her now a half   of hour
      'The book you claim to have finished reading half an hour ago ...'

(i') Cartea ce pretinzi   că   ai   terminat
      book.L ce claim.2.SG that   have.2.SG finished
      s[ă] *(?-o) citeşti acum o jumătate de oră ...
      SUBJ her   read   now a half   of hour
      'The book you claim to have finished reading half an hour ago ...'

(ii) Cartea ce ai   discutat e fără   măcar
      book-L ce have.2.SG discussed without even

246

NOTES

```
         a    fi terminat de citit    ??(*-o)...
         INF. be finished      read(SUP) her
         'The book that you discussed without even to have finished
          reading ...'
(ii')  Cartea ce ai       discutat e fără    măcar
       book-L ce have.2.SG discussed without even
         a    fi terminat s[ă] *(?-o) citeşti...
         INF. be finished SUBJ her    read
         'The book that you discussed without even to have finished
          reading...'
```

5 One instance where this factor led to confusion is in Dobrovie-Sorin (1987: § 1.3.4), where it is claimed that *ce* in constructions like those of (3.29)–(3.30) is a *wh*-element on the grounds that it uncontroversially has this status elsewhere. In Dobrovie-Sorin (1990: § 1.4.2), it is admitted, on the basis of remarks made in Horvath and Grosu (1987), that a complementizer analysis constitutes an alternative possibility, but no choice between the two alternatives is made. I hope to have shown in this section that a choice can be made, and in which way.

6 The supine is characterized by the 'prepositional complementizer' *de* (which drops after a P), and by the absence of periphrastic constructions, as well as by the inability to bear negation or clitics.

In addition to the constructions in (3.41), supines also occur without object 'gaps', for example, in control constructions and as (presumably extraposed) complements, as illustrated in (i) and (ii).

```
(i)  Maria a    terminat de mîncat.
     Maria has  finished      eaten
     'Maria has finished eating.'

(ii) E    recomandabil de citit toată cartea.
     is advisable          read all   book-L
     'It is advisable to read the entire book.'
```

For further details on the Romanian supine, see Grosu and Horvath (1987).

7 She in fact uses the term 'participe passé', rather than 'participe passif', but it is clear that she means the latter, because she imputes to the kind of participle she has in mind the property of not being able to assign Case to its direct object, something which is clearly inapplicable to active past participles, in view of acceptable data like the following:

```
(i)  Maria a    mîncat o banană.
     Maria has eaten   a banana.
```

8 Chomsky (1981: § 5.4) motivates a restructuring account of English *tough* constructions which ultimately deprives the 'gap' of Case. According to his proposal, the adjective and its right context up to the 'gap' are reanalysed as a complex adjective, and adjectives do not assign Case (in English). This analysis, however, is crucially motivated by, and relies on the fact that the matrix subject of *tough*-constructions is a non-theta position, and can thus form an A-chain with the object 'gap', thereby enabling the latter to be (re-)interpreted as an anaphor. Now, such an analysis can be applied to (3.41a), but certainly not to (3.41b), because the matrix subject is a theta-position, so that A-chain formation would violate the Theta-Criterion. Similar observations apply to adjectival constructions with a thematic subject, such as the one in (i).

NOTES

(i) Mîncarea e gata de pus   pe masă.
    food-L is ready of put(SUP) on table
    'The food is ready to put on the table.'

I also note that Chomsky's analysis of English *tough*-constructions does not really do away with NOs, since it assumes that the 'gap' arises through NO-Movement prior to reanalysis.

To sum up, Chomsky's proposals do not ensure an NO-free analysis even for constructions like (3.41a), and certainly not for constructions like (3.41b).

9 It is furthermore possible, although, as far as I can see, not easily demonstrable, that the kind of construction illustrated in (3.46), that is, one where the proposed NO-variable dependency spans two supine clauses, be subject to additional limitations, in particular, limitations on the choice of the matrix verb. Such limitations have been signalled in respect to two-clause infinitival dependencies in the *tough*-constructions of Spanish, Italian and French; illustrations taken from Aissen and Perlmutter (1976), Rizzi (1978) and Kayne (1989) respectively are provided in (i)–(iii).

(i) a. Estas galletas son casi   imposibles
        these cookies are almost impossible
        de dejar de comer.
        to-stop to-eat
        'These cookies are almost impossible to stop eating.'
   b. *Sinfonías como esa son fáciles
       symphonies like that are easy
       de soñar con componer.
       to-dream with to-compose
       'Symphonies like that one are easy to dream of composing.'

(ii) a. Questa canzone è facile da cominciare a cantare.
       this song   is easy   to-begin   to-sing
       'This song is easy to begin to sing.'
   b. *Questo lavoro è facile da promettere
       this work is easy to promise
       di finire per domani.
       to-finish for tomorrow
       'This piece of work is easy to promise
       to finish by tomorrow.'

(iii) a. ?Ce livre sera   impossible à commencer
        this book will-be impossible   to-begin
        à lire   aujourd'hui.
        to-read today
        'This book will be impossible to begin to read today.'
    b. *Ce genre de livre est facile à promettre de lire.
       this kind of book is easy   to-promise   to-read
       'This kind of book is easy to promise to read.'

Note that the matrix verbs of the two-clause supine dependencies in (3.46), namely, *a începe* 'to begin', *a continua* 'to continue' and *a termina* 'to finish', are counterparts to Western Romance verbs that may occur in the matrices of two-clause infinitival dependencies in *tough*-constructions. Whether the supinical two-clause dependencies of Romanian exhibit constraints comparable to those illustrated in (i)–(iii) is, however, difficult to investigate because the above verbs seem to be, together with some synonyms, the only ones which take supine

248

complements; furthermore, plausible two-clause dependencies consisting of a supine and an infinitival complement seem, as far as I can tell, impossible to construct, due to the rarity of infinitival complements in conjunction with other factors that I will not detail here.

Be this as it may, the existence of contrasts like those in (i)–(iii) does not necessarily mean that the dependencies in the (a) subcases are monoclausal, as Aissen and Perlmutter (1976) and Rizzi (1978) maintain. These writers propose that the infinitives in data like (ia) and (iia) undergo 'reanalysis' into a single complex Verb, something which enables them to also serve as context for the application of 'Clitic Climbing'. But Kayne (1989) points out that Clitic Climbing does not apply over infinitival sequences like the one in (iiia), and proposes an analysis for 'long Clitic Climbing' and 'long *tough*-dependencies' that does not appeal to reanalysis.

The problem noted by Kayne with respect to a reanalysis account of the restrictions on *tough*-constructions and on Clitic Climbing also surfaces in Romanian. Thus, Clitic Climbing is possible out of a 'bare' infinitival complement, which does not have functional Extended Projections, or out of the passive participle complement to the auxiliary *a fi* 'to be', which also lacks functional Extended Projections, but not out of supine complements, which do have (at least) one functional Extended Projection, that is, CP (recall that *de* is a complementizer). These facts are illustrated in (iv)–(vi) ((iv) also shows the contrastive behaviour of subjunctives, which do have functional Extended Projections, and of 'bare' infinitives, which do not).

```
(iv) a.  Nu  pot         să  -l_i  văd     e_i.
         not can.1.SG SUBJ-him see.1.SG
     b. *Nu -l_i  pot         să  văd     e_i.
         not-him can.1.SG SUBJ see.1.SG
     c.  Nu -l_i  pot         vedea   e_i.
         not-him can.1.SG see(INF)
         'I can't see him.'

(v)  Fiindu-i_i           trimisă e_i ieri,      scrisoarea
     being -him/her(DAT) sent         yesterday  letter-L
     nu -i_i       va  ajunge decît săptămîna viitoare.
     not-him/her will get    than  week-L    next
     'Being sent to him/her yesterday, the letter will not
     reach him/her before next week.'

(vi) (*Le-)    am          terminat de dat       atenţie
     them(DAT) have.1 finished of given(SUP) attention
     acestor     probleme.
     these(DAT)  problems
     'I am finished with paying attention to these problems.'
```

10 Her claim may be viewed as limited to NOs that are *moved* to [SPEC, C'] (she admits the existence of RP constructions, but does not apparently assume that they employ NOs).

BIBLIOGRAPHY

Abney, S. (1987) 'The English Noun Phrase in its Sentential Aspect', unpublished Ph.D. Dissertation, MIT.
Adams, M. (1987) 'From Old French to the Theory of Pro-drop', *Natural Language and Linguistic Theory* 5, 1, 1–32.
Aissen, J. and D. Perlmutter (1976) 'Clause Reduction in Spanish', in H. Thompson, K. Whistler, V. Edge, J.J. Jaeger, R. Javkin, M. Petruck, C. Smeall and R.D.V. Valin Jnr (eds), *Proceedings of the Second Annnual Meeting of the Berkeley Linguistic Society*, University of California, Berkeley, pp. 1–30.
Allen, C. (1980) 'Movement and Deletion in Old English', *Linguistic Inquiry* 11, 2, 261–324.
Aoun, J., N. Hornstein, D. Lightfoot and A. Weinberg (1987) 'Two Types of Locality', *Linguistic Inquiry* 18, 4, 537–78.
Ariel, M. (1990) *Accessing Noun-Phrase Antecedents*, London and New York: Routledge.
Arouoff, M. (1976) *Word Formation in Generation Grammar*, Linguistic Enquiry Monograph No. 1, Cambridge, Mass.: MIT Press.
Authier, J.M. (1992) 'Arbitrary Null Object Languages in a Parametric Theory of Linguistic Variation', in A.J. Lakarra and J.O. de Urbina (eds), *Syntactic Theory and Basque Syntax*, Supplements of the Annuario del Seminario de Filologia Vasca 'Julio de Urquijo', *International journal of Basque Linguistics and Philology* XXVII.
Babby, L.H. (1987) 'Case, Prequantifiers and Discontinuous Agreement in Russian', *Natural Language and Linguistic Theory* 5, 1, 91–138.
Baltin, M.R. (1987) 'Do Antecedent-Contained Deletions Exist?' *Linguistic Inquiry* 18, 4, 579–95.
Bayer, J. (1984) 'COMP in Bavarian Syntax', *The Linguistic Review* 3, 209–74.
Bever, T.G. and D.T. Langendoen (1971) 'A Dynamic Model of the Evolution of Language', *Linguistic Inquiry* 2, 4, 433–63.
Bever, T.G. and D.T. Langendoen (1972) 'The Interaction of Speech Performance and Grammatical Structure in the Evolution of Language', in R.P. Stockwell and R.K.S. Macaulay (eds), *Linguistic Change and Generative Theory*, Bloomington, Ind.: Indiana University Press.
Borer, H. (1984) *Parametric Syntax*, Dordrecht: Foris.
—— (1988) 'Morphology in the Lexicon and in the Syntax', paper presented at the Congress 'The Chomskyan Turn', Jerusalem, Israel.
—— (1989) 'Anaphoric AGR', in Jaeggli, O. and K.J. Safir (eds) *The Null Subject Parameter*, Dordrecht: Kluwer.
Bresnan, J. (1977) 'Variables in the Theory of Transformations', in P. Culicover, T. Wasow and A. Akmajian (eds) *Formal Syntax*, New York: Academic Press 157–96.

Bresnan, J. and J. Grimshaw (1978) 'The Syntax of Free Relatives in English', *Linguistic Inquiry* 9, 3, 331–91.
Browning, M. (1987) 'Null Operator Constructions', unpublished Ph.D. dissertation, Cambridge, Mass.: MIT.
Carlson, G.N. (1977) 'Amount Relatives', *Language* 53, 3, 520–42.
Chomsky, N.A. (1973) 'Conditions on Transformations', in S. Anderson and P. Kiparsky (eds) *Festschrift for Morris Halle*, New York: Holt, Rinehart & Winston.
—— (1977) 'On *wh* Movement', in P. Culicover, T. Wasow and A. Akmajian (eds), *Formal Syntax*, New York: Academic Press, 71–132.
—— (1981) *Lectures on Government and Binding*, Dordrecht: Foris.
—— (1982), *Some Concepts and Consequences of the Theory of Government and Binding*, Cambridge, Mass.: MIT Press.
—— (1986a) *Barriers*, Cambridge, Mass.: MIT Press.
—— (1986b) *Knowledge of Language: Its Nature, Origin and Use*, New York: Praeger.
—— (1991) 'Some Notes on Economy of Derivation and Representation', in R. Freidin (ed.), *Principles and Parameters in Comparative Grammar*, Cambridge, Mass.: MIT Press.
—— (1992) *A Minimalistic Programme for Linguistic Theory*, MIT Occasional Papers in Linguistics No. 1, Cambridge, Mass.: MIT Press.
Chomsky, N.A. and H. Lasnik (1977) 'Filters and Control', *Linguistic Inquiry* 8, 3, 425–504.
—— and —— (forthcoming) 'Principles and Parameters Theory', to appear in J. Jacobs, A. von Stechow, W. Sternfeld and T. Venneman (eds), *Syntax: An International Handbook of Contemporary Research*, Berlin: de Gruyter.
Cinque, G. (1990) *Types of A' Dependencies*, Cambridge, Mass.: MIT Press.
Cole, P. (1987a) 'The Structure of Internally-headed Relative Clauses', *Natural Language and Linguistic Theory* 5, 2, 277–302.
—— (1987b) 'Null Objects in Universal Grammar', *Linguistic Inquiry* 18, 4, 597–612.
Corblin, F. (1991) 'Are Pronouns Determiners?', Centre National de Recherche Scientifique and Université de Paris 7.
Dobrovie-Sorin, C. (1987) '*Syntaxe du Roumain*', Thèse de Doctorat d'Etat, Université de Paris 7.
—— (1990) 'Clitic Doubling, *Wh*-Movement and Quantification in Romanian', *Linguistic Inquiry* 21, 351–97.
—— (1993) *The Syntax of Romanian*, The Hague: Mouton.
Emonds, J. (1976) *A Transformational Approach to English Syntax: Root, Structure-Preserving and Local Transformations*, New York: Academic Press.
Engel, U. (1988) *Deutsche Grammatik*, Heidelberg: Julius Groos Verlag.
Fanselow, G. (1991) *Minimale Syntax*, published as *Groninger zur germanistischen Linguistik* Nr. 32.
Farkas, D.F. (1987) 'DO *pro* in Hungarian', in I. Kenesei (ed.), *Approaches to Hungarian, Volume 2: Theories and Analyses*, Szeged: JATE, 191–211.
Farrell, P. (1990) 'Null Objects in Brazilian Portuguese', *Natural Language and Linguistic Theory* 8, 3, 325–46.
Fukui, N. and M. Speas (1986) 'Specifiers and Projection', *MIT Working Papers in Linguistics* 8, 128–72, Cambridge, Mass.: MIT Press.
Gil, D. (1987) 'Definiteness, Noun-Phrase Configurationality and the Count–Mass Distinction', in E.J. Reuland and A. ter Meulen (eds) *The Representation of (In)definiteness*, Cambridge, Mass.: MIT Press.
—— (1988) 'Georgian Reduplication and the Domain of Distributivity', *Linguistics* 26, 6, 1039–65.
Grewendorf, G. and C. Poletto (1990) 'Die Cleft-Konstruktion im Deutschen,

Englischen und Italienischen', in G. Fanselow and S. Felix (eds), *Strukturen und Merkmale syntaktischer Kategorien*, Tübingen: Gunter Narr Verlag.

Grimshaw, J. (1979) 'Complement Selection and the Lexicon', *Linguistic Inquiry* 10, 2, 279–326.

—— (1987) 'Subdeletion', *Linguistic Inquiry* 18, 4, 659–69.

—— (1991) 'Extended Projection', Brandeis University MS.

Groos, A. and H. van Riemsdijk (1981) 'Matching Effects in Free Relatives: A Parameter of Core Grammar', in A. Belletti, L. Brandi and L. Rizzi (eds), *Theory of Markedness in Generative Grammar*, Pisa: Scuola Normale Superiore.

Grosu, A. (1988a) 'On the distribution of Genitive Phrases in Romanian', *Linguistics* 26, 6, 931–49.

—— (1988b) 'On an Asymmetry in the Distribution of Island Constraints', *Lingua* 74, 167–84.

—— (1989) 'Pied-Piping and the Matching Parameter', *The Linguistic Review* 6, 1, 41–58.

—— (1992) 'Une Etude de *celui* et de *cel* dans le cadre de la Théorie de la Projection Etendue', *Travaux de Linguistique* 24, 5–19.

Grosu, A. and J. Horvath (1987) 'On Non-Finiteness in Extraction Constructions', *Natural Language and Linguistic Theory* 5, 2. 181–96.

Grosu, A. and S. Thompson (1977) 'Constraints on the Distribution of NP-Clauses', *Language* 53, 1, 104–51.

Guéron, J. (1980) 'The Syntax and Semantics of PP Extraposition', *Linguistic Inquiry* 11, 4, 637–78.

Guéron, J. and R. May (1984) 'Extraposition and Logical Form', *Linguistic Inquiry* 15, 1, 1–31.

Haegemann, L. and R. Zanuttini (1991) 'Negative Heads and Negative Concord', paper presented at GLOW, Leiden, The Netherlands.

Haider (1987) 'Die Struktur der Deutschen NP', *Zeitschrift für Sprachwissenschaft* 7, 32–59.

Harbert, W. (1983) 'On the Nature of the Matching Parameter', *The Linguistic Review* 2, 3, 237–84.

—— (1990) 'Gothic Relative Clauses and Syntactic Theory', paper presented at the First Berkeley/Michigan Roundtable on Germanic Linguistics (subsequently published in I. Rauch, G.F. Carr and R.L. Kyes (eds) (1992) *On Germanic Linguistics: Issues and Methods*, Berlin: Mouton de Gruyter.

Harms, E. (1964) *The Structure of Finnish*, The Hague: Mouton.

Heim, I. (1982) 'The Semantics of Definite and Indefinite Noun Phrases', unpublished Ph.D. Dissertation, University of Massachusetts, Amherst.

Hirschbühler, P. (1976a) 'Two Analyses of Free Relatives in French', unpublished paper, University of Massachusetts, Amherst.

—— (1976b) 'Headed and Headless Free Relatives: A Study in French and Classical Greek', unpublished paper, University of Massachusetts, Amherst.

Hirschbühler, P. and M.L. Rivero (1981) 'Catalan Restrictive Relatives: Core and Periphery', *Language* 57, 3, 591–625.

—— and —— (1983) 'Remarks on Free Relatives and Matching Phenomena', *Linguistic Inquiry* 14, 3, 505–19.

Horvath, J. and Grosu, A. (1987) 'On the notion "Head": Evidence from Free Relatives and Interrogatives', *Theoretical Linguistics* 14, 1, 35–64.

Huang, C.-T. (1984) 'On the Distribution and Reference of Empty Pronouns', *Linguistic Inquiry* 15, 4, 531–74.

Jackendoff, R. (1977) *X-bar Syntax*, Cambridge, Mass.: MIT Press.

Jacobson, P. (1988) 'The Syntax and Semantics of Free Relatives', paper presented at the LSA Winter Meeting, New Orleans.

Jaeggli, O. and K.J. Safir (1989a) *The Null Subject Parameter*, Dordrecht: Kluwer.
—— and —— (1989b) 'The Null Subject Parameter and Parametric Theory', in Jaeggli and Safir (1989a).
Johnson, K. (1991) 'Object Positions', *Natural Language and Linguistic Theory* 9, 4, 577–636.
Kayne, R.S. (1989) 'Null Subjects and Clitic Climbing', in O. Jaeggli and K. J. Safir (eds), *The Null Subject Parameter*, Dordecht: Kluwer.
Kornfilt, J. (1984) 'Case Marking, Agreement and Empty Categories in Turkish', unpublished Ph.D. thesis, Harvard University.
Lamontagne G. and L. Travis (1986) 'The Syntax of Adjacency', *McGill Working Papers in Linguistics* 4.2, Montreal: McGill University Press.
Larson, R.K. (1985) 'Bare-NP Adverbs', *Linguistic Inquiry* 16, 4, 595–621.
—— (1987) 'Missing Prepositions and the Analysis of English Free Relative Clauses', *Linguistic Inquiry* 18, 2, 239–66.
Lasnik, H. and M. Saito (1984) 'On the Nature of Proper Government', *Linguistic Inquiry* 15, 2, 235–90.
Longobardi, G. (1991) 'Extraction from NP and the Proper Notion of Head Government', in A. Giorgi and G. Longobardi (eds), *The Syntax of Noun Phrases*, Cambridge: Cambridge University Press.
Mallinson, G. (1986) *Romanian*, London: Croom Helm.
May, R. (1985) *Logical Form: Its Structure and Derivation*, Cambridge, Mass.: MIT Press.
Milsark, G. (1977) 'Toward an Explanation of Certain Peculiarities of the Existential Construction in English', *Linguistic Analysis* 3, 1–30.
Paul, H. (1904) *Mittelhochdeutsche Grammatik*, Tübingen: Max Niemeyer Verlag.
Paul, H. (1920) *Deutsche Grammatik*, Tübingen: Max Niemeyer Verlag.
Pesetzky, D. (1987) '*Wh*-in-Situ: Movement and Unselective Binding', in E.J. Reuland and A. ter Meulen (eds), *The Representation of (In)definiteness*, Cambridge, Mass.: MIT Press.
Pittner, K. (1991) 'Freie Relativsätze und die Kasushierarchie', MS., University of Stuttgart.
Pollock, J.Y. (1989) 'Verb Movement, Universal Grammar and the Structure of IP', *Linguistic Inquiry* 20, 3, 365–424.
—— (1993) 'Opérateurs nuls, *dont*, questions indirectes et théorie de la quantification', in L. Tasmowsky and A. Zribi-Hertz (eds), *Hommages à Nicolas Ruwet*, Ghent: Communication and Cognition.
Reinhart, T. (1981) 'A Second COMP Position', in A. Belletti L. Brandi and L. Rizzi (eds), *Theory of Markedness in Generative Grammar*, Pisa: Scuola Normale Superiore.
—— (1987) 'Specifiers and Operator-Binding', in E. Reuland and A. ter Meulen (eds.), *The Representation of (In)definiteness*, Cambridge, Mass.: MIT Press.
van Riemsdijk, H. (1990) 'Circumpositions', in H. Pinkster and I. Genée (eds), *Unity in Diversity: Papers presented to Simon Dick on his 50th Birthday*, Dordrecht: Foris.
—— (1991) 'Complements, Adjuncts and Adjacency in Phrase Structure', MS., Tilburg University.
Ritter, E. (1988) 'A Head-Movement Approach to Construct-State Noun Phrases', *Linguistics* 26, 6, 909–29.
—— (1991) 'Evidence for Number as a Nominal Head', paper presented at GLOW, Leiden, The Netherlands.
Rivero, M.-L. (1991) 'Long Head Movement and Negation', paper presented at GLOW, Leiden, The Netherlands.
Rizzi, L. (1978) 'A Restructuring Rule in Italian Syntax', in S.J. Keyser (ed.), *Recent Transformational Studies in European Languages*, Cambridge, Mass.: MIT Press, 113–58.
—— (1982) *Issues in Italian Syntax*, Dordrecht: Foris.

—— (1986) 'Null Objects in Italian and the Theory of *pro*', *Linguistic Inquiry* 17, 4, 501–57.
—— *Relativized Minimality*, Cambridge, Mass.: MIT Press.
—— 'Speculations on Verb-Second', in J. Mascaro and M. Nespor, (eds), *Grammar in Progress, GLOW Essays for Henk Riemsdijk*, 375–86.
—— 'Residual Verb Second and the *wh*-Criterion', MS., University of Geneva.
Ross, J.R. (1967) 'Constraints on Variables in Syntax', Ph.D. Dissertation, MIT.
Rothstein, S.D. (1988) 'Conservativity and the Syntax of Determiners', *Linguistics* 26, 6, 999–1019.
Rouveret, A. (1991) 'La nature des prépositions conjuguées', MS., Université de Paris 8.
Safir, K.J. (1985) *Syntactic Chains*, Cambridge and New York: Cambridge University Press.
—— (1986) 'Relative Clauses in a Theory of Binding and Levels', *Linguistic Inquiry* 17, 4, 663–90.
Schwyzer, E. (1950) *Griechische Grammatik*, Munich: C. H. Beck'sche Verlagsbuchhandlung.
Shlonsky, U. (1988) 'Government and Binding in Hebrew Nominals', *Linguistics* 26, 6, 951–76.
Sigursson, A.H. (1991) 'Icelandic Case-marked PRO and the Licensing of Lexical Arguments', *Natural Language and Linguistic Theory* 9, 2, 231–84.
Sportiche, D. (1988) 'A Theory of Floating Quantifiers and its Corollaries for Constituent Structure', *Linguistic Inquiry* 19, 425–49.
Srivastav, V. (1991a) '*WH*-Dependencies in Hindi and the Theory of Grammar', unpublished Ph.D. Dissertation, Cornell University.
—— (1991b) 'The Syntax and Semantics of Correlatives', *Natural Language and Linguistic Theory* 9, 4, 637–86.
Stowell, T. (1981) 'The History of Phrase Structure', unpublished Ph.D. Dissertation, MIT.
—— (1985) '*Null Operators and the Theory of Proper Government*, MS., UCLA.
Suñer, M. (1984) 'Free Relatives and the Matching Parameter', *The Linguistic Review* 3, 4, 363–87.
Szabolsci, A. (1983) 'The Possessor that Ran Away from Home', *The Linguistic Review* 3, 1 89–102.
Tellier, C. (1988) 'Universal Licensing: Implications for Parasitic Gap Constructions', unpublished Ph.D. Dissertation, McGill University.
Tewarson, H.T. (1988) *Rahel Varnhagen*, Hamburg: Rowohlt.
Watanabe, A. (1991) '*Wh-in-situ*, Subjacency, and Chain Formation', MS., MIT.
Williamson, J. (1987) 'An Indefiniteness Restriction for Relative Clauses in Lakhota', in E.J. Reuland, and A. ter Meulen, (eds) *The Representation of (In)definiteness*, Cambridge, Mass.: MIT Press, 168–90.
Woisetschläger, E. (1983) 'On the Question of Definiteness in "An Old Man's Book"', *Linguistic Inquiry* 14, 1, 137–54.
Zribi-Hertz, A. (1984) 'Prépositions Orphelines et Pronoms Nuls', *Recherches Linguistiques* 12, 46–91.

INDEX

Abney, S. xi, 147, 149–51
adjacency effects 152–5, 160–2, 171–4, 192–6
amount relative constructions 5–8, 69–71, 138–9, 227 n. 1

Bresnan, J.W. 10–18, 30, 35, 90–2, 94

Carlson, G.N. 7
Chomsky, N.A. xi, 7, 57, 73, 83, 88–9, 142, 147, 151, 153, 188, 190, 192, 194, 221, 227 n. 2, 247–8 n. 8
correlative constructions 67–70, 83–4

Dobrovie-Sorin, C. 72, 162, 168, 201, 218, 224–6, 231 n. 15, 244 n. 9, 247 n. 5

Extended Projection 28, 73–5, 77–9, 150, 165

free relative constructions: anti-Pied-Piping effects in (see Pied-Piping restrictions); distribution of 3–4; headedness of 7–8, 66, 139–42, 228–30 n. 9; matching effects in 10–12, 16, 18–21, 24–5, 39–40, 113–36, 141; 'missing' preposition 13–14, 16–17, 22–3, 24, 89–106; semantics of 5–8; wh-Head analysis of 10–14, 92–3, 98–103

government as an inadequate locality construct 21–2, 24, 34–5, 37, 58, 61–2
Grimshaw, J. xi, 10–18, 28, 30, 35, 66, 73–4, 80, 90–2, 94, 149, 150, 165, 230 n. 12, 233 n. 19
Groos, A. 11, 15–19, 22, 30, 227 n. 2

Harbert, W. 19–24, 26, 30, 39, 238 n. 32, 240 n. 42
head-internal relative constructions : amount-type 50–1; restrictive 51–4

Kase: on adjectives 93; -attraction 110–13; -hierarchies 108–9; -matching (see free relative constructions: matching effects in); the notion 26–8

-L morpheme: as Case-assigner 160–2, 163–4, 166–7, 171; as Case-recipient 159–60, 168–9; as euphonic element 179–180; as reanalysed determiner 176–8

Larson, R.K. 23, 90–9, 106

Null Operators (NOs): (non)existence in Romanian of 201, 207–8, 212–17, 220, 222, 223, 224–6; see also Pied-Piping restrictions with NOs; pro as NO

Pied-Piping restrictions: with Null Operators (NOs) 46, 76–7, 106; in wh-free relatives 34–5, 37, 38–9, 40–3, 77–9, 83, 141–2, 235–6 n. 23, 237–8 n. 29; in wh-interrogatives 73–4, 233, 234 n. 21
PRO-headed analyses for free relatives 19–20, 24, 43
pro: adjectival 105, 238 n. 30; as Head/external nominal of a relative 19–22, 24–5, 28–41, 69, 80–3, 103–5; locality domains for identification of 61–4, 80–3; as Null Operator (NO)

85, 87; theories of 59–65, 84–9

van Riemsdijk, H. 11, 15–19, 22, 30, 173–4, 195–6, 227 n. 2
Rizzi, L. 57, 58, 61, 62, 63, 70, 71, 74, 80, 84, 87, 231 n. 18, 249 n. 9
Srivastav, V. 67–70
Suñer, M. 23–31, 33–39, 228 nn. 5–7, 240–2 n. 44